Tattooed on My Soul

Number 149 Williams-Ford
TEXAS A&M
UNIVERSITY
Military
History Series

TATTOOED ON MY SOUL

Texas Veterans Remember World War II

EDITED BY STEPHEN M. SLOAN,
LOIS E. MYERS, AND MICHELLE HOLLAND

Texas A&M University Press
COLLEGE STATION, TEXAS

FIRST EDITION

THIS PAPER MEETS THE REQUIREMENTS
OF ANSI/NISO, Z39.48-1992
(PERMANENCE OF PAPER).
BINDING MATERIALS HAVE BEEN
CHOSEN FOR DURABILITY.
MANUFACTURED IN
THE UNITED STATES OF AMERICA

Library of Congress Cataloging-in-Publication Data

Tattooed on my soul: Texas veterans remember World War II / edited by Stephen M. Sloan, Lois E. Myers, and Michelle Holland. — First edition.
pages cm — (Williams-Ford Texas A&M University military history series; no. 149)
Includes index.
Summary: "For more than forty years the Oral History Institute at Baylor University has dutifully gathered the flesh-and-blood memories of the World War II generation in the state of Texas to ensure that the personal experiences of those pivotal years would be preserved—for them, for their families, and for future generations. Tattooed on My Soul brings together seventeen of the most compelling narratives from Baylor's extensive collection of more than five thousand interviews"—ECIP Data View summary.
ISBN 978-1-62349-307-3 (cloth: alk. paper) — ISBN 978-1-62349-308-0 (ebook) 1. World War, 1939–1945—Veterans—Texas—Interviews. 2. World War, 1939–1945—Veterans—Texas—Biography. 3. World War, 1939–1945—Personal narratives, American. 4. United States—Armed Forces—Biography. I. Sloan, Stephen M., editor. II. Myers, Lois E., 1946– editor. III. Holland, Michelle, 1982– editor. IV. Baylor University. Institute for Oral History. V. Series: Williams-Ford Texas A&M University military history series; no. 149.
D810.V42T48 2015
940.54'81764—dc23
2015006407

All royalty payments from
Tattooed on My Soul go to support
the continued research work of
the Institute for Oral History
at Baylor University.

To those who served

You know, that kind of stuff is tattooed on your soul.
You're never going to forget it.
— Frank Curre Jr.

CONTENTS

ILLUSTRATIONS

PREFACE
REFLECTING ON THE MEANING OF WORLD WAR II

ON WORLD WAR II

World War II was a watershed in US and world history. The conflict dramatically affected the cultural, political, and economic fabric of society at home and abroad. Changes brought by the war were the impetus for major movements to come, from domestic social reform via the civil rights movement to global diplomacy through the United Nations. Its political wake generated the international standoff between the United States and the Soviet Union known as the Cold War. Domestically the war enhanced the role and power of the federal government. Federal spending reached levels inconceivable even during FDR's Depression-era relief efforts. And the high production and employment of the war years did much more than kick-start a sluggish economy. Consumerism and suburbanization boomed, for the most part, throughout the remainder of the century. For the first time the nation enjoyed a middle-class majority. The war provided unprecedented opportunities for women as well as for Hispanics and African Americans. There was a significant shift in population, from the rural center to urbanized industrial areas near the coasts, particularly in California. Despite combat deaths and the rigors of wartime, the overall health of the nation improved considerably. The birthrate rose quickly, the death rate declined sharply, and median life expectancy increased by five years. Virtually no facet of American life was untouched by the war.

This volume, however, does not focus on global political power struggles, reformed economic landscapes, or national demographic shifts. The precise manner in which the war was prosecuted against the Axis is not to be found in these pages. Rather they contain personal stories telling how the events of World War II were made manifest in the living of a life. Those who speak here represent the more than 16 million men and 250,000 women who served in the US military from 1941 to 1945. Thrust into extraordinary circumstances, they lived to tell others what they experienced. Oral history offered a vehicle for these individuals to record, preserve, and share their experiences during war.

ON ORAL HISTORY

The following stories were shared in one-on-one recorded interviews transcribed and preserved since the 1970s by the Baylor University Institute for Oral History (BUIOH).[1] The interviews chosen for this volume are characteristic of hundreds in the Baylor oral history collection that relate stories of World War II from the battlefield and the home front. Built upon an interdisciplinary foundation, the Baylor oral history collection in its early years highlighted the lives of twentieth-century men and women who made contributions in the areas of economics, the judiciary, religion, and medicine as well as those whose experiences touched on events and persons related to the history of Baylor University and its surrounding community. Whether the focus of the research was the rise and fall of the Texas cotton culture, the controversies of Baptists, the varieties of Texas art and music, or any number of other topics, every encounter with a narrator who was alive during the 1940s, as a child, teenager, or adult, naturally included questions about the war.

Many of the narrators chosen for this volume were lifelong Texans, and all but one lived in the Lone Star State at the time of the interview. The narrators signed a release form granting the Institute full rights to their stories. The Institute offered each narrator the opportunity to review the transcript, and most did. For this volume the editors retained the first-person narrative of the original recording, allowing the reader to catch the cadence and timbre of each witness's voice as nearly as possible.

The nature of oral history fundamentally impacts the ways in which the stories here are told. Being spontaneous, oral history seldom captures memories in strict chronological order. As the narrator tells a story, the mention of a person, place, or event at one point in time may call forth a tangential memory from an earlier or later time. Transcripts, then, often call for the reader to accept shifts in the story timeline. For this anthology the editors reordered misplaced stories when necessary to keep the narrative flowing.

Narrators may, of course, also confuse times, places, and people or collapse several events into one, especially when recalling incidents that happened repeatedly over a long period. With a topic as widely researched and broadly published as World War II, aspects of the war learned from books, film, and television may integrate into veterans' personal memories and become part of their narrative without being part of their experience. The editors have tried to recognize occurrences of confusion, collapse, and integration and to correct them when possible or omit them when unverifiable.

Oral history editors face constant tension in discerning the accuracy of oral history transcripts. Stories that contradict accounts in other historical resources may stem from a narrator's faulty memory, personal biases, or misspoken words or from a transcriber's misunderstanding of recorded dialogue. On the other hand, the contradiction might represent new information or an undocumented perspective that actually corrects or supplements the received historical record. One major motivation to do oral history is to capture previously untold memories. In doing so, oral history might complicate accepted, traditional accounts. We editors placed our veterans' stories on the balances piece by piece, weighing each memory for accuracy and validity. When we could neither confirm a detail nor justify it as fresh information, we removed it or created an explanatory note for the reader. We accept responsibility for errors we might have missed.

We editors want to stand aside and be forgotten while the reader meets the narrator. We therefore impose ourselves sparingly. We use endnotes to define words or phrases not in a standard dictionary or not readily understood from the context, and we use brackets when we add a word or phrase to clarify a meaning.

In each oral history interview, multiple factors combine to create a unique interchange between the interviewer and the narrator. The oral histories selected for this anthology represent some of those variables. The reader will notice that some stories have greater depth and richer detail than others. Narrators with outgoing personalities share memories differently from those who are reserved. Some narrators were more practiced than others in telling their war stories. In some interviews the primary purpose was to record the veteran's military experiences; in others the military stories were but a chapter in a full life-history interview series. In this volume, nine witnesses shared their stories in a single interview focused on their military experience. For eight, the war years were part of life histories recorded in multiple sessions.

Differences among narrators and purposes explain some variance of detail in the edited stories, but the principal explanation lies in differences among interviewers. The degree of rapport between the interviewer and the witness and the ability of the interviewer to ask questions that facilitate recall and elicit details directly affect the outcomes. First-time interviewers often miss more opportunities with narrators than seasoned interviewers. A few oral histories in this volume are products of students in university history courses, but the majority resulted from the work of professional oral historians.

As one reads these stories it is important to remember the enduring truth about oral history best articulated by the master oral historian

Alessandro Portelli: Oral history "tells us less about *events* than about their *meaning*."[2] Within these pages are new perspectives on the events covered. And new facts surface. But this volume makes its greatest contribution by conveying the *meaning* of those events, the way they were experienced by each individual, and the manner in which they have come to be understood so many years later.

Notes

1. Full transcripts of these Institute for Oral History interviews are available through Baylor University Library Digital Collections, available at http://digitalcollections.baylor.edu. Hereafter references to the transcripts and supporting materials are cited as BU Digital Collections.

2. Alessandro Portelli, *The Death of Luigi Trastulli and Other Stories: Form and Meaning in Oral History* (Albany: State University of New York Press, 1991), 50.

ACKNOWLEDGMENTS

As editors of stories told by others, we are acutely aware of our debt to the storytellers. Because of their willingness to share their memories of wartime service, future generations will have the opportunity to read and hear eyewitness accounts of personal encounters with history. Baylor University's Institute for Oral History is a preservation partner with the narrators and also with the interviewers. Interviewers conduct background research, make contacts, ask informed questions, dutifully record the interview sessions, and obtain the proper legal releases. The interviewers who co-created the interviews in this volume are diverse—from undergraduate history students to longtime professional oral historians—and we appreciate each of them for their diligent work.

Our Institute staff brings the recorded interviews to life, and we gratefully acknowledge their contributions. Undergraduate and graduate students and staff editors carry our oral history recordings through technical processing, transcribing, abstracting, editing, and, eventually, dissemination to the public. Help in identifying hundreds of interviews containing World War II experiences and selecting a handful for inclusion in this volume was given by then-graduate assistant Steven Sielaff, whom we also thank for finding many of the images. Elinor Mazé, Becky Shulda, and Jaclyn Jeffrey read and edited the manuscript in its various versions. Our appreciation extends across campus to the staff of Baylor's Ray I. Riley Digitization Center, who partner in digitizing our print, audio, and video collections, allowing us to include in this volume interviews originally done in the 1970s and 1980s.

Outside grants made possible the recording and processing of many of the veteran stories included here. We gratefully acknowledge funding from the Texas Historical Commission and the Texas Holocaust and Genocide Commission. Other veteran stories represent the ongoing work of the Institute, which is made possible by generous support from Baylor's academic affairs office. We are grateful for the encouragement and validation of our work by Dr. James Bennighof, Vice Provost for Academic Affairs and Policy.

Tattooed on My Soul

THERE AT THE START
1941–1942

THE PACIFIC

EVERY DECEMBER 7 THE UNITED STATES COMMEMORATES that date in 1941 when the shocking news spread of Japan's raid on Pearl Harbor, Hawaii, and the Empire's ensuing declaration of war on the United States and the United Kingdom. Americans going about their usual routines that Sunday remember where they were, what they were doing, and whom they were with in that life-changing moment.

The takeover of the Japanese government by military leaders, the subsequent compact with Germany and Italy, and an increase in the number of incidents of Japanese aggression in the Pacific had put US forces on alert by mid-November. A strike was coming, but where? In answer, Japan sent almost four hundred fighter aircraft and bombers over Oahu in two waves, an hour apart, destroying or damaging twenty US ships and about three hundred fifty US aircraft and killing or wounding more than thirty-five hundred American service personnel and civilians. Torpedoes also fell that day on ships at Honolulu and San Francisco, demonstrating clearly the strength of the Empire's threat. Within twenty-four hours, reports came of Japanese air strikes against Malaya, Hong Kong, Guam, the Philippines, Wake Island, and Midway Island.

The goal was clear: Japan intended to expand its empire to include all US, British, and Dutch holdings in the Central and Southwest Pacific and on the Southeast Asian mainland. Discouraging months passed as the Allies witnessed loss after loss, including Wake Island, Malaya, Borneo, the Dutch East Indies, and strategic sites in the Philippines—Luzon, Manila, and the Bataan Peninsula. Japanese submarines lurking off the western coast of North America made several successful strikes against US, Canadian, and Mexican ships. By the end of August 1942 the Empire had reached its zenith. In the Pacific it claimed Corregidor Island, the Caroline Islands, the Gilbert Islands, the Marshall Islands, the Mariana Islands, parts of New Guinea, and portions of the Solomon Islands. In Southeast Asia it controlled Burma and Singapore.

Amid the ominous reports pouring in through the first half of 1942 came hopeful hints that the tide would turn. In April spirits rose with news of the audacious bombing of Tokyo by the Doolittle Raiders. In May and June, successes in the Coral Sea and at Midway Atoll proved that the United States was gaining the expertise and assembling the machinery needed to slow the spread of the Empire. In August, US forces took the offensive at Guadalcanal in the Solomon Islands, eventually forcing out the Japanese in February 1943. The war in the Pacific during the next two and a half years was a grueling, unrelenting struggle to regain control over those territories lost in the first eight months after the bombing of Pearl Harbor.

THE WITNESSES

The first two of the following accounts come from veterans who were members of the US armed forces when the nation entered the war. One was a navy seaman; the other, an air force pilot. They speak for thousands of service personnel who experienced firsthand the opening months of the war in the Pacific Theater. Survival of the attack on Pearl Harbor launched one narrator into subsequent naval battles in the Pacific, and the Doolittle Raid on Tokyo became for the other narrator the first of many harrowing flights to curb Japanese ambitions in the China-Burma-India Theater.

Eighteen-year-old Frank Curre Jr. was working in the mess hall aboard the USS *Tennessee,* docked next to the USS *West Virginia* in Battleship Row, Pearl Harbor, on December 7, 1941, when the Japanese attacked. He quickly assumed his position as ammunition handler in Gun Turret II just minutes before a bomb hit the middle gun and spread shrapnel onto the *West Virginia,* mortally wounding that ship's commanding officer. Curre was an eyewitness to the sinking of the *Oklahoma* and the bombing of the *Arizona,* and he assisted with rescue and recovery operations aboard the *West Virginia.* Indelible memories of his experiences that day sustained him later as he took his place at the guns time after time in strategic Pacific naval battles. Before the war's end, Curre saw action at Tarawa, the Mariana and Caroline Islands, Luzon, the Leyte Gulf, Iwo Jima, and Okinawa.

Richard E. "Dick" Cole was an experienced air force pilot when, on April 18, 1942, he climbed into the cockpit of a B-25 aboard the USS *Hornet* as copilot to Jimmy Doolittle. The success of the Doolittle Raid in bombing industrial and military targets in Tokyo and other Japanese cities deflated Japan's confidence and bolstered US hopes for ultimate victory. Later in the war, Cole flew C-47s over the Himalayas in Southeast Asia, transporting supplies and personnel from India to China. In March 1944, as a member of the 1st Air Commando Group, he flew troops into Burma in the first all-aerial Allied invasion behind enemy lines.

FROM NORTH AFRICA TO EUROPE

On December 11, 1941, the United States and the Axis powers, Germany and Italy, mutually declared war. The Germans took the offensive immediately, wreaking havoc on US merchant and naval shipping down the full length of the Atlantic Coast. In the first year the Allies lost more than a thousand vessels to German U-boats within the US defense zone. At stake was keeping the waters passable for ships carrying not only the supplies, personnel, fuel, and equipment required for combat but also basic resources needed to sustain life in the besieged United Kingdom. By mid-1943, having devised alternative routes, formed massive convoys, increased intelligence gathering, developed new weapons and equipment, and improved air-power defensives, the Allies had gained the upper hand in the Atlantic. Nevertheless, until Germany surrendered, any American aboard a ship in the Atlantic recognized the threat of U-boats.

In the early stages of planning for the war in Europe, the United States favored sending troops across the English Channel into France right away to distract Germany from its invasion of the Soviet Union. Britain, however, needed help freeing North Africa of Axis occupation. Since June 1940, Britain had fought to maintain its base on Malta in order to secure the Mediterranean Sea and defend the future invasion of southern Europe. At the same time, Britain had to protect its control of Egypt in order to maintain command of the Suez Canal and Middle Eastern oil supplies. Offensives and counteroffensives throughout 1941 pitted armies from Britain, India, and Australia, aided by the Free French Army, against the German Afrika Korps and six Italian combat divisions. In early November 1942, in the Second Battle of El Alamein, British forces finally pushed the Germans and the Italians, commanded by Gen. Erwin Rommel, out of Egypt.

At that point Operation Torch began under the command of Gen. Dwight D. Eisenhower. The goal of the three-pronged Allied amphibious invasion of French North Africa was to trap Rommel in Tunisia. On November 8 the Americans arrived on the northern shores of Africa—the western task force in French Morocco, at Safi, Fedala, and Port Lyautey; the center near Oran, Algeria; and the eastern at Algiers. From there Allied infantry and tank troops, supported by British and US naval and air power, advanced eastward into Tunisia. At the same time, the British Eighth Army, under Gen. Bernard L. Montgomery, pushed Rommel westward through Libya into Tunisia until they cornered his forces in the port of Tunis. The Axis launched a strong counteroffensive against US forces in mid-February 1943, driving them through and beyond the Kasserine Pass, south of Tunis. A final, massive response from the Allies drove the Axis forces back to the coast, where they surrendered in May. With North Africa secured as a staging ground, the Allies immediately turned their attention to southern Europe, beginning in Sicily and advancing into Italy.

THE WITNESSES

The following accounts are from veterans who were in the US Army when the nation entered the war. All three—a career officer, a reservist, and a draftee—saw action in North Africa. After the invasion of Italy, the career officer completed the war in administrative service in Washington, DC. The other two eventually joined US troops in France in the push toward Germany, remaining in action through the end of the war in Europe.

George C. McDowell, a 1937 graduate of West Point, was a specialist in ordnance and logistics for the US Army Air Forces. As a member of Gen. George S. Patton's team, he oversaw the transport and delivery of ordnance for air support during Operation Torch and the Battle of Tunisia. From November 1942 to the summer of 1943, he served in French Morocco and Algeria. Then, under Gen. John K. Cannon, he oversaw ordnance supplies for air operations in Corsica and Italy. Called back to the War Department in Washington, DC, in July 1944, McDowell served at the Pentagon until 1947.

Frank Morrow Pool, a petroleum engineer and proud alumnus of the Texas A&M Aggie horse cavalry, was called from the reserves into active service in January 1942. In November he commanded a company of the 1st Armored Division during their Operation Torch landing near Oran on the Algerian coast and on their dangerous trek across Algeria into Tunisia. In February 1943 he returned to the United States as aide to Gen. Lunsford E.

Oliver. After the June 1944 Normandy invasion, Pool took command of Company B, 10th Tank Battalion, in the 5th Armored Division, which followed the infantry into Europe. Company B engaged the Germans in tank warfare through France into Belgium, across the Siegfried Line into Germany, and over the Rhine River to the Elbe River, where they spent VE (Victory in Europe) Day, May 8, 1945, giving thanks that the fighting was over.

HERBERT U. STERN, drafted into the army in the summer of 1941, was placed in medic training a few weeks before he became a US citizen. A German Jew whose father had been imprisoned by the Nazis in 1934, Stern immigrated to the United States at the age of seventeen in 1936, just two days after his father's release. During Operation Torch, his division landed at Port Lyautey, in French Morocco, where he was separated from the other medics and made an interpreter and interrogator for army intelligence. He moved with the troops across Morocco and Libya into Tunisia and was among the first troops to land near Palermo, in Sicily. Before the invasion of Italy, he was shipped to England, where he attended British Intelligence School. From D-Day to VE Day, he was a field interrogator of German prisoners. In April 1945 he was a member of a patrol that helped liberate the German SS extermination camp at Nordhausen.

FRANK CURRE JR.

Frank Curre was born on August 10, 1923, in Waco, Texas, and grew up in a house across the street from Cameron Park, one of the state's largest municipal parks, which stretched along the banks of the Brazos and Bosque rivers. When he was not in school or selling newspapers, Curre spent countless hours in Cameron Park hunting for squirrels, observing the imported exotic ducks, catching fish on trotlines, playing on seesaws and swings, splashing around in the springs, and swimming in the rivers. In the 1920s and '30s the park was teeming with children, and many of the friends Curre made there joined the military around the time he did—soon after he graduated from Waco High School in 1941.

I COULDN'T FIND A JOB, so I went and told Mama, "I've been talking to a man up here at the corner about the navy, and I'm going to join the navy. He told me all I have to do is get you to sign the papers, that at seventeen I can get in on what they call a minority cruise: you're over seventeen, under eighteen."[1] I talked her into it and went up there. I passed the physical and went to Dallas and then passed the physical up there. Then I went to San Diego. They sent me there from Dallas with all Texas and Oklahoma boys. I had to pass another physical, and if I passed that one, I was in Uncle Sam's navy for good. I took my oath June 5, 1941.

We didn't have quite enough boys to form a company, so we had to wait a week or so to get enough. Our DI, drill instructor, had us go around barracks fixing up the bunks, making hammocks, because back there then, aboard ship, you slept in a hammock, not a cot or a bunk. We slept in hammocks that had billet hooks on the overhead. You hook them up, and that's what you sleep in at night. So we got in there, and I got through with that boot camp.

I came home from boot camp somewhere around the end of July, first part of August, because when I go back, I'm assigned to the ship. What the DI did was put a bulletin board up there with a list of ships, and he had the *Tennessee* and the *Texas* together. Well, the boy who went in with me, Angelo Arcivar, he was a boy from Fort Worth. We said, We'll take the *Texas*. The DI said, "No, that one's up there by mistake. It's an East Coast battleship, and you're going to have to go aboard one of the West Coast battleships." *T* for Texas; we'll take the *Tennessee.* And that's how we got aboard the *Tennessee.*

Sometime in August they told us we was getting under way, and I said, "Where we going?" They said we're going to Pearl Harbor. I ain't never heard of it. We ain't out but a few days, and we hit a ninety-knot gale. That's wind and water coming at you at over one hundred miles an hour. It washed our seaplanes off the catapults. It took the dogs on our hatches and twisted them like pretzels.[2] We had a foot and a half of water on the main deck. We set watertight, got pumps going pumping the water off, put tarps around the hatches, latched them down, and went on into Pearl. When we got in, they started working on those ships, repairing them.

When we first got over there, we had three battleship divisions. You had three battleships in each one. We'd stay out at sea two weeks, come into port one week, three of us at a time. And then Roosevelt began to economize. We're going to stay out one week, two weeks in port. Then all at once, all of us go in at the same time. I ain't got a answer to that yet. It had to be spies to know all of those battleships were going to be in there at the same time. The only one attached to the Pacific Fleet that wasn't there was the *Colorado.*[3]

Each one of us had yard periods on the West Coast. When your yard period had come up, you'd go into dry dock and they'd paint, scrape the hull, minor repairs and all that—and give you your annual leave. The one outboard of us, the *West Virginia,* was due to go in when the *Colorado* come out, and it had a lot of boys. Their enlistment was up, and they was due to get discharged, but they was waiting to get to the States so they'd be in the States when they got discharged. Some of them lost their life that day. All of them didn't make it.

Here comes the seventh. When the Japs attacked, they attacked us at seven fifty-five that morning. I was mess-cooking on the ship. And when you're a mess cook, back there then, you didn't eat cafeteria-style. You eat family-style. You swung tables on your overhead. You'd break them down, put them up three times a day. You'd go to the galley, bring your food down. And whenever they were through eating, then you do what we call mess. We clean up our mess. We washed our dishes in salt water with saltwater soap. Freshwater soap won't suds in salt water. And that's the way they'd make us clean them. Then, when you get through cleaning all them, you put them in racks, and you take them to the scullery. It's a sterilization process.

Well, just as I got my racks back there and set them up on that counter is when I heard the first blast of that day, a tremendous blast.

A big heavyweight wrestler on the ship come running through that passageway. I don't know where he was going, but he was knocking everybody out of the way and he was getting there in a hurry. And then, instantaneously, we hear another one. There was a chief petty officer coming through this time. He'd been in the Asiatic Fleet and spent time over there, knew all those countries, all their flags. He started hollering something about a meatball.[4] Well, to me, I thought he was talking about something to eat. But when he come through we hear another giant blast, and then we go to general quarters.

I'm in a second-division forward deck force. First division mans number one turret. We man number two, fourteen-inch gun turret. My battle station is in the lower ammunition-handling room. That's right in the bottom of the turret. Next to your turret is your magazine. The boys working in the magazine go in there, close that hatch, and they got a scuttle that they put a bag of powder in, switch it on your side. You take it out, go and put it in another one, send it up to your gun pit. We wasn't down there long when all at once that turret shook like something mad. Boy, it really rattled. We took a 1,760-pound bomb hit. It didn't penetrate, or I wouldn't be here. It hit a glancing blow; hit the middle gun, knocked it out. When it exploded, it killed a captain on the *West Virginia* next to us, blew him almost half in two.[5] We secured all fourteen-inch gun turrets.

As I come out of the overhang, I seen the first of the two god-awful sights I witnessed that day. When I looked over to the right, there's that giant battleship, the *Oklahoma,* already hit and capsized. She was hit so quick with around six torpedoes and went over so quick they didn't have time to flood nothing on the starboard side.[6] I had a chief warrant boatswain by the name of Adkins.[7] He was wanting all us out of number one and number two turret to come aft.[8] He's going to tell us what he wants us to do.

As we're going aft, that's when I watched that bomb that sank the *Arizona.* It come down on the starboard side just right behind turrets number two and number one and exploded. And when that ship exploded, it went twelve to fifteen foot in the air, and the bodies was scattered all over that harbor. If you'd have took a bag of popcorn, went out there in the breeze, come up in the air, that was like the bodies going out all over that harbor.

When she exploded, she caught our fantail on fire, caught the *West Virginia*'s on fire. Both ships is burning. There's a chief petty officer on the *West Virginia.* He's trapped in his quarters. And you can see that fire; it's a roaring inferno. He's got the hatch jammed in there. He can't get out; they can't get to him. He's going to try to get through about a

Rescuers pull a survivor of the USS *West Virginia* from the water. The USS *Tennessee* is inboard. *Courtesy of Library of Congress.*

twelve- or fourteen-inch porthole. The old battleships have portholes; the new ones didn't. He got one arm and a head through, and that's all. He couldn't come one way; he couldn't go the other way. Boatswain Adkins had already sent a bunch of us on the *West Virginia* and told us, "Go over there and help them boys, whatever they need. Fight fires. Check below decks. Do whatever the officers tell you."

While we was over there, we hear the old boatswain holler, "Somebody take that man out of his misery," talking about that chief. Somebody took the man out of his misery. Didn't see who did it, didn't want to see who did it, don't care who did it. But I've always said to this day it could not have been one of us teenage kids because I don't think we was mature enough in age to understand fully what that man was asking to be done. Now, at my age, yeah, I know fully what he was asking.

Then you get to banging on the hull. We went below; we checked with the officers on the *Wee Vee*. That was the nickname for the *West Virginia*. One says, "Bang on the hatch, and wait for a response. If you don't get a response, go on to another one. If the ship starts crickling and crackling, come topside," because it's listing pretty good on this port side[9] as it is. It was pretty low to the water. It'd already took several torpedoes. I watched one go in before we got on her. I didn't see the torpedo; I see a wave coming at it.

Later on, sometimes we had a working party in the area where it turns out to be three men trapped below decks on the *West Virginia*.

They're pounding on the pipes, bulkhead, and you can't do nothing to them. The flood is already on top of them, so you can't get to them. When they raised it, it was three of them trapped down there. They claim they lived up to December 23, when their water and oxygen supply run out.[10]

Then we get out there. The *Solace* motor launch was in.[11] She'd already dropped her barges in the water, and she's picking up dead and wounded. One guy tells us when he's in his barge he goes to pick up one, and the boys in the water is begging him, Don't touch him. He says, "I got to touch him. I got to get him medical help." When he reached to grab him under the arm, what he grabbed ahold of come right out in his hand. Just like you took that body and cooked him. That's what you had to do all during that day, is pick them boys out of that water.

We picked up a survivor that the *Solace* motor launch brought over to us, and he saved his life. He was trapped below decks in the *Oklahoma* in the shipfitter compartment. He'd been on the ship a good while, and he memorized the frames in that ship; that's your ceiling joists. He knew, being in the shipfitter shop, that was frame number so-and-so. And he's in there with another sailor, and you can't see each other. Below decks on a ship you can't see. It's absolute, total darkness. He tells him, "If I can go to frame so-and-so and hold my breath and come back, then we can hold our breath and go all the way. The time we get there we'll be where the lifeline should be, and we'll give ourselves a shove to top of the water." Well, he does what he says. He comes back. He makes it. But he can't get the guy to go with him. He's hysterical. So he leaves, goes on his own, gives himself a shove, and a *Solace* motor launch come by just as his head popped out of that water, bleeding out of eyes, ears, nose, and mouth. Picked him up, and they brought him aboard our ship. He taught me a lesson about them frames.

The *Arizona*, she was a roaring inferno for two and a half days. We had a tug called *Holga*. She pumped water on the *West Virginia*, fantail and everything,[12] and also on the *Arizona*, continuously. When them fires went out, some of us went aboard the *Arizona*, crawled up on there to see what we could find. You could see melted coins—copper, silver. If you got up around a superstructure and went into an area where the wind couldn't have got to, you see piles of ashes where them bodies was cremated right where they stand. They list 1,177 entombed. Many of them, when that bomb blew—spfft!—they turned to dust, disintegrated. Them poor souls didn't even know they left this earth when that magazine went.[13]

I met a boy ashore the night before, Saturday night, December 6. In the process of shooting the bull, he said, "Where you from?" I said, "I'm from Waco, Texas." He died laughing and said, "That's where I'm from! Where'd you live?" I said, "Well, temporarily, we lived on 1910 North Fifth, but we were staying with my aunt and uncle and grandma at Twenty-Fifth and Alexander." He said, "I lived on Alexander." I said, "Where'd you live?" It was right up there by that North Waco Elementary School. He said, "What do you do on there?" I said, "Right now I'm mess-cooking." He laughed again, said, "That's what I'm doing on the *Arizona*. Say, let me ask you. Can you get somebody to watch your mess tomorrow?" I said, "Yeah. I volunteered to help a boy ahead of me before I took over. He'll watch it for me." He said, "How about coming over and have noon chow with me? When we get through, we'll clean up the mess, we'll sit around and shoot the bull about Waco." Well, here comes the seventh. He's on that row[14] back there. He's still on there.

You react. That's what you do. In no matter what you do, you react. We had three men trapped in the water, burned bad, and we're on the *West Virginia*. They're going to be burned alive because the oil and fire off of that ship and *Arizona* is going to overtake them. I was a excellent swimmer because I grew up in them two rivers down here. I hollered at two guys. I said, "Y'all swim good?" "Yeah." I said, "Let's wet ourselves down, cover up our eyes, and we'll dive through the oil and fire and swim underwater. When we clear it, we'll get them boys out because it's going to catch them, burn them up." They said, Come on, let's do it.

Somebody throwed a hose on us, wet us down. We dove through, went over, and each one of us got one. We was going to try to put them up on our bow and get them in our ship. God, we get around; it looks like it's four miles up there. So we hollered for help on Ford Island. Some boys come down, got them, took them up, put them in their sick bay, but we got them out of the water. Now, whether they lived or died, that we don't know. But, to me, I couldn't live with myself if I didn't get in and try to help them. It was going to overtake them.

If a guy goes out here and does something right quick and earns him a Medal of Honor, he didn't do it for the medal. He did what his own conscience dictated him do. He reacted to the moment. He didn't have time to plan nothing. You just do it.

Later in the war, when we'd go to our battle stations, my old heart could beat ninety miles an hour. But the minute I got on that gun and I could see them kamikazes, that bitterness of December 7 set in, and I forgot about being scared. I hated them devils so bad, I couldn't wait

Bound for Pearl Harbor, a Zero takes off from *Akagi,* a Japanese aircraft carrier, on December 7, 1941. *Courtesy of National Archives and Records Administration.*

to shoot at them. That's the reason I didn't want below decks on a ship. I said, "If they're going to get me, we're going to be looking at each other eyeball to eyeball."

Them guys that come on December 7 wasn't much higher than this ceiling. They'd be in that cockpit, look down, and laugh and smile at you. But when they'd get over to the ships, did their damage, they'd turn and shoot straight up. We ain't figured out yet how they cleared them masts. Them masts on our ships stood 110 foot high. But they'd turn and go straight up. That Zero was a good plane.

For several days you're in a daze, more or less. You still can't figure out what you're looking at has happened.[15] Then you're thinking, What else is going to happen after this? You automatically think about home. You're wanting to be home, and you know you can't. But after that day, you're never a teenage kid again; you're a full-grown man. You create a new sense of values and priorities about your life immediately. You may not know you're doing it, but you do it. You just automatically think different because what you're going through and what you're going to go through is mean stuff.

We got under way from Pearl Harbor on the twentieth of December. The *Maryland* was free. The *Oklahoma* freed her when she capsized. The *Pennsylvania*'s in dry dock. They blew two destroyers together, forward of her, in dry dock, just bombed them together. Well, the *Pennsylvania* could get out when they flooded. They had to take underwater demolition, get down and dynamite the quays—that's what they call what we tied up to. Then they put some powerful sea-going tugs, fishtailed us out.

Three of us was able to get under way on the twentieth of December, and we headed for the States. We had our first Christmas at sea, and they took wrappers off of turkeys marked "World War I," but they was good turkeys. Starting with Christmas 1941, I spent Christmas at sea in the Pacific, aboard ship, '41, '42, '43, and '44, never ashore. The war was over in '45, and I was ashore then. My wife and I, a couple invited us for Christmas dinner, so we went and we ate Christmas dinner with them.

When I left the *Tennessee,* they transferred me. "New construction," as they called it back there then. In February of '42 they took most of the crew and sent you to new ships because the *Tennessee* was going to be in there several months for repairs. They give me orders to go to Seattle. I got on the ferry, go over there, go in a office building, get my orders, come back. I had two days to show up for this new ship. I was broke and out of money, so I went back to *Tennessee* and stayed there till time to go so I had a place to eat and sleep.

When it's time to check in to the new ship, I go down there to the chief petty officer on duty, and I showed him my orders. I said, "Where is this ship, Chief?" He said, "Go down to the end of the pier. It's right down there." Well, YMS-102 is on the bow of this thing. It stood for yard minesweeper. I didn't go far enough to see that, so I go back and tell the chief. I never got over that. I said, "Chief, you're mistaken. There ain't nothing down there but a fishing boat." He come back to me and said, "I tell you what you do, son. You go get all your fishing gear together and you come back because that's the one you're going on." Man, that thing wasn't much bigger than our motor launches on that battleship. I stayed on there '42, '43.

Then they transferred me to the escort carrier USS *Petrof Bay.*[16] I got on that carrier and finished out the war. A lot of people don't know, but we gave fuel oil to Franklin Delano Roosevelt Jr.'s little destroyer escort.[17] A little while later we got the word President Roosevelt had died,[18] and then they flew his son off, back to the States.

The last fourteen months of the war on that carrier, we went nine months in combat out of the fourteen. In the process we were awarded the Presidential Unit Citation on that ship. There was more of the little carriers earned that than the other two class of carriers put together. I think it was six of us or seven, and we was awarded that. The Philippine government awarded us a presidential citation, too.

I remember Iwo Jima because Edwin was on it, my brother, and we hit it February 19, 1945. We went through the Luzon operation, Western Caroline Islands operations, the Leyte Gulf operation, Iwo Jima, Okinawa, Tarawa, and the Marianas. Man, we covered everything. I stayed a year and two weeks on the carrier, never stepped foot off. And Charlie[19] that was on the *Tennessee* with me, they took him off, put him on a destroyer in September of '42, and he stepped off twice in two years. Now, he's got a story. He come home, met his wife one day and married her the next. They just celebrated their sixty-fifth wedding anniversary. The other day I said to him, "Y'all was desperate, wasn't you?"

Now, as to how I got married. We'd invaded Okinawa April 1, Easter Sunday, '45. We'd cleared April, and we was into latter part of May. We come down with engine trouble, and they told us we was going to have to get major repairs. The floating dry docks over there were full, the ones in Pearl Harbor were full, so they sent us into San Pedro.[20] I was standing on the fantail one day, and the skipper come down. We got to talking, and while we was talking, I said, "Man, I wish I could go do something I'd like to do." He said, "What is it you'd like to do?" I said, "I wouldn't do it earlier, but I'd like to go home and get married."

He said, "How you know she'll marry you?" I said, "Well, about three months ago I mailed her a letter and told her I didn't know when I'd get home, and it's a possibility I may not make it home. But if I get home again, we're getting married." And I said, "I ain't had a negative reply yet, and I've received lots of letters." He says, "Go up and tell the yeoman to give you a ten-day emergency leave home. You're going to have to fly." So I flew home, we got married, and I took her back to California with us.

You know, the war is tattooed on your soul. You're never going to forget it. You might forget small details and dates. But the one thing that I liked that we ain't got now: the whole nation was one family. Part of the family had to go to war and fight the war and win the war. The rest of it stayed here: made, produced, melted, made all the sacrifices, had all the victory gardens, and built what it took for us to win the war.

Following his marriage to Alma Louise "Toots" Head in Waco in 1945, Curre continued his love affair with Cameron Park. Toots was the daughter of J. W. Head, who worked for the park for almost five decades. The couple had two daughters and had been married forty-nine years at the time of Toots's death in 1994. In the fall of 1946, Curre embarked on a sixty-year career as pressman with the Waco News-Tribune *and the* Waco Times-Herald. *(The two newspapers merged in 1973 to form the* Waco Tribune-Herald.*) In his* *later years, Curre spoke at area schools, honestly recounting his war experiences so students would have more than a textbook understanding of World War II. He passed away on December 7, 2011, the seventieth anniversary of the attack on Pearl Harbor.*

Frank Curre was interviewed by a graduate student in the Baylor University Department of History as part of a master's thesis project on Waco's Cameron Park. The student went back a second time to gather Curre's memories of the attack on Pearl Harbor. Frank Curre Jr., *Oral Memoirs of Frank Curre Jr.*, interviews conducted by Mark Firmin, January 29 and May 23, 2009, in Waco, Texas, BU Digital Collections.

Notes

1. A minority cruise was typically a four-year hitch.
2. In navy lingo, *dogs* are metal levers used to secure hatches, or doors, against water and fire.
3. Indeed, spies were very much involved in the attack. After May 1940, when the United States based its fleet at Pearl Harbor, the Japanese Foreign Office kept tabs on the US Navy and its ship movements by asking the Japanese Consulate in Honolulu to cable regular reports. In March 1941, Japan even sent a trained intelligence agent, Takeo Yoshikawa, to its Honolulu office. For four years prior to his arrival, Yoshikawa had studied the English language, the US Pacific Fleet, and the US bases at Guam, Manila, and Pearl Harbor. In 1941 he routinely scouted the area of Oahu, making detailed notes and charts until he detected a pattern that allowed the Japanese to carry out their attack successfully. Gordon W. Prange, *At Dawn We Slept: The Untold Story of Pearl Harbor* (New York: McGraw-Hill, 1981), 70–77.
4. The rising sun insignia, a solid red circle, painted on Japanese aircraft.
5. Capt. Mervyn Bennion of the *West Virginia* sustained fatal wounds from that bomb when a large piece of shrapnel entered his abdomen, but he remained conscious for a time and refused attempts to move him from the bridge. While dying, Bennion asked for updates on how the *West Virginia* was faring and voiced his concerns about fires on board and about the oil covering the surface of the water. He was awarded the Medal of Honor posthumously. Bill McWilliams, *Sunday in Hell: Pearl Harbor Minute by Minute* (New York: E-reads, 2011), 313, 318.
6. When standing on a ship facing the front, "starboard" is the right side.

7. In his official report on the attack, the commanding officer of the *Tennessee,* Capt. C. E. Reordan, commended Lewis W. Adkins for his actions on December 7: "In charge of the after repair party, his leadership and heroic conduct while fighting the fires contributed much toward saving the ship from destruction. Throughout the attack he was in an exposed position and continued to fight the fires until they were brought under control." "USS *Tennessee,* Report of Pearl Harbor Attack," C. E. Reordan, Department of the Navy, Naval Historical Center, published online May 23, 2001, http://www.history.navy.mil/docs/wwii/pearl/ph89.htm#anchor415563.

8. Toward the rear of the ship.

9. When standing on a ship facing the front, "port" is the left side.

10. Navy salvage divers had hammered on the *West Virginia* hull on December 12 and heard no response. The position of the ship made it impossible to hammer on all sides, and the extensive damage the ship sustained likely prevented the divers' sounds from traveling through the hull. The trapped men had access to battle lanterns and marked on a calendar the days they survived below decks. Edward C. Raymer, *Descent into Darkness: Pearl Harbor, 1941: A Navy Diver's Memoir* (Novato, CA: Presidio Press, 1996), 124–25. The navy never informed the families about the experiences of these three men, and their headstones record their last day as December 7, 1941. Family members and friends who learned the truth usually kept it to themselves, to protect others from the grief. "Pearl Harbor: 16 Days to Die—Trapped by the Memories—Few Knew the Secret of the Sunken Battleship; Families Weren't Told of Sailors' Lingering Deaths," Eric Gregory, the *Seattle Times,* published online December 7, 1995, http://community.seattletimes.nwsource.com/archive/?date=19951207&slug=2156455.

11. The USS *Solace,* a hospital ship, was stationed at Pearl Harbor at the time of the attack and played a crucial role in the aftermath. Her crew cared for many of the wounded, and her two motor launches rescued dozens of men from the stricken battleships and the oily, burning waters. The Japanese did not strike the hospital ship, which was painted white and bore red crosses. McWilliams, *Sunday in Hell,* 547–50.

12. The fires aboard the *West Virginia* took thirty hours to extinguish and caused extensive damage to the interior. The sheer fury of the blazes was attributed to the oil-based paint used on the bulkhead. Not long after Pearl Harbor and horrendous ship fires in the Solomon Islands, the navy ordered the removal of all oil-based paint and other combus-

tibles from warships. Raymer, *Descent into Darkness,* 113; Rick Atkinson, *An Army at Dawn: The War in North Africa, 1942–1943,* vol. 1 of *The Liberation Trilogy* (New York: Henry Holt, 2002), 33.

13. Jack Kelley, a shipmate on the *Tennessee* who also stepped onto the *Arizona* after the attack, remembered, "I wished I hadn't gone aboard after I went aboard because there were pieces of burnt bodies and little dabs of clothing, helmets, and, well, just half-charred bodies all over the place. They gave off quite an offensive odor." Robert S. La Forte and Ronald E. Marcello, eds., *Remembering Pearl Harbor: Eyewitness Accounts by US Military Men and Women* (Wilmington, DE: Scholarly Resources, 1991), 58.

14. Battleship Row at Pearl Harbor.

15. The attack on Pearl Harbor was a surprise to Americans, but evidence suggests that officials in Washington, including President Roosevelt, knew the attack was coming and even provoked it, wanting a reason to enter the war. See George Morgenstern, *Pearl Harbor: The Story of the Secret War* (New York: Devin-Adair, 1947); Percy L. Greaves Jr., *Pearl Harbor: The Seeds and Fruits of Infamy* (Auburn, AL: Ludwig von Mises Institute, 2010); Robert B. Stinnett, *Day of Deceit: The Truth about FDR and Pearl Harbor* (New York: Touchstone, 2000); Prange, *At Dawn We Slept.*

16. For more on the *Petrof Bay,* including some of Curre's actions while serving on it, see Rick Cline, *Escort Carrier WWII: War in the Pacific on the Aircraft Carrier USS* Petrof Bay (Placentia, CA: R. A. Cline, 1998). Cline interviewed Curre and other crew members for the book.

17. Lt. Cmdr. Franklin D. Roosevelt Jr. commanded the USS *Ulvert M. Moore.*

18. President Roosevelt passed away on April 12, 1945, during the Battle of Okinawa.

19. Charlie Boswell.

20. *Petrof Bay* arrived at Terminal Island, San Pedro, California, on June 19, 1945. Cline, *Escort Carrier WWII,* 194.

RICHARD E. "DICK" COLE

Born in Dayton, Ohio, in September 1915, Richard E. "Dick" Cole grew up watching flight tests at nearby McCook Field, an aviation experimentation station located in a narrow floodplain between the Great Miami and Stillwater Rivers. He rode his bicycle to a levee above the field and watched the planes take off and land. Having seen a Curtiss Hawk airplane flying security over an armored car that made monthly payroll runs between the airfield and a bank, he grew up wanting to chase bad guys in an airplane. He fed his interest in flying by keeping a scrapbook of everything he could find on aviation and by talking to the test pilots who were customers on his paper route at the airfield. Later, at Ohio University, in Athens, Ohio, Cole signed up for the Civilian Pilot Training Program. He completed ground school by taking night classes at Wittenberg University, in Springfield, Ohio. While taking flight lessons, he worked for one of William Powell Lear's companies that manufactured radio compass equipment in Vandalia, Ohio. His boss allowed him to take off work during the daytime to complete his flying hours and earn his pilot's license. In 1940 Cole enlisted in the US Army Air Corps. He completed primary training at Parks Air College, East St. Louis, Illinois, and flight school at Randolph and Kelly Fields in San Antonio, Texas. Upon graduating from Kelly Field in July 1941, he was commissioned a second lieutenant and assigned to the 17th Bombardment Group of the 34th Bombardment Squadron at Pendleton Field, in Pendleton, Oregon.

When we arrived at Pendleton, the group was on maneuvers up at Spokane, Washington. So right away I was TDY[1] up there. But I joined it at Spokane, and the airplanes we had were the B-23 and the B-18. In about a month we got the first B-25, and the B-25 was an airplane that was bought off the shelf. It was never given any kind of test program. So we went to the factory and picked up all the aircraft that we were authorized for and left Spokane, flew to Jackson, Mississippi, and Augusta, Georgia. The B-25 was speedy, easy to fly, handled nice. It was fun to fly it. They carried six people: had an upper turret and a lower turret, a navigator, a bombardier, and the two pilots. We operated out of Augusta on war maneuvers with the army, flew up into North Carolina and South Carolina. We did that until about

Thanksgiving of '41. Then we got orders to return to Pendleton, and we flew to March Field in Riverside, California, and arrived there on December 5.

When we arrived in March Field, Colonel Peck[2] gave everybody what they called "open post," which meant that we could go anyplace we wanted to go as long as we were back by midnight on Sunday night. So everybody went to Hollywood, and we were in the Hollywood Plaza Hotel when I heard about Pearl Harbor. I was probably apprehensive of what was going to happen, maybe a little bit scared. What have I got myself into? But you're there, and you've got to put up with it.

We flew right back up to Pendleton and did some modification on the bomb loading we had and flew over to Portland, Oregon, and to Everett, Seattle, and Tacoma, Washington, and went on submarine patrol. We were stationed at Portland and Tacoma. They worked out a grid map, and we would fly so far out and then turn around and come back and go back and forth. Nobody in our group or squadron ever saw anything. We saw a lot of whales. But Everett "Brick" Holstrom, who was one of the Doolittle Raiders, was in the 95th Squadron—they were up at Everett, Washington—he sank a sub.[3] The rest of ours was just looking at the water. We had to put up with bad weather, too. They had a big sleet storm when we were at Portland, and all the aircraft got frozen to the ground.

We did that until the latter part of January, and we got orders to be transferred to Columbia, South Carolina. On the fourteenth of February—and I remember it well—we left Pendleton and headed out toward Columbia. On our way to Columbia, the guy that I was flying with upgraded me to first pilot. In Columbia we heard that there was to be a special mission, and I signed up for it. I was probably thinking about getting more flying time because becoming a pilot is in steps. First, you get to be a pilot, and then you see these people with wings with a wreath around it. Then you see one with a star. And you start to try and upgrade yourself, and you have to do that by length of service and amount of flying time.

They didn't tell us anything about the mission. The guy who had upgraded me wanted to know if we could go together. I talked to the rest of the crew, and they were willing, so we went there with him. We went down to Eglin Field, in Florida, and after we got down there, we did some local flying and so forth. Colonel Jimmy Doolittle came and gave us a briefing, said it was dangerous, and if you volunteered and changed your mind, nothing would be said about it. You could back out. But after you think about it awhile, we were the only group that had B-25s and the only ones that had been flying them. So it didn't make any difference whether we volunteered or not, we were going to go. I don't know of anybody who backed out. The whole group volunteered, even the group commander. I know that later, on board the carrier, some of the reserve crews that went down to Eglin and trained with us were offering five hundred bucks to trade seats.

My individual thought was we were going to be taken some place in the Pacific, take off, and go to a predesignated airfield that they had selected and fight the war there because you had a squadron commander, you had a squadron airplane, and you had the necessary crews. It wasn't till we left Alameda, California, and were two days at sea that they told us, "This force is bound for Tokyo." That's when you started thinking, Eek!

While we were on the carrier, the USS *Hornet,* Colonel Doolittle divided up the pilots targetwise. He gave them their permission how they wanted to fly it and so forth. Actually, we were supposed to take off on the nineteenth of April. We were to take off at dusk, bomb Tokyo, fly all night, land at Chuchow in China, and gas up and go on into western China. That way Colonel Chennault[4] would have a B-25 squadron.

Well, a lot of flip-flops. They had planned to have a portable homer[5] at Chuchow, but the airplane carrying the homer crashed, killed everybody on board, and never got there. They never told Chennault we were coming. They told somebody in the Tenth Air Force, or somebody in the Tenth Air Force knew, but they didn't tell Chennault.[6] We got picked up by the Japanese early, by a fishing boat, so that screwed that up. We had to launch early, about a couple of hundred and fifty miles farther out from Japan than we wanted to be, and right away fuel became a problem. But we had to launch, so we launched on the morning of April 18.

We were the first plane to take off. We were what they later on called a pathfinder airplane because we had nothing but incendiary bombs. Doolittle was the pilot; I was the copilot; Hank Potter was navigator; Fred Braemer, bombardier; and Paul Leonard, engineer/gunner. Our target was northwest Tokyo. The weather was pretty lousy when we took off. Early on everybody thought that the takeoff was going to be the most challenging thing, but actually it was easiest. We got off in good shape. We circled back over the carrier. They held up a big chalkboard with the heading to Japan on it, Tokyo. So we flew maybe a hour out. We saw a big four-engine Japanese flying boat pass overhead, but apparently they didn't see us. And we saw some surface vessels, and we tried to avoid those.

The USS *Hornet*, with US Navy escorts, carried the sixteen North American B-25 medium bombers that on April 18, 1942, successfully completed the first Allied air raid on the Japanese home islands. *Courtesy of US Air Force.*

We're about, oh, three hundred feet. The whole thing was flown at low level. The only time we were higher than that was when we made the bombing run at fifteen hundred feet and when we climbed up to bail out. Anyway, flying into Japan was pretty uneventful. We got over the coast, and I thought it was very pretty, nice and green. Everything was horticultured, in rows. And we could see Tokyo Bay. So we flew in maybe ten miles and turned south. As we approached Tokyo, Doolittle pulled up to fifteen hundred feet. They had given Fred Braemer photos, and he picked out his aiming point, and we dropped our bombs and were right back down on the deck.

While we were on the bombing run, antiaircraft fire popped up all around us and jostled us around. It wasn't accurate, but it was pretty intense. And as soon as we dropped the bombs, we went back down on the deck and flew out about seventy-five miles parallel to the [Japanese islands] chain, where we could see it all the time. But I don't think anybody saw us.

After a couple of hours, Hank Potter, the navigator, passed a note up saying we're going to end up a hundred and eighty miles short of the China coast based on his fuel figures. So at that time, we went through ditching procedure. Nobody was anxious about ditching, particularly because when we were flying lower there, you'd see these sharks laying up on top of the water. But Doolittle got on the interphone and said that if we have to ditch, we're going to ditch by a friendly vessel, and they'll take us aboard and we'll get to a friendly port. If we have to ditch by a enemy vessel, they'll take us aboard. And if we can, we'll take over that vessel and get to a friendly port. But as it happened, lucky, we didn't have to ditch.

Well, while we were flying toward China, there was a big warm front over China that created a tailwind, which made it so every airplane could get to China except the one that went to Russia. The tailwind was about thirty knots, and that's what we needed. I don't know whose lucky star was doing the guiding, but somebody's was. Everybody thinks the airplane that went to Russia did so on purpose, but you'd never get anybody to admit it.

But all this time we were flying over the China Sea, we were dead reckoning.[7] We had no navigation aids. The navigator couldn't take a drift meter because everything was low level. We were most of the time below three hundred feet, and it was very choppy and windy. The drift meter got covered up with salt spray, so we couldn't measure our drift. With the high overcast, you couldn't take a sun shot, so we were dead reckoning. The navigator, Hank Potter, did a real good job. There's an island at the end of the Japanese chain called Yakushima. It's nothing but a big old volcanic thing sticking out of the water. It wasn't armed, and we took a beam of it about, oh, maybe ten miles. We could see it. From there he plotted a dead reckoning thing toward Chuchow, and he did an excellent job.

But instead of getting there at the time that we wanted to, we got there at dusk on the night of the eighteenth. The Chinese, on hearing our engines, shut off all electricity because they thought we were Japanese. The weather was bad, so we had to climb up to nine thousand feet and go on instruments and fly until we ran out of gas and jumped out. We landed in an area about sixty miles north of the place we were supposed to be. After bailout, the big problem was the weather was socked in. You couldn't see the ground with the big thunderstorms and lightning, rain. The big apprehensive point I guess was, how am I going to hit, and where am I going to hit?

Fortunately my chute drifted over a pine tree, and I never hit the ground. So I pulled the chute in and made kind of a deal like a hammock so I could rest my legs instead of having to hang down. I spent the night there in the tree. I was too scared to sleep, but I know I dozed off. There was a hook to that, because you were afraid you were going to fall out of the tree. But fortunately I didn't. Next morning when you could see the ground, I was about twelve feet high off the ground. I climbed down and started walking.

The five-member crew of the lead plane in the historic Doolittle Raid over Japan in April 1942 pose in front of their B25 aircraft aboard the USS *Hornet*. Left to right: Lt. Henry A. Potter, navigator; Lt. Col. Jimmy Doolittle, pilot and mission commander; Staff Sgt. Fred A. Braemer, bombardier; Lt. Richard E. Cole, copilot; Staff Sgt. Paul J. Leonard, flight engineer/gunner. *Courtesy of US Air Force.*

The only preparation we had for China was that on the carrier they had a navy officer that had been an attaché to Japan.[8] He's the one that got the Japanese medals that you see in the picture of Doolittle tying them on the bomb. He could speak fluent Japanese and some Chinese. He said, "If you are accosted by someone, say, 'Lushu hoo megwa fugi,' and say, 'I am an American.'" So we got that down pat. The only problem was, it was the wrong dialect. The other thing we went by was, if you're accosted and the individual smiles, he's Chinese. If he's very stern-looking, so forth, Japanese.

I met a woodcutter who looked at me, and I looked at him. He didn't say anything; I didn't say anything. I kept walking. But there were two young men that accosted me. I don't know whether they were Chinese or not. I eventually ran them off with my .45 and kept walking. I found Doolittle. China still had warlords then, and the provinces had their own military. Apparently we were in occupied territory and were picked up by warlord personnel. We didn't care who it was, though, as long as they weren't Japanese. It was about ten days before we got to a place called Hengyang, where the Flying Tigers had a couple of airplanes and a couple of pilots and maintenance people. A C-47 came in and picked us up and took us to Chungking.

After Chungking, they gave us a debriefing. Everybody had lost everything. We only had the clothes we had on. We went to Calcutta, in India, and got new uniforms and got paid. And one of the deals, a carrot, that they offered when you volunteered for the mission: If you survive the mission, you'll get to come home. Well, there were twenty of us that didn't get to come home. Orders were in File 13[9] or someplace, but we didn't get to come home. In the case of the twenty, some of them went to outfits there in India. There were, I think, twelve of us who went back to China to Kunming. They had four B-25s. We were there for maybe a month.

But in the meantime they had an influx of a whole big boatload of aircraft crews. They ended up with something like thirty-seven crews and four airplanes. Nobody was getting any flying time. The conditions weren't too good, and the morale wasn't that great. So they put out a feeler that they were looking for pilots to fly the Hump between India and China.[10] So I think five of us volunteered to do that. I got checked out in a C-47 and the next day started flying the Hump. We did that till late June of 1943. I left there the last week in June 1943. But during that time we flew C-47s, and in December of '42, they brought over some C-87s, the cargo version of a B-24, and we flew those until we got to come home. It was only a six-hour flight, and in a C-47, you could carry about eight and a half hours of fuel. One good thing about a C-87 is it had turbo and you could go to thirty thousand feet. You were pretty much limited to twenty thousand in a C-47. Jake Sartz was my roommate while we were on the Hump. And you may have heard this story: the last airplane that left Rangoon before the Japanese took it took off with seventy-two people. When it landed in India, there were seventy-three. A baby was born on board. Anyway, he flew that airplane.

In June 1943 I got transferred back to the States. I was sent to Love Field up at Dallas. From there I was sent to Tulsa, Oklahoma, to the Douglas Aircraft Plant, as what they called a ferry control officer. My job was to accept the airplane from the factory. And when the pilot came in to pick up the airplane to take it to Salina, Kansas, or someplace—because they were making B-24s then—he would sign for the airplane. Another part of my job was the acceptance test pilot, so that I could go out on the flight line and select any airplane that the contractor had turned over to the military and take it up and test to see if they were doing there what they were supposed to be doing, which was a good job. In addition to that, they had a modification center on the other side of the field. They had all kinds of airplanes: A-20s, DB-7s, B-25s and B-17s, P-61s, SNJ, and the dive bomber. Had all different kinds there. So I got to fly those, and I was happy.

I got married in the meantime. I'd met a gal there in Tulsa. We hit it off, and so I got married. My wife's name is Martha. She had signed up and was taking flying lessons at Spartan Air School[11] to go into the WASP[12] program. She'd already soloed and was just about finished to get ready to be transferred up to Sweetwater.[13] Well, we met each other, and we got married in two weeks. I was there till the middle of September 1943, and I got a call from a guy by the name of Johnny Alison.[14] He was a fighter pilot, and he was with the Flying Tigers. I got to know him, and he wanted to know if I wanted to go back overseas with the 1st Air Commando Group. I said yeah. I left there in October. Martha and I had our honeymoon between Dallas and North Carolina.

We got to Goldsboro, North Carolina, in the 1st Air Commando Group. We did a lot of training with the gliders. When they got the gliders and everything ready, why, we went to India and did more training over there. I went in a C-47. I was the engineering officer and led a flight of five over there to India. And then in March of '44, why, we invaded Burma. I was the third airplane in. The commander of the transport, the glider corps, was a guy by the name of Bill Cherry. He was the pilot on that B-17 with Eddie Rickenbacker. Bill was also an American Airlines pilot, and he was the commander. The operations officer was a guy by the name of Jake Sartz, who was my roommate while we were on the Hump.[15] I stayed there till the end of July in 1944.

When I came back, I got sent back to Tulsa to test planes again. I stayed there until the fall of 1945. With the war's end, they reduced people there at the plant, so I got assigned to Victorville Army Air Field in California, which later became George Air Force Base. They were receiving all the B-29s coming from the Far East, taking out all the unnecessary equipment and so forth, and then flying them from there down to Arizona, which was another good job. And then they had the big exodus, where all the reserve officers were put on inactive status, and so I started back to college. We had a child by then. I went to Corvallis, Oregon, and enrolled in a school of forestry there while I was waiting to get in and go to school. I got a job working at a sawmill.

I don't think I ever got any news about the reaction to the Doolittle Raid back home. Actually, we never even knew, though, what the raid was intended for. The two reasons which came out later was that, number one, it was to let the Japanese people know that their island wasn't invulnerable to air attack, and the other was for the morale of the Americans and the Allies. Fortunately it did that. It did one other thing: when the raid happened, right away the Japanese thought there were going to be more. So they pulled in forces that were down by

Australia, and they definitely had plans to invade India. But when they pulled those things back to the homeland and concentrated more in the Pacific, they sent two carriers to Alaska. For what reason, nobody knows. They had seven, and that made them only have five in the Battle of Midway. That evened up the odds with the navy, and the navy was able to beat them. That was one of the few turning points in the war.

In June 1947 Dick Cole was recalled into service and sent to Wright-Patterson Field, Ohio, to fly special missions, transporting VIPs to and from Air Mobility Command headquarters. In 1952 he entered the Armed Forces Staff College in Norfolk, Virginia, and after graduation was assigned to the training office of the Far East Air Force headquarters in Korea. Next he worked at the Pentagon, and while there he went to jet school. After becoming jet qualified, he rounded out his peacetime military service as a command pilot, serving in Ohio, Washington, DC, North Carolina, California, and Venezuela. He retired in 1967 as a lieutenant colonel. Cole earned the Distinguished Flying Cross with two oak-leaf clusters, the Air Medal with one oak-leaf cluster, the Bronze Star, the Air Force Commendation Medal, a Presidential Unit Citation, and the Chinese Army, Navy, Air Corps Medal Class A First Grade. After his military retirement he settled in Comfort, Texas, where he had a construction business.[16] *On Memorial Day 2014, ninety-eight-year-old Dick Cole accepted the Medal of Honor from President Barack Obama on behalf of the eighty original Doolittle Raiders, of whom only four still survived.*[17]

Dick Cole was interviewed for the project Here and There: Recollections of Texas in World War II, funded by a grant from the Texas Historical Commission. Richard (Dick) E. Cole, *Oral Memoirs of Richard (Dick) E. Cole*, an interview conducted by Stephen Sloan, July 16, 2009, in Comfort, Texas, BU Digital Collections.

Notes

1. Temporary duty.
2. Walter R. Peck commanded the 17th Bombardment Group March 1941 to February 1942. "17th Bomb Group WWII," 17th Bomb Group, accessed June 30, 2014, http://bombgroup17.com/17th_bg_wwii.
3. Ted W. Lawson, *Thirty Seconds over Tokyo* (New York: Random House, 1943), 14, gives an eyewitness account of Holstrom's sinking of a Japanese submarine near the mouth of the Columbia River.
4. At the time of the Tokyo raid, Claire Lee Chennault led the all-volunteer Flying Tigers in support of the Chinese against Japan. See

Robert Hotz, ed., *Way of a Fighter: The Memoirs of Claire Lee Chennault* (New York: C. P. Putnam's Sons, 1949).

5. Homing device.

6. Martha Byrd, *Chennault: Giving Wings to the Tiger* (Tuscaloosa: University of Alabama Press, 1987), 148, confirms Chennault's ignorance of the mission.

7. "Dead reckoning" is using only the compass heading, air speed, time, and estimated or known drift to plot the aircraft's course and location on a map.

8. The former naval attaché was Stephen Jurika. James H. "Jimmy" Doolittle and Carroll V. Glines, *I Could Never Be So Lucky Again: An Autobiography* (New York: Bantam Books, 1991), 10–11, 265.

9. Military slang meaning "the trash."

10. The "Hump" refers both to the rugged Himalayas mountain range between India and China and to the airlifting of personnel and supplies over the mountains to support China's defense against Japan. John D. Plating, *The Hump: America's Strategy for Keeping China in World War II* (College Station: Texas A&M University Press, 2011).

11. Spartan School of Flight, Tulsa, Oklahoma.

12. Women Airforce Service Pilots.

13. WASPs trained at Avenger Field in Sweetwater, Texas.

14. The 1st Air Commando Group, co-commanded by John R. Alison and Philip G. Cochran, led the first Allied all-aerial invasion behind enemy lines. R. D. Van Wagner, *Any Place, Any Time, Any Where: The 1st Air Commandos in World War II* (Atglen, PA: Schiffer Publishing, 1998), 21–23, 42–57.

15. After the B-17 Flying Fortress piloted by William T. Cherry Jr. ditched in the Pacific, the crew drifted in life rafts for twenty-four days. The ill-fated plane was carrying former World War I flying ace Eddie Rickenbacker on a tour of Pacific air bases. James C. Whittaker, *We Thought We Heard the Angels Sing* (New York: Dutton, 1943). On Cherry, Sartz, and Cole's roles in the 1st Air Commando transport section, see Van Wagner, *Any Place,* 26 (photo), 44.

16. "Biography of Richard E. Cole," Richard E. Cole Collection MSS #191, Robert E. and Jean R. Mahn Center for Archives and Special

Collections, Ohio University, Athens, accessed August 9, 2013, http://www.library.ohiou.edu/archives/mss/mss191.pdf.

17. Antonio Olivo, "'Doolittle Raiders' Receive Congressional Gold Medal," *Washington Post,* May 25, 2014, accessed November 24, 2014, http://www.washingtonpost.com/local/doolittle-raiders-awarded-congressional-gold-medal/2014/05/25/de05e9aa-e27e-11e3-8dcc-d6b7fede081a_story.html.

GEORGE C. MCDOWELL

George McDowell was born in 1913 in Detroit, Texas, the son of a traveling salesman and a teacher. While growing up in the Oak Cliff neighborhood near Dallas with his sister and two brothers, he earned money delivering packages for a drugstore, delivering newspapers for the Dallas Morning News, *and working at a Texaco filling station. McDowell participated in ROTC at Oak Cliff High School and North Texas Agricultural College, graduating from the latter in 1932. Next he enrolled at a senior college but could afford to stay only a few weeks and returned home, where he continued to take classes at NTAC. Because of the bleak job market, McDowell's goal was to stay in school, and he knew he had to go where tuition and expenses would be covered. In 1933 he won a competitive appointment to the US Military Academy at West Point, where he met such luminaries as Omar Bradley, who taught him how to fly-fish. After graduating with the class of 1937, McDowell was stationed at Fort Sill, Oklahoma, where he was assigned to the 18th Field Artillery, one of the last horse-drawn artillery regiments. While McDowell was at Fort Sill, William Childs Westmoreland introduced him to Rae Woods. They married in 1939.*

I WAS AT FORT SILL ABOUT A YEAR AND A HALF. I took an assignment in the ordnance department from Fort Sill and thought it was going to be temporary. It turned out to be permanent. The air corps was wanting to get aviation ordnance people to handle bombs and fuses, so the army established a school at Aberdeen Proving Ground.[1] I went up there for three months, and then the last three months were at Langley Field, Virginia. Then I stayed on as an instructor for about six months to the subsequent classes coming through. But that's where we started developing techniques for handling bombs for airplanes, and that's what I got involved in.

The B-17s had just come into being about that time. And you had to have a way of hauling bombs from a bomb dump on some kind of vehicle, to put it underneath the airplane and hoist them back up into the bomb bays. So we developed trailer type of things that could be hooked on behind two-and-a-half-ton trucks, and then the bomb hoist in the plane hooked on to the bombs going up there. The equipment we developed would only accommodate up to one-thousand-pound bombs. Later on we should have been handling two-thousand-pound bombs, but the airplanes wouldn't have carried it anyway. Later on we didn't have any planes that would carry two-thousand-pound bombs. The British did, but we didn't.

I left Langley Field to go to Bowman Field, Louisville, Kentucky. They were opening up that as a new airfield.[2] I took my ordnance organization, together with a bunch of air corps members. I was in charge of the truck movement of the whole thing from Langley Field to Louisville, Kentucky. That took about three days. We had about a hundred and twenty vehicles of different kinds. I'd call ahead and make state troopers escort us. We were moving people and vehicles.

We opened up Bowman Field, and I was there on the seventh of December, 1941. By that time we already had an A-20 group move in there. They were practicing air support. I remember we had a big party the night of sixth of December. About nine o'clock in the morning I got a phone call. My wife was going down to visit her folks at Fort Sill with our son, who was only three months old at that time.

So I got a phone call and says, "Have you turned your radio on?" I said no. They said, "Well, turn it on." I wasn't quite comprehending what had happened. They didn't say battleships had been sunk or anything like that. They just said the Japs had struck and were attacking. My West Point roommate was at Schofield Barracks:[3] Colin Kelly. He was the first one of our class that got killed. He was flying a B-17 in the Philippines and got shot down. He got all his crew out, but he didn't get out himself. He got the Distinguished Service Cross for that.[4] His son later on was a chaplain in the army. Colin Kelly and I used to sit next to each other in the choir.

So about noon the next day, I got a call from base to come out there. We had a brigadier general there, Junius Wallace Jones.[5] I'll never forget him. Junius Wallace Jones had the whole staff out there. He walked out and says, "Gentlemen, today we go to work." That conference took place around the eighth because that was after Roosevelt's speech.

We got orientation at Mitchel Field.[6] They had a week of flying in AT-10 bombers. I was all for it. I wanted to go to flying school, but the flight surgeon at Fort Sill, the one that passed everybody on tests, said, "I'm not going to pass you." I don't know why. He had some reason. I think he said deviated septum of the nose or some thing. So I didn't get to go to flying school.

But later on in World War II, I did a hell of a lot of flying. In Italy we had about three C-61s, single-engine monoplanes that the British had. They were manufactured here, but the British bought them, and we had some of them down there with us. It was a hell of a nice airplane. I had all these pilots working for me. They said, "Hell, you might as well learn to fly this damn thing." So I did. I got about five hundred hours flying until my boss, General John Cannon,[7] caught me. Oh, he gave me hell.

Before December 7 we were sitting here looking at the war in Europe and thinking, One of these days we're probably going to have to be involved. Everything we did was oriented in that direction. It changed your perspective in thinking. We didn't know quite how we were going to get involved in it.

After December 7 the security became much more tight. That A-20 group started training more in earnest. I was ordnance officer. I had to start getting live ammunition and some other bombs and other stuff like that so that we could practice over Fort Knox, Kentucky, which was close by. They got ordered out down in Florida someplace where they could maneuver faster.

After I left Bowman Field I came to New Orleans, and we were creating a task force to go to Northern Ireland from all over the airfields in Louisiana, about four, including Barksdale and Alexandria. We were assembling these things by the day with headquarters we had in New Orleans. And all of a sudden they decided we weren't going to Ireland. I think the British said it's not necessary. It was too early. The cross-channel invasion was months and months away, and that was basically what it was supporting. All were bomber groups, B-25 and B-26. They said they'd be more useful in the Pacific and also in other places. They broke this organization up. One group headed for Egypt; one headed for the Pacific. They scattered them all over.[8]

I got ordered to Fort Leavenworth[9] to go to school for a few months. I trained in how to be a logistics officer, and that served real well. I ended up doing more than just planning for the ordnance aspects. I had to figure out vehicles and other things, mainly because nobody else around there knew how to do it.

Then from there I went to Birmingham, Alabama, and that was a air support command. I was only there about six weeks or two months when they decided to take us to Washington to become the air support section of General Patton's headquarters going to French Morocco. There were about thirty of us that were out there. We were told to report to the Munitions Building on Connecticut Avenue.

We get over there, and we've got the end of one building, upstairs and down, and General Patton had been designated as the commander of this force. He had a glass-enclosed office on the corner down there, and everybody else had desks. We were going to have about fifty-odd freighters in New York and about a comparable number down in Norfolk, and we were prepared to take all the supplies and everything clear across Africa, as far as we thought we were going. Of course we resupplied. But we were going to have to fight our way into French Morocco, and we didn't know to what degree the Germans had put the bite on the French down there.

We found out later they had some control, but the whole fighting operation ended in a few days.[10] From there on it was a case of pushing stuff across, because Eisenhower's force had come in through Algeria, right by Spanish Morocco, and they were pushing up toward Tunisia to intercept Rommel as he was coming around.[11] So working with Patton was a sporty operation.

At that time Patton wasn't known. I mean he was only a major general. When I first went there, in August of '42, at the Washington Munitions Building, Patton, he'd come out of his cubicle and walk around all the time and talk to people. My wife had come to visit me up there in Washington for a couple of days, and I was going to put her on a train going back out to Wright-Patterson[12] about six o'clock. About three o'clock I was bent over this desk, big charts of what I was putting on different ships and different places and what fuses and bomb loads and things, and hear a screech right beside me. It was a chair. I looked around; it was Patton.

He said, "Son, what are you doing?" I was a twenty-nine-year-old lieutenant colonel at that time. I had to explain to him what we were doing: laying out bomb loads for ships up in New York and Norfolk. He didn't say a word, kept looking. Finally he gets up and says, "Just be goddamned sure we got enough." He couldn't say anything without putting cusswords in it. And that movie, *Patton,* that George C. Scott made, I've seen that about three times. It was a very good portrayal of Patton. But they had to clean the language up.

In planning for Operation Torch, we weren't running into too many shortages. We were just running into knowing where we might tell somebody to start shipping it. The arsenals around — Watertown Arsenal and Watervliet Arsenal and some of them — they had better handles on where stuff was. I was dealing with them mostly, telling them to get some shipping orders on fast going to the ports to start loading that stuff. What we were really running into shortages of was signal trucks.[13] We wanted a lot more signal trucks than I could get hold of. I put a load of fifty jeeps on one freighter. I was cramming decks with everything that we could find, even in my own bag.

I was going on the *Conte Biancamano.*[14] It was following right behind the battleship *Texas* in a support convoy. I had ordered a whole

An Allied armada heads toward Morocco for Operation Torch, which began on November 8, 1942. *Courtesy of Associated Press.*

case of .50-caliber automatic pistols, put them in my room so that I could hand them out to anybody needing them. After we'd been over there about a year, I got a stack of paper wanting to know what I had done with those pistols. I thought, This is the most asinine thing I have ever seen in my life. I decided, I can be just as—I said, "The people that I gave these pistols to, they ran out of ammunition. In order to kill Germans, they threw the pistols at them."

When we got out on the ocean, as far as you could see there were ships. The navy destroyers were out because the German submarines were out there. That reminds me of a story about Patton. One day while we were in the Munitions Building, he wanted everybody assembled in one room. There were about a hundred and fifty people that were involved in planning: the officers; he had a few civilian secretaries in there. They were lining the walls and sitting around. At four o'clock Patton comes out and says, "Now, I can't impress on all of you the importance of the secrecy of what we're planning. If one word leaks out and those German submarine commanders get word of it, I want you to know you're sending seventy thousand men to their death." He turns around and starts walking. He comes back and he says, "And thirty-five thousand of them are going to hell."[15]

But anyway, we left in the dark. When we got outside the New York port, I thought, My God. As far as you could see were ships. This was the biggest convoy that the navy had ever pulled off. This is the support convoy. The assault convoy was delayed, and the fighting, it was going for nine days. It wasn't supposed to be but about three. The support convoy was encroaching too close on the tail of the assault convoy, so this admiral had us going between Cape Verde Islands and Canary Islands.[16] He turned this whole convoy around.

And right in the midst of it, here this typhoon comes. My gosh! This ship I was on, they couldn't steer from the bridge. They had to depend on the auxiliary steering from the fantail. I got to where I had to go back there where that helmsman was, watching for submarine periscopes. But when we were back there we ran into this cloud of rain. You couldn't see anything. We were probably in it an hour. When we broke out of it, here's a minelayer coming right close to us. He wasn't more than a hundred feet away. He didn't see us. All of a sudden there was a frantic maneuver, him pulling out, getting away. Visibility was such that you couldn't see anything, and we pitched around a lot.

Some other things. We were bunked about four officers into a bunk, into a real cramped space. We had five thousand troops on that ship, and the navy crew was running it. We were only serving two meals a day. I took a dim view. I was one of the senior army officers, and so I got about three or four others same rank as I was. We went up to the skipper. I said, "Look, we need to serve three meals a day on this thing. I know that there's enough food here to do it." He said, "We don't have the manpower." I said, "My God, we've got cooks galore, so let's start doing it." He agreed. We used some of the cooks out of our units to man the mess. It gave them something to do.

I went into Casablanca right soon as we could get off the ship: into a motor sailer,[17] get in dock. My job was to figure out where headquarters would be. We already had some advance notice of what potentially we could use: buildings and other things there. We knew that a lot of it had been sabotaged. But I found the Transatlantic Hotel was right around the corner from where Patton wanted to put his headquarters, so we combined that as a headquarters for the task force. I went in there, and we took over the Transatlantic Hotel. We found there was a French bar down the street from us, but the only way we could go was as an armed patrol because the Germans, they still had snipers on tops of some of these buildings. So we'd go as an armed patrol down each side, one watching the line on the other side and one on the other, tommy guns at the ready.

The Germans didn't have a big force down there. It was some contingent. As soon as they got wind of what was going on, they got the hell out of there. I don't know how they got out, but they did. There weren't any Germans in there when we got over there. It was French Moroccan goons.[18] And French Foreign Legion was there for a while.[19]

We'd only been there about three or four weeks when they decided to use French Moroccan airfields around there, about four or five, as a training base, indoctrination for crew training. And so our mission, instead of heading on for Tunisia, was to come back here and support this training operation right there, which is what we did. Eisenhower's forces moved on to Tunisia. We set up a supply line. But also our mission was to support this training operation that was going on there down at Marrakech.[20]

In fact, I was on my way down to Marrakech one day by myself in a jeep. This is across the boondocks. I looked, and there was a cloud of dust behind me. I thought, Boy, who the hell's coming like that? I slowed down right as he went by. Two stars on the front of that command car. I thought, Oh, I know. This is Patton. He pulls up in front of me. I stop. I get out, salute. He says, "Where's your helmet?" I said, "Well, sir, it's on the floor of my jeep back there." I was wearing a flight cap. He says, "McDowell, don't you know that I put out the order everybody has to wear a helmet?" I said, "Yes sir." He says, "You're fined ten dollars." Theater commander had authority to fine you, and we had scrip. We didn't have regular money. I pulled out ten dollars and handed it to him. He puts it in his billfold, starts walking back to his command car, turns around, laughs like hell, says, "Now, dammit, McDowell, wear that helmet!"

After we got into Casablanca, I had to brief Patton a lot of times. One time, after we'd been there about ten days' worth, we began to bring ships into where we could unload them at docks. Patton called General Cannon, who was my immediate boss, says, "I want somebody out of your section to go with me. I'm going on about a three- or four-hour look-see around here." Cannon says, "Yes sir." Then he says, "You're it." So I go down and get in this command car with Patton, and he's got a lieutenant colonel aide and a driver. We go down to the docks, and here we've got five-hundred-pound bombs; we've got fifty-five-gallon drums of aviation gasoline all interspersed. A German bombardier's heaven.

Patton said, "What's all this?" I said, "Well, General, you remember, back in the Munitions Building you told General Cannon that he was limited for air units to no more than 10 percent of the authorized vehicles for each unit, and General Muller[21] would be responsible for clearing docks and that type of thing." "Yeah, I remember." He tells his aide, "Get Muller going on cleaning this out," because we had designated a cork forest behind Casablanca—several square miles of cork forest back there, with roads in it—and it was a perfect ammunition dump. So they had to start clearing that up right away.

From there on we drove over to the airfield, and we've got these cantonment buildings[22] going up. Patton says, "What's all this?" I said, "Well, General, here you remember, last week we got a Teletype from Washington wanting to know if you would accept about two hundred women coming over here in a company of WAACs,[23] and you said yes." "Yeah, I remember." I said, "Well, General Muller called me and wanted to know where are we going to put these gals. I said, 'Hell, I don't know, General Muller. You know that the Germans sabotaged most of the office buildings or any buildings around here with pumping concrete into the sewer lines, so we can't use them as dormitories. But we do have two engineer battalions sitting out here just doing some superficial training. Why don't we put them to use and build some cantonment buildings right there?' And Muller said, 'That's a hell of a good idea.'" So we had three thousand engineer troops building about twenty cantonment buildings, one-story buildings. They scrounged lumber from everywhere they could for a hundred miles' radius of Casablanca.

We had twelve-foot concertina wire[24] going all around this thing, twelve foot at the bottom, twelve foot high. And General Patton says, "What's the meaning of all this wire?" I said, "General Muller and I thought we better put some kind of protection around these gals." And, oh, Patton didn't bat an eye. He turned to his aide and says, "Anybody in this command that starts in that wiring and don't get through is going to get tried." We get in the car and keep going.

Patton was excellent in dealing with the French in Casablanca because he'd been over in France. He knew a lot of French officers.[25] He negotiated the end of the fighting right there. He said, "There'll be nothing written. Gentlemen, you're professional soldiers; so are we. That's it." Nothing was ever written.[26]

General Cannon was a brigadier general when we went into Morocco. He was later a lieutenant general, commanding all of the British and American tactical air in Italy. He had four of us he always took with him, and I was one of those. You never knew what job you were going to have. We went into Morocco in November '42, and I was there until summer of '43 because we had this training operation going on, crew training. But also the 1st Armored Division had been pulled back from Tunisia and was back being rehabilitated. They were in a forest right above Rabat-Salé.[27]

Another time General Cannon was ordered to find some airfields on the other side of the Atlas Mountains over there in Morocco, in case the Germans decided to make a drive down through Spain, jump across from Gibraltar and down that way, so that we could pull back and still fight from over there. And Cannon, he got on me and said,

"I want you to take an armed patrol and go over there and find some airfields, some area that we could convert to airfields real fast." So I got about fifty-odd guys, and we started out, went over those mountains and got over there. We found about two or three areas.

We were coming back, and here on the skyline was this string of Arabs on camels. I looked through the glass, and they all had guns sticking up on their backs. Some of those Arabs were friendly to the German forces, and I wasn't quite sure what the hell they were up to, so I just halted. We had about twenty vehicles, two-and-a-half-ton trucks and jeeps. I said, "Let's make a circle here." As that column turned and turned toward us, I said, "Everybody get under these trucks. The first guy that pulls a rifle off of his shoulder, let him have it." They kept coming along on camels — slow, plodding, no rifles — so I walked out. I had a flag on my shoulder.[28] I walk out to see who the hell this was. And this Arab leader, he looked up and he saluted, turned around, then walked away. They headed out back the other way. So we didn't have any problems.

I was eleven hundred miles away from Tunisia, but we were feeding people up there all the time. The air support was limited wholly to P-40s and B-25s. But there wasn't much of that. Rommel was coming around pretty damn fast. That spring is when Eisenhower called Patton up forward to take command of the whole force up there, and that was when Patton began to make a name for himself.[29] Up to that time he was just another two-star general.

By that time Cannon had been made in charge of all American air units in North Africa. And then later, when we went to Italy, he was commanding all of the British as well as the American. So we moved from Casablanca to Constantine, Algeria. That was when Cannon was in charge of air support for the Tunisian operation. He was supporting Patton on that, too.

In Constantine I was primarily on ordnance. Staff meetings. Basically we were marking time, I think, more than anything else. We knew we were going up to Italy somewhere, and we didn't know to what degree we were going to be involved in the operation in Sicily. Sicily had to come first. So we had a fighter training field and a bomber training field right there that we sort of had moved from French Morocco. The workload was such that we could have only two fields, one for each: fighters and bombers. Basically that's what we were doing, and it was very light load.

On one occasion there, the air unit over in Italy had just gotten done supporting Salerno.[30] We found a big German diesel generator, and they wanted it over in Italy. So we loaded it on a C-47, and it would just barely fit in the thing. We were just within the load limits of a C-47. We took off and started over there. Ran into bad weather, and you didn't have any navigation aids. You had dead reckoning in time. But we ran into a hell of a thunderstorm, and it pushed us out on top at about fourteen thousand feet. We were on our back at one time. I looked out there, and the right wing was bent up, the last six feet of it. We were out clear in the desert, and we said, "Well, what do we do?"

Buckshot Taylor,[31] a good friend of mine, he was flying the thing then. I said, "Buck, what do you want to do?" Everybody had a parachute on. I said, "Think we ought to abandon this thing?" He said, "Let's see what it lands in." So we practiced landing on top of clouds. He said, "This thing don't stall out until you're just below a hundred miles an hour." The normal stalling speed is about seventy-eight to eighty, somewhere in there. So we flew that thing on a red diagonal[32] for about six weeks. It kept on going. Everybody who flew it had to know that it was a hot-landing airplane till I could get a wing panel—I finally got one put on there. But we delivered the generator.

I was in that plane another time going back to Algiers. And this British Spitfire, he was patrolling down on the Mediterranean like they did all the time because the Germans had Ju 88s they were running out there, too. But this Spitfire came alongside of us, pointed at that thing. We said, "Get away!" He couldn't believe that we were flying with a wing bent up like that.

We were number one getting supplies up until the sixth of June of 1944. Everything shifted to England. I'll never forget that day. We got a Teletype saying, "Sorry, we just sent this to England." We knew then that we were not number one on the supply chain. By that time Mark Clark was commanding the Fifth Army. But Cannon had established his headquarters about fifty miles north of Naples at Caserta Palace. That was about a thousand-room palace. The Fifth Army headquarters was there. Our support was there. The Eighth Army, they were on the other side.

But this was starting in the fall of '43. After we got to Italy, there were staff meetings every night where the operation orders were going out in support of both Fifth Army, American, and Eighth Army, British, going up Italy. We got to where every night at midnight, the operation orders went out to the groups at various places what operation was going to take place the next day, bombings and other things. I was responsible for seeing that we had the right bombs and fuses and everything for all of the support we had over in Corsica and in Italy.

The British insisted on bombing Monte Cassino Abbey that overlooked this valley about ten miles. I had information that the walls on that thing were eight feet thick in some places, and it was on the side of this mountain up there, a very imposing place. It had tunnels underneath it. The Germans were using it for an observation point, controlling that whole valley right there, and were dealing misery to the Fifth Army trying to get up through there.[33] I said, "All we've got is thousand-pound bombs. I mean, that's all we can put on. They're not going to touch these walls. All we're going to do is knock the roof in." Well, they insisted we put an airplane raid on that thing.

This master sergeant I had with me, I said, "Let's go up. We're going up there, and we're going to watch this raid." So we drove up there at night and found a sunken road where we could put our jeep down and get out of it. The bombing operation started right at daylight on February 15, 1944, and it did just what I said.[34] But in the meantime, there was a B-24 group of our own that I looked up there and I said, "My God, they're bombing short." They had mistaken a village right close to us for the one that was ten miles away. I thought, Oh Lord. I told the sergeant, "Get up. Let's get on our hands and toes. Don't put your belly to the ground. If there's any shaking, it'll knock the breath out of you." That string of bombs landed about—the last one was about three or four hundred yards back behind us. But it went through a British truck park, and those guys opened up on the B-24s. It did kill some people in that British park. All kinds of mishaps take place like that. Then passions take over, and they shoot. Now, the British later on had Halifaxes and other things; they could handle two thousand pounds.

As a matter of fact, when I was back in Casablanca that summer, a guy came into my office: "There's a British ship captain down here who's got six two-thousand-pound bombs that he wants to unload off of his ship." I said, "Tell him don't unload those damn things because we've got no way to handle them and no airplanes to carry them. I don't want to see them." I go down two days later, there's six two-thousand-pound British bombs sitting there. "Sergeant," I said, "What the hell are we going to do with those things?" He says, "Colonel, don't worry about it. I'll take care of it." I said, "What do you mean you're going to take care of it?" He says, "I'll take care of it." I go down about two days later. I don't see the bombs. I said, "What the hell did you do with them?" He says, "Well, we got forty feet of water out here right off that dock. Four Arabs[35] per bomb, push them off." I don't know whether they're still there or not.

Over in Italy we were using TNT bombs. All of a sudden they started sending us RDX bombs. They were much more fragile, and they'd go off. We warned everybody, "Don't let those things drop!" because the

Allies approach the rubble of Monte Cassino Abbey, on May 27, 1944. *Courtesy of National Archives and Records Administration.*

fuse and booster weren't necessary to set one of those off. We had a colored ammunition company over there that was hauling bombs and dispersing them at the locations where planes were in revetments. We'd put out notice, and one of those damn guys rolled one of these off the back of a two-and-a-half-ton truck. Of course, it blew the hell out of all those on there, and I had to break that ammunition company up. I had to scatter the men all to different organizations.

Another time over in Italy, this British army captain came into my office. I said, "How long have you been over here?" He said, "I've been here about two and a half years." He'd come around from Egypt around our way. He was an ammunition disposal guy. But he's sitting there, and he started shaking lighting a cigarette. I said, "You're a little nervous. How would you like to go to England, back home?" He said, "Oh, I'd love it." I said, "Goddamn, you're a menace to yourself and everybody around you. I'm going to put you on that Mosquito[36] flight." We had a Mosquito flight running right out of Naples, right over the Alps to England every night, go to about forty thousand feet. We had space for about two or three people on there. I said, "I'm going to get you on that thing." And I did. I almost got sent to the naval bomb disposal school at Yorktown, Virginia, right before the war. I was sure glad later I didn't go. Oh Lord.

The Germans had the capability of a five-hundred-pound canister that had bomblets[37] in it—2.2-kilogram things, about a hundred or something of them. They could drop them out; they had a vane on them that would come out and either arm them for instant explosion or short delay or antidisturbance. They had three different kind of fuses on them. They were deadly because if you hit one of them, you weren't sure what the hell was going to happen. They were demoralizing truck convoys, too.

So Cannon told me one day, "Get a crew together and go back over to North Africa and see how many of those damn things are in German bomb dumps." I went back for about two weeks, flying from Casablanca. We went down to Marrakech. We went about seven or eight places where the Germans had had bomb dumps, particularly after we got toward Egypt. I came back and told General Cannon, "I think we've found enough for one whole group mission." Cannon says, "That settles it. We're not going to let the bastards know how effective they are. We won't use them."

This air vice-marshal on the staff, he wanted to skip-bomb[38] tunnels that the Germans were using to run trains down through because northern Italy is full of tunnels. He thought that would be a good way to block their movement. I told him, "We haven't got anything that will do anything to those things except knock the bricks down inside of them. As a demonstration, I'll show you what'll happen." We took a five-hundred-pound bomb out at a tunnel right out of Naples. Everybody got around, out of the way, and we set that thing off. It blew all of the bricks off of that end of the tunnel. This major I had used to be a maintenance man with the New York Central Railroad. I said, "How long would it take you to get this thing cleared out so the trains can move?" He says, "Give me five hours." I finally convinced the air vice-marshal that let's don't try that, trying to stop these Germans from coming through those tunnels.

We had this combined British-American headquarters. Every section of the headquarters there had both RAF types and American types. In my own ordnance section, I had probably fifty people, which about half and half were British and American. Because they were used to using fuses different from ours, it worked out well.

The Fourth of July of 1943, we were a hundred miles north of Rome, at Lake Bolsena, on bivouac. The RAF types in our section, they said, "We're going down and celebrating Fourth of July with you Yanks." They had Beretta pistols firing up in the air. About that time, General Cannon came out of his trailer and said, "What the hell's going on down there?" I told him, and he says, "For God's sake, go down there and stop them. The night fighters[39] doing strafe invasions are using Lake Bolsena to check their guns before they keep going. They'll think we're right there on the front lines." So I had to get in my jeep and go down there. I said, "Boys, the celebration of Fourth of July is over."

In Italy, it was just day in and day out. We had a gigantic wall map in the operations headquarters there in Caserta. We had a green tag on the intersection of a road if that intersection had been bombed in the last three days and we thought it was unusable. After three days it turned red. This was the way that you kept track of where you were trying to interdict the traffic of the Germans coming down. Keep it green as much as possible. That dictated what the next strikes were going to be.

I was on the Teletype to Washington all the time wanting something. We developed these spikes where anyplace it hit, it was three prongs down and one up.[40] That would puncture German tires. We did have some of those, but we didn't use them too much.

At Anzio Beachhead in early '44, it was just slow, gradual fighting. The Eighth Army was going over those mountains on the other side over there, and Fifth Army was going up the west coast of Italy. There was just slow grinding until the Germans started trying to move fast. The Germans evacuated Rome real fast. It took me about ten hours to get through Rome because everyplace wanted to hand you a bottle of vino when you were going in your jeep. The surgeon on our staff, Hubert Johnson, he and I were traveling with a trailer on the back of my jeep up there, and we had a heck of a time getting through Rome.

Rather than getting in tents, I'd found out that we could get some big live-in-type trailers. They were going to be manufactured in California. I was talking to somebody in Washington about it: "Put them on a baby flattop.[41] Run them around over here, and send them over here," which they did. They put them on high-speed baby flattops, and they came into Naples. I had the job of allocating them, where they were going. Of course, I got General Cannon one and then got the air vice-marshal one. We scattered them out a little bit. But that proved very effective. We didn't have to live in tents. And the British liked that too, because they'd been used to living in tents coming across the desert there. We had enough trailers to where that made life a little more pleasant.

Well, about that time is when I got ordered back to Washington. It was in July of '44, and Colonel Mechling had been over there.[42] He was in G-4,[43] and he said, "I'm going to ask for you to come back here." When the orders came in, it was subject, of course, to General Cannon releasing me. So I went up there and talked to General Cannon. He said, "You've been over here as long as I have. You got a replacement?" I said, "Yeah, I've got one in the replacement pool back here." He was a class ahead of me at West Point, Bill Davis, but he got late into the aviation ordnance business. Cannon said, "Get him up here, and after you've oriented him for about two or three days, you can go," which is what I did.

I flew back down to Naples and got on a C-54 and got to Washington and landed about seven o'clock at night. I called my wife—she was at Wright-Patterson—and I said, "I don't think I want to keep going. I haven't slept for a little over twenty-four hours. I think I'll take an overnight train, come out there and see you in the morning." My wife and son and my daughter—at seventeen months old, I had never seen her. Rae had her in her arms, and my son was about two and a half. They were down at the station to meet me. I start walking up to put my arms around them, and my daughter puts out a big stiff arm. She don't know who this guy is. My son didn't know. He was hanging on to Rae's arm.

We moved to Washington, DC. I was in G-4 of the War Department for four years. I was the chief final approving authority for all small arms that were being planned to be thrown into production. I had a lot of other things like that that were involved that were very interesting.

I was the youngest colonel sitting on a twelve-man budget advisory committee because Congress said they wanted to know how much they could withdraw in spending authority. They wanted the answer by the first of December. We started in late August. And every day, even Saturdays and sometimes Sundays, we were listening to what all we should continue to support and what can be cut away. This one colonel, he was sitting next to me. I think he'd been in World War I. All of them were older colonels, a lot older than I was. Finally he leans over and says, "How much is a billion dollars?" because we'd talk in terms of billions all the time. I started, "Well, let's see." He says, "Don't bother. It's 476,320 Cadillacs. Get it down to something you can understand."

It was most interesting. Eisenhower had come back as chief of staff at that time, too. Of course there was so much variables. It was so undecided as to what should be done.

They wanted a petty cash fund or something that they could call on. We decided that was pretty good. We created a $50 million fund that we labeled top secret, a need-to-know basis. RFSC, that's what we labeled it: Reserve For Santa Claus. And it went through Congress. If you look at the 1946 appropriation bill in the army, you'll see in there RFSC.

Each one of the twelve of us had advisors, depending on what we were going to hear that day. This one lieutenant colonel there in the Pentagon, he was walking down to lunch, and he says, "How much money did you make yesterday on those hearings?" I said, "What do you mean? What are you talking about?" He said, "You mean you didn't go out and buy stock in that company?" I said, "No sir, I didn't. And I hope you didn't." You had to be very circumspect in what you were doing there.

I was in the Pentagon when I heard the news of surrender. I thought, Thank God, because we were planning here the invasion of Japan. Every casualty forecast was somewhere of a million, and it was going to be fantastic. We were probably going to use atomic bombs to do it somehow.

McDowell left the Pentagon in 1947 and entered Harvard Business School, graduating in 1948 with an MBA. He returned to the Pentagon and transferred to the air force, which had recently separated from the army. He was soon stationed at Wright-Patterson Air Force Base, in Ohio, and took the lead in establishing the first computers used by the government and military, communicating with computer corporations what they needed to build. Later, after attending Industrial College of the Armed Forces, McDowell entered the missile program and was in charge of installing the Thor Missile Force in England. He returned again to the Pentagon in 1960 as part of the Secretary of Defense Weapon System Evaluation Group. In 1961 he retired from the military. Afterward he moved to Houston to take a job with the Corporation for Economic and Industrial Research (C-E-I-R) and later formed a successful real estate company.

George McDowell, a 1937 graduate of West Point, was interviewed for the project Here and There: Recollections of Texas in World War II, funded by a grant from the Texas Historical Commission. George C. McDowell, *Oral Memoirs of George C. McDowell,* an interview conducted by Stephen Sloan, December 11, 2009, in Houston, Texas, BU Digital Collections.

Notes

1. In Aberdeen, Maryland.

2. Bowman Field was organized in 1920 as a commercial airport; two years later a reserve air squadron moved on site. McDowell likely is describing the field as it transitioned to a full-scale military training facility in anticipation of US involvement in World War II. During the war thousands of members of the military trained at Bowman Field. It earned the distinction as the busiest airport in America. "Bowman Field History," Louisville Regional Airport Authority, accessed December 20, 2013, http://www.flylouisville.com/bowman-field/history/.

3. In Honolulu, Hawaii.

4. When Colin Kelly died on December 10, 1941, he became the first hero of World War II and a household name. Legends took hold concerning his last mission and the circumstances of his death. Some reports erroneously stated that he had been posthumously awarded the Medal of Honor for his heroism. Gene Eric Salecker, *Fortress against the Sun: The B-17 Flying Fortress in the Pacific* (Conshohocken, PA: Combined Publishing, 2001), 67–68.

5. At the time of the attack on Pearl Harbor, Jones was commander of the 16th Bombardment Wing at Bowman Field. "Major General Junius W. Jones," US Air Force, accessed December 20, 2013, http://www.af.mil/AboutUs/Biographies/Display/tabid/225/Article/106596/major-general-junius-w-jones.aspx.

6. In Long Island, New York.

7. Gen. John Kenneth Cannon.

8. The United States was facing a shortage more of shipping than of aircraft or troops. In early 1942 the principal reason for downsizing US convoys planned for Northern Ireland, and for Iceland, was to free up US ships to take sorely needed aircraft and men to the Far East. Wesley Frank Craven and James Lea Cate, eds., *The Army Air Forces in World War II,* Vol. 1, *Plans and Early Operations, January 1939 to August 1942* (University of Chicago Press, 1948), 242–43.

9. In Leavenworth County, Kansas.

10. Operation Torch took place November 8–16, 1942.

11. McDowell is referring to the Center Task Force, which landed at Oran, Algeria. Cdre. Thomas Troubridge led the Royal Navy components, and Maj. Gen. Lloyd Fredendall commanded US air and ground forces. Eisenhower was commander-in-chief of Operation Torch. Wesley Frank Craven and James Lea Cate, eds., *The Army Air Forces in World War II,* Vol. 2, *Europe: Torch to Pointblank, August 1942 to December 1943* (University of Chicago Press, 1949), 25, 68.

12. Wright-Patterson Air Force Base, near Dayton, Ohio. During WWII, Wright Field and Patterson Field had not yet merged.

13. Vehicles used by the US Signal Corps.

14. The United States took possession of the Italian *Conte Biancamano* in the Panama Canal Zone in March 1941 and soon after converted it into the troopship USS *Hermitage.* During World War II, the ship's capacity was 6,107. Following the war the United States returned it to the Italian Line. William H. Miller Jr., *Picture History of American Passenger Ships* (Mineola, NY: Dover Publications, 2001), 81.

15. The combined British and American efforts for Operation Torch involved approximately 300 warships, 400 transports and cargo vessels, and 100,000 troops. About three-fourths of the troops were American. Rick Atkinson, *An Army at Dawn: The War in North Africa, 1942–1943,* Vol. 1 of the Liberation Trilogy (New York: Henry Holt, 2002), 22, 30–31.

16. Cape Verde and the Canary Islands are off the northwest coast of Africa.

17. A boat equipped with sails and an engine.

18. What Americans called Moroccan goums. These tribesmen sported beards and striped robes and supposedly collected bounties for human ears. Atkinson, *An Army at Dawn,* 503, 531.

19. During World War II, members of the French Foreign Legion fought on both sides, either for the pro-Allied Free French Forces or for the pro-Axis Vichy Government. The legion troops in North Africa were Free French. Alan Axelrod, *Encyclopedia of World War II* (New York: Facts on File, 2007), 364.

20. Roughly 150 miles south of Casablanca.

21. Gen. Walter J. Muller.

22. Temporary quarters for troops.

23. Women's Auxiliary Army Corps.

24. Barbed wire formed into large coils.

25. Patton was a Francophile and proficient in French. He studied swordsmanship at the French Cavalry School in Saumur in the summers of 1912 and 1913 and served in France in World War I. Carlo D'Este, *Patton: A Genius for War* (New York: HarperCollins, 1995), 136, 140, 195–96. D'Este details Patton's World War I activities in Section V, 185–282.

26. D'Este notes that the decision to take the Vichy French officers at their word could have been a fatal mistake for Patton's career had their commander, Auguste Noguès, double-crossed him. D'Este, *Patton,* 439.

27. German troops in Tunisia surrendered in mid-May 1943.

28. Possibly referring to his American-flag shoulder patch.

29. Patton replaced Lloyd Fredendall as commander of the US II Corps on March 6, 1943. D'Este, *Patton,* 461.

30. Operation Avalanche, the landings at Salerno, was part of the Allied Invasion of Italy on September 3, 1943.

31. B. B. "Buckshot" Taylor.

32. A red diagonal mark on a form that indicates an airplane is flyable but has a problem.

33. The destruction of the abbey is viewed as one of the most tragic mistakes of World War II. The belief that German troops were inside the abbey was based on several reports from dubious sources or overactive imaginations. For instance, a US colonel reported having seen the glint of field glasses in a window. In reality, German forces steered clear of the abbey to avoid angering the Vatican. Rick Atkinson, *The Day of Battle: The War in Sicily and Italy, 1943–1944,* Vol. 2 of the Liberation Trilogy (New York: Henry Holt, 2007), 433, 436, 440–41.

34. On the day of the operation, about 250 bombers dropped close to 600 tons of explosives and incendiaries on the abbey, in conjunction with heavy artillery. Atkinson, *The Day of Battle*, 437.

35. Locals employed as dockworkers.

36. A British combat aircraft.

37. The bomblets were commonly known as butterfly bombs because of their shape when deployed.

38. A low-level bombing technique in which aircraft crews skip bombs across the surface of land or water toward their targets. In this case, the targets would have been the insides of tunnels, to inflict maximum damage.

39. Fighter aircraft meant to be flown at night or when visibility is poor. It is unclear if McDowell is referring to aircraft flown by Germans or Americans.

40. Weapons known as caltrops.

41. Nickname for an escort carrier.

42. Maj. Gen. Edward Pont Mechling had served in the Mediterranean Theater as an ordnance officer and then as a supply officer for the air force. "Major General Edward P. Mechling," US Air Force, accessed December 20, 2013, http://www.af.mil/AboutUs/Biographies/Display/tabid/225/Article/106143/major-general-edward-p-mechling.aspx.

43. Logistics division of the general staff at the War Department.

FRANK MORROW POOL

Born on the family ranch in Johnson County, Texas, in 1918, Frank Morrow Pool spent his childhood in Grandview and his teens in Waco. He graduated with an engineering degree from Texas A&M University in May 1941, earning his way through with summer jobs in Texas oil fields. The required military science courses and rigid discipline of the cadet corps taught him leadership and confidence. During summer 1939 Pool trained as a private with the 7th Cavalry Division regular army at Fort Bliss, and the next year he received his commission as a second lieutenant in the army reserves. After graduation he worked for Humble Oil Company in offshore drilling and directional drilling along the Texas Gulf Coast. As he carried in the drilling report on December 7, 1941, he heard about the Japanese attack on Pearl Harbor. Petroleum engineers had been exempt from active duty because of their essential work in producing oil and gas for the Allies, but the army now required all its trained officers.

In February 1942 Pool reported for his physical exam at Camp Wolters, Texas, and from there went to Fort Knox, Kentucky, for tank gunnery school with the 1st Armored Division, Combat Company B, under Brig. Gen. Lunsford E. Oliver. In May 1942, when the 1st Armored and 1st Infantry Divisions disembarked in Belfast, Ireland, they became the first American ground troops on British soil.

In Ireland we maneuvered with the British 77th, an infantry division. We had a lieutenant colonel who was a graduate of West Point. In fact all the officers in the 1st Armored Division were either reserve officers or graduates of West Point. He was a brilliant officer. We were on maneuvers, and I had my tanks up there in Northern Ireland, and there were coke fields where they cut out the coke. A tank can sink out of sight in a coke field. I had about ten tanks. They were having the Mosquito bombers — British two-engine, light bombers — come over and drop flour sacks on us as if they were bombs, training us, teaching us. They caught me on this narrow road, and this lieutenant colonel came by. We were really getting worked over with the flour sacks. He told me, "Lieutenant, you're going to be a corporal, a private, or you're going to be an officer. You do something and you do it right now, or

First Armored Division M7 is unloaded on the North African shore in Operation Torch. *Courtesy of US Army Signal Corps.*

you're going to lose everything you've got." I thought that guy must be crazy. There were peat bogs on my right and on my left. What was he thinking about? What he was thinking was to teach me I must do something. I did something because he told me he was going to break me from my rank if I didn't do something. They have hedgerows. I thought, I can get one tank track up on the hedgerows, and I'm going to lose some tanks but I'm not going to lose all of them. So I turned my column off down the hedgerow, about a 45-degree angle. I remember one or two that fell over in the bog, but I saved the rest of them so I didn't have to be demoted. The lesson was you must take some positive action at times in your responsibility.

From Ireland, the 1st Armored Division moved to Scotland, where its tanks were equipped for beach landings to prepare for the Operation Torch invasion of North Africa. Loaded onto modified oil tankers, the division embarked from Liverpool and headed for Oran, on the coast of Algeria. To land the tanks on the beach, the troops constructed an inflatable pontoon bridge of General Oliver's invention. Pool's tanks went ashore near Arzew under cover of night on November 8, 1942.

My mission was to be on the force to secure the Tafaraoui Airport. Daylight came and the German planes appeared, and the only support we had was from Gibraltar, the nearest airfield. They put American pilots in British Spitfires—the Spitfire was known for its range and its capabilities—to come to support us. The problem was they couldn't carry enough fuel to fly back to Gibraltar, and so we were to take Tafaraoui Airport so they could land.

Come daylight, we were on the outskirts of Oran. The group that I was commanding were the flank, and we were experiencing the fight, not against tanks but against antitank guns. We met small arms, machine guns, and the like, nothing real bad. We lost a few men. They had the barracks and the fort there, and I was carefully going into the fight. We just had so much to work with, secure what you can, but the target was the city of Oran, the harbor of Oran, and Tafaraoui Airport. We had surprised the enemy totally.

We were able to get down there five or ten miles to the airport. It was a rather large base with grass runways. The Germans had bales of hay where you could pull the fighters up in for protection, rather than hangars. We got down to Tafaraoui by fighting, and the artillery was shelling Tafaraoui when our planes, the Spitfires, came to the point they had to land. We had secured the airfield, but we hadn't overcome the artillery that was shelling the airfield. We were just going to take our tanks out and pick up the pilots, then taxi the plane up into the shelter of these stacks of hay until they could overcome the artillery fire. The problem was—and it was a heartbreaking scene—as the first squadron of Spitfires came in to land, it was getting late in the day. A plane slows down as it comes to land, and just about that time a German flank hit them as they were in this approach. Those that were not hit out of the sky landed very well, and that was most of them, and we'd go out and pick them up. It was terrible, but as a leader, you just see your people are secure, go on with your job, get on with the show. Don't show any fear, don't show any frustration, don't act like you don't know what to do. Just let them know what we're going to do next. People are all waiting for you to say what we're going to do. That got to be old shoe before it was all over.

Shortly after we secured the airport, the French surrendered in Oran. We were out on the outskirts of Oran. We had overcome all resistance, and we were preparing to load on freight cars. We had secured the railroad, and the old railroad was going to carry us through. You'd put one tank on one railroad car because the trains weren't very strong. We started our trip out to the Algerian–Tunisian border. We unloaded at an Algerian point right on the border, then it took awhile to move that many tanks. A tank can go only so many miles before you can't use the tracks anymore. They have rubber blocks and they're good for about a hundred miles and that's all, so you have to load them on something whenever you can to save that track. When we got over there within reach of the German fighters out of Tunis and Sicily and Italy, they began to hit us pretty hard with the Stukas, the dive bombers, but we got over there and got formed up to proceed to face Rommel as he came.

We were fairly safe. Come Christmastime, we were on the Tunisian border in the Atlas Mountains, which run parallel to the seashore between there and the Mediterranean. We were getting British rations. Things you must have every day: water, food, gasoline, and ammunition. You had to have that and you had to have it every day, particularly gasoline. You could get by on the water and the food. You'd just stretch it out, and you'd find villages and things to get the water. We had chlorine pills and that sort of thing. The food in the desert was a serious matter. It's not like in Europe. We had the compact rations, K-rations, C-rations, mostly British rations, which were cheese and little cans of something. We were surviving on our rations. The supply officer was just as critical as a gunnery officer. The truck drivers were just as important as the tank drivers because they had to find us. They had to supply us, or we were out of business.

Christmas, though, I decided we would do something else. Some of the men told me about a Catholic monastery back in the Atlas Mountains away from the combat area. The sergeants and a couple or three jeeps went with me back in the Atlas Mountains, and we took mattress covers and all sorts of things that we had been issued that we didn't use to trade for some food for Christmas. We got back there, and they had a bountiful supply. They had gardens, they had cabbage, they slaughtered pigs. I traded for the whole deal, enough for the whole company, and we went back with Christmas dinner and left them with more than they ever dreamed they could have. That was a win-win situation. We went back and had Christmas dinner from this monastery.

Those were pretty dark days for us because we were fighting the German tanks in the valley between Medjez and the port of Tunis. I was attached to the British Coldstream Guard Battalion, the elite soldiers, the guys that guard Buckingham Palace. They had to be six feet tall. They've got to be the best soldiers. They were at the Medjez railroad station. I was ordered to go give them tank support. I decided that I would go at night because I was afraid I would lose my tanks in daylight. We got up there close to where this command point was, and the Coldstream Guard Battalion was facing the Germans that were up toward the city of Tunis. It was a black, dark night, and the sergeant and I were going to walk up to where the railroad station was to report to this lieutenant colonel. We were in the bar ditch, walking in the dark. As I approached it, all of a sudden these men stepped out. They were Senegalese, big blacks with knives about two feet long they held under your chin. We all had American flags on our sleeves. The Senegalese didn't speak English, and I didn't speak Senegalese, but the black officer finally got the point that I wanted to see their commander. I went up there and this commander was very leisurely sitting there, reading a *Reader's Digest.* He lays it down and takes all the excitement out of me.

Shortly after that, we were called back. General Oliver had his command at Medjez. The French had wheat fields—they were good farmers—and silos. I don't know who dreamed up the orders that we were to go ahead to advance toward that German strongpoint, but I took my tanks up and, sure enough, we didn't get started good till here came a flight of German 109 aircraft. They can work a tank over in short order. One of them singled out my tank. The silo is standing in the middle. Here came this 109, and I knew when he was going to start bombing and shooting, and I'd just move around the silo. He'd come back in, got right down to where he was going to pull the trigger, and I'd just go around the silo. We did that till finally he came by—and this is a true story—and leaned over and waved to me. He was out of gasoline.

In North Africa, I learned that tank warfare is just as much of an art as physics. You had to learn to defeat the enemy without losing your own people and your own tanks. There was no glory or no victory in being destroyed. The object was to achieve what you had been instructed without destroying your command, and you learn over and over the necessity that you must make a decision. You must take an action. It couldn't exist that there isn't any decision, there isn't any action to be taken. It might not be the best, but there's some action to be taken. You're not in a position to take no action because somebody was depending on you to take some action.

When you see your colleagues being killed, you think, What could I have done? At the next action and the next action and the next action, you think about that, and you let the men know that you're thinking that. That's the key to the whole thing of leadership. They must know that you're concerned about them coming out whole more than anything. The men have to know that you're the guy out there that's going to save their life, too. Knowing you're killing other people didn't bother me. In tank warfare that's not quite like putting it in your sights because you really don't see the person. We never followed the practice of seeing how many machine gun shells we could put out into a village or into a house or into something. I have strong feelings about this. I conveyed this to the men: "You don't ever, ever, ever injure older people, children, or women. No, never. If you think they're there, don't pull the trigger." And it worked for us.

In February 1943, as Rommel battered the Allies in the Kasserine Pass, General Oliver chose Pool to serve as one of two aides to return with him to the United States in his new assignment as commander of the 5th Armored Division. Before reporting to Washington, DC, Pool visited his family in Waco, and while there he met his future bride, Elizabeth Ellen Hughes. As the general's aide, he took part in initiating Oliver's plan for streamlining all army ground forces in preparation for the invasion of Western Europe. Tank, artillery, and infantry battalions replaced the former regimental structure. Each battalion was independently commanded, but its separate companies were flexible, allowing the commanders to "marry" or unite them as needed into a single combat unit. After accompanying General Oliver to the stateside bases of every armored division to describe the new structure, Pool joined the 5th Armored Division in training with Sherman tanks at Camp Cook, California. There he took command of Company B of the 10th Tank Battalion and was soon promoted to captain.

In February 1944, after completing maneuvers in Tennessee and gunnery training at Pine Camp, New York, Company B, 10th Tank Battalion, departed for Europe. In Cornwall, on the southwest tip of England, they conducted target practice and "married" with Company B of the 47th Infantry Battalion, creating a joint force of four hundred soldiers. For the remainder of the war Pool served as co-commander of the married tank-infantry company.[1] *In the weeks leading up to the June 6 D-Day invasion, Company B personnel moved to Plymouth, on England's east coast, to help provide food, lodging, and general care for the assault troops who would precede them into France. In early July, with their tanks and armored infantry vehicles loaded onto LSTs, Company B crossed the English Channel. Pool's troops landed at Omaha Beach and encountered their first combat action at Saint Lô. After the breakthrough, the entire combat command, including the tank-infantry company, with its reconnaissance, artillery, engineering, and air support, moved ahead day and night toward Le Mans, beyond the German lines. They were to meet Canadian and British forces at Argentan and cut off the German Seventh Army at Falaise. On the way they encountered stiff German resistance.*

When I got to Alençon, the Germans were laying out protective screens of tanks. My artillery officer and I got out of the tank and went into a little brick barn, and with my glasses I could see German tanks, a half dozen. They had taken dozers and dug out, and the tanks were down in with nothing showing but the gun in this big open field. I asked the artillery officer to lay fire on the tanks. He did. We had the battalion of artillery ready, so boom, boom, they came over on those six tanks. Not a tank moved. Every time we made a move, bang, bang, bang, bang! Oh well, I'll get the planes; they can spot those guys. Well, here they came, bang, bang, bang! Not a tank moved. Not a one budged.

Then, General Oliver or the combat commander sent word up to me to move, move now. We could not stay there at dark because the German infantry was in the woods. Do something now. Oh me. I tried to remember what I'd learned. The Lord helped me. I wasn't going to throw my tanks out there because they'd kill more of us than we'd kill of them. They would win the game. I spread all the tanks out in the woods. We had every tank and every half-track out in the flank, out in the woods, staying where you can't get hit, because if you stuck your nose out, you were dead in the water. Those German tankers, they're good tanks, big tanks, Tiger tanks. They've got the same sighting devices we've got, and that's crosshairs in the periscope. I thought, When they can't see their crosshairs, they can't hit us. I told all the officers, "Just watch my tank."

When I came out firing, I wanted them to fire every gun they had. When you fire a machine gun or any gun, every fifth round or something has a tracer in it, a tracery. You get a red streak so you can see where you're shooting. I told the infantry commander, "You tell every man that's got a rifle or anything, when we move out of this wood, I want everybody to fire. Whether he sees anything or not, fire in the direction of the enemy." Just at dusk I looked down in my periscope and I could not see the crosshairs. I gave the signal. Every vehicle, forty-four of them, all firing, moved out of that woods. Those Germans backed their tanks out and got out of there. That whole valley was full of tracer bullets. They had nothing to shoot at. I lost one tank. Bingo, they backed out and departed. We did that and unplugged the cork, and the whole division began pouring out.

That night I circled the tanks. The infantry always dug in around the tanks. The tanks couldn't fire at night, couldn't see the crosshairs. The infantry would get in front and pull out their guns. During the night some German trucks came down the road across from where we had our defenses set, and of course the guns whacked them. They were payroll trucks, and money went everywhere. The next morning there were German marks all over the landscape. True story.

We went on to Alençon, right up at the edge of the Falaise Gap. The German Seventh Army, about 150,000 men that had opposed the attacks on the beaches and had sought to counterattack and cut off the thrust down into France, were there. The strategy of our commanders was to bring the British and Canadians in. My orders were not by any circumstances to advance further than Argentan because then we would be firing on our own troops. It was very difficult to sit in my turret and see the dust columns as the Germans were withdrawing, escaping out this road, but a command is a command. I was not to take my tanks any further than this point. I sat on the top of my turret and watched those dust columns. My wife-to-be had sent me milk cartons cut in half full of fudge. I sat on that turret that week eating that chocolate. The air force was just absolutely riddling those columns, but had we moved out, we'd have run into the Canadians, and first thing you know, we'd be firing on our own people.

We set up roadblocks further on, just outside of Argentan. They were seeking to go other ways, and we went and captured, in one case, a whole company of German infantry, armored, and so on. Having prisoners was difficult for the commander to handle. Here you have all this sentiment built up, emotional things about the terrible enemy, and they're not the terrible enemy. They're men that have families. They're doing a job to honor their country. We always had a stand-pat rule that you protect children, old people, and prisoners. They're all three terribly vulnerable. They're not armed, they're helpless, they're scared. Your prisoners, after they're taken, that was the job of the infantry that was with us. They would disarm them. But a commander had to fight hard to see to it that no one abused prisoners because they are completely helpless. I've seen the prisoners come out of wherever they are, the ditch or whatever, behind something, and often hold up a picture of their children or their wife.

The Germans were fleeing to Paris, and our next orders were to go towards Paris. We didn't follow the main roads, just small roads or open fields. We had a firefight at Dreux. It was mid-August, thereabout, and that's where I lost my hearing. In tank warfare whoever got the first hit survives. You have a clash against antitank guns and artillery and other tanks, and you see where they are by the flash of their gun. A tank gun shoots very effectively a mile away. The early morning air was full of moisture, and with the high-velocity tank gun, this flash of fire comes out the barrel and it condenses the atmosphere. It looks like smoke. The tanker has got to, what we call, "sense the shot." He's got to see where that shot went a mile away to make the next shot go. You've already disclosed where you are. Then the enemy's going to shoot at you. Sensing the shot is the critical thing. That particular morning it was high humidity, no visibility, and the first round that I fired, that thing hit us so quick I couldn't sense my shot. I got out of my tank to the side where I could sense the shot. The tanks had what we called flash deflectors on the barrels, and when I fired, the flash deflector sent the sound and it ruptured my left ear. I got the target and we moved on ahead, but that's where I lost my hearing.

We came in at Saint-Germain-en-Laye, on the outskirts of Paris. The Germans were across the Seine from Saint-Germain. We were held at that point because the high command had concluded that they wanted the Free French, the 1st Armored Division of France — in our tanks, of course — to move into Paris to make that triumphal entry. The Free French had gotten semi-control of Paris, but the Germans were still there. The French 1st Armored Division went into Paris. Our division was going to move through Paris in a blaze of glory — girls, roses, the works. I had received a new tank because my other one had been hit, and I was quite proud of that thing. Turned onto the Champs-Élysées, the big avenue right before the Arc de Triomphe, and I'll declare, that motor sputtered about twice and quit. Wasn't that a fine blaze of bravery? I just stepped on the tank behind me and moved on. I came right down the Champs-Élysées, all the way down. That was good. While I was going down that beautiful avenue, I thought, Boy, now we get some rest. Well, I got on my earphones, and I heard that I was given the command to immediately move on, to forget about the parade, that the Germans were moving into Compiègne Forest from Holland.

Late that afternoon we got to the flanks of the Compiègne Forest with a task force — infantry, tanks, air force guys, artillery guys, the reconnaissance. As we approached, the Germans had blocked the American 4th Infantry Division. An infantryman cannot move in the face of antitank guns and tanks, so I was told to move right through the 4th Infantry Division troops and to hit the Compiègne Forest. There's nothing worse for a tanker than forest, but that was the orders. I started spreading my tanks out and was going to make an assault. With a group of tanks and infantry on my left and tanks and infantry to my right and I was in the middle, away we started down, and when we did, flashes came. The show began. I could see that we weren't going to be able to successfully penetrate that forest by a frontal assault. I ordered immediately to have the tanks withdraw. We moved back, and as we moved back, I took a hit on my turret, but it hit the slope and just gouged a big piece of steel out. It didn't penetrate.

The German infantry had been dug in so I asked the artillery officer if he had artillery out from Paris to give us air bursts. They could do that, time the shells. Gave them air bursts and the artilleryman, he corrected it and fired. I told him to go to the right, go to the left, and go all through the front of that forest. During the night I told the infantry

American armored car passes beneath the Arc de Triomphe after the liberation of Paris, August 1944. *Courtesy of National Archives and Records Administration.*

commander to send in squads of good patrolmen to determine the condition of the German gunners. They came back about daylight and said all the gunners were dead. The artillery had mauled them. So here it goes. Through the forest we went. The 4th Infantry, then, came by in trucks with tarps on and went right through where we had cleaned out. Our job was to help the 4th Infantry get through, and they did.

We then proceeded to go on exercising our privilege with our one-way ticket to Berlin. At the end of the day you're out of gasoline and low on ammunition. Your men didn't have food. You need food and drinking water, so you have a good supply officer. During the night, every night, here would come the six-by-sixes, we called them, the trucks, and they would bring jerrycans, a five-gallon GI can that held water or gasoline. You'd stop at a tank and you'd tell him how many cans you would need. He would unload them in the dark, fill up the tanks with gasoline, and leave the five gallons or two gallons of water, and leave a box of either dry rations or something for the crew of five men. Five men could eat a lot of food in twenty-four hours. He'd leave that and be out before daylight. The next morning at daylight we were ready to go. So you'd do all that at night and get a little rest. I usually didn't go to bed till I was sure that we had the essentials.

We're through at Compiègne, and we've got about a week's break while all the military forces get organized. They'd bring the kitchen trucks up, two trucks with ranges in them and the mess sergeant, and we'd have hotcakes and fresh eggs during this break. Because you had your forces out there in front of you, you could get your breath. Got the mail. They'd send the trucks up, and the tankers would all get in the trucks and go back about twenty-five or thirty miles to a shower point, which was duck tenting put up to break the wind, and they had boilers and they had showerheads out in the open. You'd take off all your clothes, didn't worry about any rank assemblage ever, because everybody knew who the captains were. We'd been doing this a long time. You'd take off all your clothes, tie them in a bag, and put them in a huge pile. We're talking about four hundred men. We'd go through and have a big hot shower. I mean a *big* shower tank, soapy hot water, all we wanted. This is usually by a river. When we'd come out of there, we wouldn't get the same clothes, but they'd ask, you know, what's your waist size and what is your neck size. That's all. Length didn't make any difference with your tucked-in boots. They were fresh, clean clothes. They'd do that for thousands and thousands of troops. We'd come out clean, get back in our trucks, and go back to our tanks.

At night we would sleep in the mud if it was muddy, but when we were sleeping in mud, a tanker had some advantage. In the daytime we'd put our bedrolls in a tarp, roll it up, put it across the tank. At nighttime we'd take the tarp and hang it off the side of the tank and fold it under so you didn't have to lay down in the mud. Put your boots in the track where it's dry. The company commander had a tarp of his own he'd pull off the tank, and that's where you would get your rest if you lay down that night. You could shave, and you could bathe. The water cans would always give us enough to put in our helmets and you could sponge off your body from the helmet. Every tank had a little stove, about three inches in diameter and about ten inches high, and we could set that and heat water for shaving or sponging or making coffee.

The men played poker, but I spent my time studying maps. You have to realize the Germans took away every road sign, the name of every town, anything that identified anything they had destroyed. As you moved, you had to be absolutely 100 percent pure map readers to know where you were, when you were, how you were. Your maps are so critical. A military map shows a church with a cross, it shows a cemetery, it shows a school, it shows everything. So you pick those points up all the time as you go along. I had it in a waterproof case, and it hung right with me.

Moving forward, helping push the Germans back behind their own borders, Pool's combat team rolled through France, Belgium, and Luxembourg, reaching Diekirch, on the German border, by early September 1944. To keep going they would have to break through the formidable Siegfried Line.[2] *While other US forces fought along the Belgian-German border to penetrate the heavily fortified German city of Aachen, the 5th Armored Division concentrated farther south along the rivers on the eastern border of Luxembourg.*

Our combat command got into Diekirch. There were a couple of US divisions taking terrible, heavy losses at Aachen. I was called up to the colonel's[3] headquarters, and he told me to take my command and make a feint attempt to cross the Siegfried Line at a place called Wallendorf, where the Our and the Sauer Rivers come together. The point was to draw the Germans down that way. Not only that, I was supposed to take a whack at Bitburg, where the SS[4] headquarters was. Nobody had crossed the Siegfried Line! The Siegfried Line was pits, dragon teeth,[5] antitank ditches. You couldn't take tanks across the Siegfried Line anywhere, all the way across Germany for hundreds of miles.

I didn't know what to do. The first step I did was fortunate. The Lord helped me on that. There was a priest, or a white-collared man, a Christian minister, who lived on this side of Luxembourg and was going across the Siegfried and holding services at Wallendorf, a small, agricultural village just at the base of a cliff. I knew he knew about what's over there, so I asked him if he'd go with me, and I went down there close to the river. We laid on our stomachs, and I took my field glasses, and he showed me where the pillboxes were. He told me about the whole deal, this priest. He was my reconnaissance manager.

The commander[6] of the 10th Tank Battalion, who was a great friend and a petroleum engineer, a colonel, had someway authorized for a battery of 155 mm guns to get in front of me. Following the priest's advice, I knew where to point my 155 guns, and I took the guns up on the high ground where the Our and the Sauer came together and they flat fired all those places that I had been told about. The tanks were ready to go immediately after the fire of the 155s. I stayed on the high ground because they had a lot of forces there, a lot going on. Lieutenant Rollins, nicknamed "Pork Chop," was the assault commander, and the second, Lieutenant McCauley. Behind Rollins, we went down, and we had no trouble fording the Sauer River. Got into Wallendorf following the fire of the big guns. I was there with my field glasses observing Lieutenant Rollins's movement. Lieutenant Rollins was the hero. He says, "Hey, I believe there's a feed road in behind Wallendorf going up that cliff." I took my glasses. "Yes, I see it. I see it very well." In West Texas we have feed roads that go down to a windmill where you put out feed. It's just a path, so to speak. The Germans put their cattle around their houses at night, and they'd have hay meadows up this tremendous cliff. Well, the dragon teeth came up to the cliff but stopped there. "Pork Chop, lay your tank on that path and call me back and say if it'll support your tank, wide enough." He called back and said, "I've got my tank on it and there's just the width of my shoe before my tank would fall over." I said, "We've got it made. Up you go. I'm on the way." I dropped off the high ground where I was across the Our, and up that little road we went with that entire task force, all those tanks, all that infantry. We were through the Siegfried Line by dark without one casualty.

That night we circled the wagons, and the infantry dug in. We were right in the heart of the German forces. Sure enough, that night, here came the Krauts. They were bringing big pots of food to the bunkers for the German troops, so the boys captured a hot supper. I just remember those trucks with that food. The next morning we were through the Siegfried Line a couple of miles on some high ground. Next morning we knew we had to move and move fast because there was no support behind us.

The next morning early—it was September, about the tenth—as we came off this high ground, there was a row of apple trees along the farm roads, and it was foggy down by a creek. It was Lieutenant McCauley's day. I was about three tanks back. I was watching everything. We got down there, and just as we started down I looked at the road on the other side of the creek. There was coming a German tank column with a half-track, a command vehicle, in the front of the column, coming down the same road we were on towards the Siegfried Line. Lieutenant McCauley couldn't see that because he was already down close to the creek. I immediately told everyone to hold their fire, and I waited till that column got down pretty close to the creek and stopped to look things over, as I hoped they would.

McCauley is just about to the creek, Niedersgegen Creek. He's almost there, but he's down in the fog. They couldn't see him. As soon as the fog was up and rising, visibility improving, I spread the tanks out immediately. As soon as we could see, I gave the orders to fire and we really did tear into them. Somebody hit that lead half-track, and through the glass I saw a woman jump out of it. They were carrying their own woman with them. So we went by, and, lo and behold, immediately McCauley went to cross the creek on the bridge, and the bridge fell in, and down his tank went to the bottom. The men came out and got in somebody else's tank, but we didn't stop. Tanks never stop. We went around that, forged the stream, mud, some sticking, some getting across. That didn't matter, just so you keep going. They let the tank receiver recover vehicles, do all of that. We were a striking force. Like a fighter in a plane, that's all he thinks about, nothing else.

We hit a couple of the German tanks. They hit a couple of our tanks, nobody killed. On up we kept going until we were within five or six miles of Bitburg. We were getting short on gasoline because we weren't fueled up the night before; nobody could get to us. I got on a piece of high ground, and I didn't see a soul. They did get the trucks in at night in a couple of days, but no other troops, no other relieving tank companies. We were in there about five or six days. But they did refuel us and gave us what we needed. The battalion commander someway got a platoon of antitank guns, bigger guns than we had, but they had open turrets. They got through on the same crossing, up like we did, and got to us, so I had more strength. I had antitank, infantry group, tank group, so we stayed up there. You couldn't get any more fuel except what I had. There was a village down below us. When we got there, we could see the soldiers with their girlfriends walking the streets. They didn't have any idea we were through the Siegfried Line.

After about six or seven days, the outpost infantry radioed that they could hear tanks moving. Tanks make a noise: clank, clank, clank, clank, clank, the tractor treads. They called back, and they could hear more troop movement. My command was, "Stand to," which means everybody wake up and get alert, but don't do anything. Come daylight they spotted a tank column of German infantry and tanks coming towards our position. As the daylight came, I could take my glasses and see all of it: a bunch of German tanks in formations on the whole slope of the ridge. I had moved part of my command on the flank, and they thought that was us, Sergeant Novello with a platoon of tanks. I had the tank destroyers and our guns all in defilade, where the ground rolls and you stay just behind the roll, then you can roll up just a little bit and your guns clear.

Everybody stays tight. I could see the whole thing like it was on a screen. The German officers got out of their tanks, opened their maps, talked to one another. I stood there and watched that as it got brighter, got daylight. They were deciding how they were going to attack us. I had this whole thing on their flank, big tanks, lots of stuff. So they all went and got back in their position and started moving up the slope because Sergeant Novello's tanks were up at the head of this where they were going. They thought this was where I was, where the task force was. Their tanks were very vulnerable on the side like ours were, but you can't penetrate in the front because their armor's thick. I waited till they all got to moving, got to going up and way up high. Then poor Sergeant Novello, just pleading, said, "I can't stop them." He was firing but not stopping anything. He didn't have any idea what I was going to do. Then, when they got to the right point, the critical point before they got to him, we all rolled over the hill. Fire! We knocked out twenty German tanks. It was unbelievable. The minute we started firing, they would turn to fire on us. I radioed to Novello and he would hit them in the side as they turned. Not a tank got away. One half-track got away and that's all out of that whole entire force. We didn't lose a man.

About that time the word came on my earphones that I was to withdraw completely back across the Sauer River. Orders had come from corps to withdraw all the forces back. The trouble was that the US forces had been committed to Operation Market Garden, the big one, where Montgomery brought airborne divisions and tanks up through Holland. They were going to come down and meet that group that was coming from Aachen. Well, they didn't get through Aachen. That was a disaster. But all supplies had been diverted to them, so there couldn't be a major thrust. You know when we got to the Rhine River? First of March of the next year. Next year! September, October, November, December, January, February, March, all of this cold winter. That's when all the deaths occurred in the prison camps and so forth. We came back across and sat there the next morning looking across the Sauer River. The Germans were moving en masse up at Wallendorf, and we stopped and fired every round we had.

Through October and early November 1944, the 5th Armored Division moved into the Forest of Ardennes, taking defensive positions for a time. By mid-November they resumed the offensive with the goal of breaking through to the Ruhr Valley and moving on to the Rhine River. Company B of the 47th Infantry was separated from Company B of the 10th Tank Battalion to join the assault on the German-infested Hürtgen Forest, where it suffered the loss of almost two-thirds of its troops. On November 25, at seven-thirty in the morning, Pool's tank battalion began moving through dark, cold rain toward Hürtgen. The tank in front of his dropped into a deep crater in the road, and when Pool stopped to determine the best way to get past the obstacle, he attracted heavy enemy fire and sustained wounds to his shoulder and back. Medics removed him to the 2nd Evacuation Hospital at Eupen.[7] *General Oliver granted Pool's request that he be permitted to convalesce at the evacuation hospital so that he could stay close to his troops.*

I was ambulatory pretty soon, getting along very well in my recovery, still strapped up. One night, about December 15, out the window I saw flares being dropped. Wow! Flares being dropped, and paratroopers. It was the Bulge beginning. I went immediately, gathered what little gear I had, and shanghaied a jeep driver to take me to corps headquarters, which was in Eupen, to see where the 5th Armored Division, the 10th Tank Battalion was, and then from there I could go to Company B. That night I took command back of B Company. They were not far, less than five miles from Eupen. They had already gotten orders to move out. I couldn't get in the turret, but I got in a half-track, put my radios in there, and away we went that night. We moved out that night to face the Germans that were making what became the Bulge. Technically, it was December 16.

We were in the woods right out of Eupen, in Belgium, and our orders were to move out to the west of Malmédy, where the Germans had come through Saint-Vith and Malmédy. Our orders were not to take Malmédy but to form a stopper there so the Germans could not go further. We made our strong position about ten miles north of Malmédy. Well, the next morning the orders were to stay in contact with the Germans, keep the pressure on. We went into Malmédy after the massacre there on the seventeenth. There were no Germans there. They had orders to kill, not take prisoners, so they had killed all the troops, the US prisoners, when they were in Malmédy. They were laying in the snow, all the bodies laying in the snow. At Christmastime we were still just outside of Malmédy. We did have turkey at that place in the forest there. We were close to Bastogne, but we were not in that. We had our hands full where we were.

The Germans were defeated, and the end of December came. Then we came back to a defensive position again and moved further north and became a part of the Ninth Army under General Simpson, a Texas general.[8] We changed from Patton, who had the Third Army, to the Ninth Army, under Simpson, and then we moved up and went under Montgomery, the British army. The Germans still had a force between the Rhine and the Siegfried Line. We were in that area. We were fighting up to Krefeld, and I was given the mission of taking a river crossing on the Rhine at Orsoy, which is north of Krefeld, right across from

Duisburg. We were right on the Rhine, across the Siegfried but not across the Rhine. It was cold, very cold. The turrets would freeze.

I reconnoitered some and found that all along the Rhine was lined with 88 mm guns, which was the Germans' main antiaircraft and antitank weapon, which turned the tide in the desert in Africa. Here were these 88s all lined up where I was supposed to go. On close examination of it, I found that there was a mound around those guns. When they lowered the guns, the wall around them would not permit the guns to come down to the level of my tanks. That's all I needed to know. In we go, wide open. They showered us with a blanket of shells whose bursting almost blackened the sky, but they couldn't get them down, and the shells were bursting above us. In fact, shrapnel was coming in, cut the back of my coat, but we never slowed down because the guns could not come down to hit us. Into Orsoy we went like a birthday party. It was a piece of cake.

In Orsoy, we took the crossing, which had been blown up by aircraft. We completed our mission, but after we got down there, I looked up the Rhine and I could see between the levee and the Rhine here came some German *big* tanks. I said, "Well, there we go again." I felt that I just had to have air support. The tanks were out in the open; they weren't dug in. There was a flight of P-47s close by. Boy, they came down and worked those tanks over, and they withdrew. I could see across the Rhine. I could see the streetcars in Duisburg.

We moved on up the river under Montgomery and crossed the Rhine near Wesel. We had a bridgehead already, put the pontoons in, and I got to see Montgomery. That was a treat. I was in my turret. He was a great commander in his turret. He saluted me, and I saluted him. We came on up out of Wesel a ways and ran into stiff German opposition. It was not a favorable position. I decided to have a look at it before I took my tanks down in there. I had a real good jeep driver named Pishko. Anytime I needed to get up and go, not take a tank, I'd holler for Pishko, and he'd come and pick me up. Well, I went up to take a look. Pishko had always been so careful, but it was on a gravel road. The Germans had crossed that river and must have seen us because they laid a shell right alongside the jeep. It scared Pishko, and he jerked the jeep and away we went—kaflip. Broke some of my eye up here, hit my knee. Anyway, got back and got in the tanks and handled that matter the next day, but I was about running out of gas.

The next week we were going east. My objective was to go on past Münster, Germany, towards Hanover. We moved on toward our objective by Minden towards Hanover. Before we got to Minden, I had another kind of a hiccup. We came into this big valley, and there was a tank company from the 8th Armored Division. They were supposed to be on my flank. I rolled up to this company captain, and he said they'd been there two or three days, and there was a German parachute battalion down in that valley with guns and that's as far as he could go. I thought I could handle it. I told him we were going on by and we would not disturb his troops there. So I took every tank and every vehicle I had on the rise, same deal, and we just went all over the side at the same time. I knew they couldn't hit all of us. Well, that sight, I guess, frightened them.

At that time I didn't have any experienced officers, so I was the lead every day, which is natural, because we were moving fast and things were happening fast. First tank hit was my tank. Hit my tank and gouged a big lot of metal out of it and went past my head with the metal off the tank and just filled underneath my throat full of little, tiny, tiny pieces of metal. I thought my head was shot off, and I could see the blood all over my shirt. We went right on through the German forces. I think I got a couple of tanks hit, but nothing bad. This was our job, and away we went. We didn't even slow down till dark. The battalion medics that night picked stuff and laughed about it till everybody was just about exhausted. They got it all out. Just a few days before they had sewed up where I cut my eye, so I was wearing out my welcome.[9]

The Germans had a lot of guns back around Münster, and on out on the flank by Münster on Easter morning, the first day of April 1945, they opened up on the flank of our column. It was a pretty quick assault. I picked up the mike to give my orders to turn the tanks to the fire. I couldn't breathe. I was blacking out. I dropped down to the bottom of the turret and another officer took command. We wheeled, and we fought the guns, overcame the power. I got over it after a while so I could breathe again.[10] On about the fifteenth or something of April, my objective was Wittenberg, the bridge across the Elbe River. I was not at the front of the division, so I got to Wittenberg and thought, We'll scoot across that thing and see the lights of Berlin before the sun sets. We were only about fifty miles. Got to the bridge at Wittenberg, and just as I got there, it blew up in my face. They had it all set. It was a stone bridge, an arch. I asked the engineer officer if he would bring up his pontoons to cross the Elbe River. I told him we'd cross it about four o'clock in the morning. I remember that because about two o'clock in the morning I got this call from Colonel Cole,[11] who was the chief, old-timer, full colonel, warrior. He sent word up there to tell me not to even think about crossing the Elbe, that I wasn't going to cross it and nobody else was. That's where we're going to meet the Russians.

For all practical purposes, when we got to the Elbe it was over. There was disappointment. We had so much momentum and had been making a major effort in the war so long from the time we first began training and certainly wanted to go to its conclusion. I felt like we could have helped materially if they had not agreed to stop at the Elbe. We could have been a threat to that flank and maybe saved many, many Russian lives by bringing the force to bear on the west side of eastern Europe, but that's not the way it went. We moved north because there was still some German strength on the west side of the Elbe. We fought at Dannenberg for several days until we'd overcome the forces and met the British who were coming down from the north. After the German forces were destroyed on the west side of the Elbe, the division moved back to Magdeburg, which was on the Elbe, a sizeable city. That's where we were when the final VE Day occurred, Victory in Europe Day. We got the company together and just had a period of thanksgiving and relief. No parties. We weren't in that sort of location. To the guy that had been on a long period of fighting, he was so pleased and happy just to be quiet and thank the Lord that it's over.

My war service was the greatest training period of my life. The impact was one that gave me a great value of comradeship, friends, of discipline, and a respect for the capabilities of our country, which were profound.

By VE Day, Frank Pool had achieved the rank of major and was operating officer over the 10th Tank Battalion. His troops acted as a police force in the area of the Harz Mountains during the occupation and enjoyed some time off in southern France. Because of his injuries, Pool was ordered back to the United States to McCloskey Hospital in Temple, Texas, where his knee was repaired. The shoulder wound sustained in the Hürtgen Forest was inoperable, and the bullet remained there for the rest of his life.

Discharged from service on January 28, 1946, he married Elizabeth Hughes on February 16. In addition to campaign medals for the European, African, and Middle Eastern Theaters, Pool received the Bronze Star, Silver Star, and Purple Heart, each with one Oak Leaf Cluster, and the Distinguished Service Cross.

In 1948 Pool left Humble Oil Company and moved to San Angelo, where he established his own well-servicing and drilling contract company. From one oil derrick the business grew into the multinational Pool Energy Services Company. Pool retired from the company board at age seventy-five but continued as project consultant. He founded the Association of Energy Services Companies and served on numerous school, college, church, and bank boards.

In 1997 Pool was inducted into the first class of Texas A&M University's Petroleum Engineering Academy of Distinguished Graduates.

Frank Morrow Pool's life story was gathered in seven oral history interviews for the longstanding Texas Economic History Project. His war experiences are included in his second, third, and fourth interviews. See Frank Morrow Pool, *Oral Memoirs of Frank Morrow Pool,* a series of interviews conducted by Rebecca Sharpless, June 2, 1998, to December 2, 1998, in San Angelo, Texas, BU Digital Collections.

Notes

1. Company B, 10th Tank Battalion, and Company B, 47th Infantry Battalion, formed a task force within the 5th Armored Division's Combat Command R. Vic Hillery and Emerson Hurley, *Paths of Armor: The Fifth Armored Division in World War II* (Nashville, TN: Battery Press, 1985), 44.
2. A mesh of impregnable antitank traps and devices, laced with explosives, connecting defensive pillboxes and bunkers for almost four hundred miles along and inside the German border.
3. Col. Glen H. Anderson, a veteran of World War I, commanded Combat Command R. Hillery and Hurley, *Paths of Armor,* 332.
4. The *Schutzstaffel,* Adolf Hitler's police and security forces.
5. Pyramid-shaped pillars of reinforced concrete set up in multiple rows to deter tanks.
6. Lt. Col. William A. Hamberg. Hillery and Hurley, *Paths of Armor,* 338.
7. Hillery and Hurley, *Paths of Armor,* 159, records what happened: "Heavy artillery and mortar fire rained on the engineers as they worked. Capt. Frank M. Pool, B Co., 10th Tank Bn., commander, was hit by a German burp gun while standing in his turret directing the bridging operations, but refused to be evacuated. He climbed out of his tank to help the engineers and while on the ground was wounded again, this time by mortar fire. He again refused to be evacuated, but was soon so weak from loss of blood that evacuation was necessary."
8. Gen. William Hood Simpson, born in Weatherford, Texas, in 1888, fought in World Wars I and II. "William Hood Simpson, General, United States Army," Arlington National Cemetery Website, copyright M. R. Patterson, 1994–2011, accessed September 10, 2012, http://www.arlingtoncemetery.net/whsimpson.htm.

9. For his March 3–5, 1945, service leading his tank battalion to the Rhine River, Pool received the Distinguished Service Cross. The award citation states, "Exposing himself to all types of enemy fire, Captain Pool, riding in the leading vehicle, directed the attack of his tank company which swiftly advanced nine miles and overran six villages. . . . He led his men in a bitter fight which culminated in the capture of an enemy town and cut the enemy's last escape route in that sector . . . across the Rhine River." "Frank Morrow Pool," Military Times Hall of Valor Awards and Citations, accessed September 10, 2013, http://projects.militarytimes.com/citations-medals-awards/recipient.php?recipientid=22561.

10. Long after the war, doctors concluded that an injury to his adrenaline gland sustained with the shoulder wound he suffered in the Hürtgen Forest was the cause of blackouts that Pool experienced first in combat in Germany and later during his work in Texas oil fields.

11. Col. John T. Cole, a 1917 West Point graduate and veteran of World War I, commanded Combat Company B of the 5th Armored Division from September 1943 to the end of the war. Hillery and Hurley, *Paths of Armor*, 331.

HERBERT U. STERN

Herbert U. Stern was born in Germany in 1919 and spent his childhood and adolescence in Berlin. He learned some English from his father, a successful businessman working internationally. Stern attended gymnasium, or secondary school, until what would be considered his junior year, when state policy declared that nobody of Jewish descent was allowed in any school.[1] *The rise of the Nazi Party in the early 1930s created a deteriorating climate for German Jews that manifested bitterly in the Stern family. In 1933 Stern lost his mother to suicide amid circumstances, Stern remembers, in which a "number of people in Germany that were different ages . . . just felt that there was no way out to anywhere to do anything."*

Just a year later the secret police, the Gestapo, arrested Herbert's father on a train to Switzerland and imprisoned him. Officials accused the elder Stern of violating a German law against taking reichsmarks out of the country. Following his imprisonment, the hardships of the family increased with the loss of income and the auctioning off of family belongings to cover the expense of his legal defense. Stern's father received a two-year sentence. Unbeknownst to Stern, his father began to make arrangements with distant cousins to get his son out of the country before he too was incarcerated. It took two and a half years for the teenaged Stern to get his visa. His father was released in 1936, only two days before his young son fled Germany, sailing to live with relatives in the United States.

Arriving in the States on August 26, 1936, Stern was taken in by his father's second cousin, who became like a mother. He flourished in his new home, Cincinnati, Ohio, and he excelled in his studies at the University of Cincinnati before being drafted into the military in 1941.

In that summer of 1941 I found myself needing one credit, so I went to the draft board and asked, "Can I get a deferment for about a month and a half?" to finish a course that I had to take during the summer. After that I was drafted and sent to a place called Camp Lee, outside of Petersburg, Virginia, which was brand new at the time. I found myself in the medics.[2] I couldn't tell you why. You learn a lot about what you were supposed to be doing in the field and how to treat wounded people. I thought, Well, so I'm in the medics. After about two or three weeks there, I got a message that I had to come get a pass back to Cincinnati, Ohio, because they had a federal district court there and that I was to get my citizenship papers. I was interviewed by a couple of the newspapers at the time because I was in uniform and they had never seen anybody in an American uniform that was sworn in to become a United States citizen.

After four or six weeks at Camp Lee, many of us were transferred to the 9th Infantry Division at Fort Bragg. I thought to myself, you know, What the hell am I doing here in a place called Fayetteville? It was called "Fatalburg." Just a terrible town, really. Typical army town. It was a huge camp and was known as an artillery-training camp primarily. At Fort Bragg they announced that a specific number of what we called "cadres" from each company in the division, of all units, were taken out to form a brand-new division, which turned out to be the 82nd Airborne Division. I found myself with, I would say, 80 percent Brooklynites, really a bunch of tough guys, many of Italian or German descent. Some from New Jersey, mostly from the East. All with either a high school education or men who had been in the regular army, including some of the officers. Many of the officers were from the South, and most of the enlisted men were from eastern states: New England, New York, New Jersey, Pennsylvania, and so on. I was one of the few people from Ohio at that particular time. So I learned basically a new language altogether. It was fascinating. We all became, sooner or later, very close friends, including the officers for that matter. I remained in the medics, in the medical battalion of the division.

Later on, in the summer of 1942, most of us were shipped to Chesapeake Bay to get involved in amphibious maneuvers, as we were destined to go overseas. Many of us had no idea whether it would be the Pacific or Europe. Certainly one of the things we never thought of is that we would go into Africa. In mid-October 1942 we were taken to Norfolk and placed in a convoy of about a hundred ships. I was very fortunate to be on the commodore's ship, which was very protected. The convoy was defended by destroyers and cruisers throughout the journey because of the activity of German U-boats during that period. We were at sea almost four weeks before they told us that we would be landing on the French Moroccan coast in an amphibious landing. Our landings were actually covered by the battleship *Texas*. We disembarked north of Rabat, which was then the capital of French Morocco.

We were in a bivouac area in a place called Port Lyautey, French Morocco. Again, this was a fascinating period because, if you were at all in any contact with the natives, the women all wore veils, and it was very primitive in many ways although the French had settled that part of Morocco since the 1870s. Port Lyautey was named after a General Lyautey.[3] The French were very smart in colonizing Morocco in the 1870s. They induced—through tax situations and various other incentives—a surprising number of French Jewish people, merchants, to move there to start businesses, to grow orchards, to do a lot of exporting from those areas. All sorts of materials. So, when we got there, the Vichy French were the ones that opposed us and our landings. They had native troops, French noncommissioned soldiers, and some officers. In Safi they marched right in. There was no opposition. At Port Lyautey we had three days of fighting. We landed at a sea-resort place that had cabanas and swimming pools and everything else and a lot of dead bodies around there—our first wave or first two or three waves. We were strafed by French planes when we landed. It was amazing. They had a huge mountain area at the entrance of the river that was going in. Here's the beach, here's the mountain, here's a small river, and right above the river on the embankment were railroad tracks, and they had a naval gun that was moving back and forth on these tracks shooting at us. This mountain was called the Kasbah. The site is now an American cemetery for some of our soldiers. We had between thirty and forty casualties during that fighting. Interesting thing, they had a big stadium at the edge of town, and all the Jewish people were assembled and stayed out on the grass of the stadium. They were herded there. They were rounded up there by the Vichy French. What they were going to do with them, I don't know.

When we housed in buildings in Port Lyautey, the Assistant G-2, intelligence officer of the division, came to meet with me and my company commander and said, "I want him. We have an idea that we need people that can do interpreting and interrogation work and whatever. We're all new at this. We've never done it before. This is kind of a new concept. Could he be on detached service with us?" So that's when I went to Division Headquarters of G-2 and became, for the rest of the war basically, out of the medics.[4] I would, on many occasions, be housed with my old medical company. I was doing a lot of clerical work when I was free to do so for them. I handled all the insurances, the GI insurance, payrolls, and there were a lot of, you might say, personnel files that I had to take care of along with our first sergeant, who also was from Long Island. He called me "Stern" with a thick New York accent. My nickname became "Gestapo." Everybody in the division knew me as Gestapo because of what I was doing. The idea was, if you spent a lot of time with the medics, then the first thing that you want to do if you have wounded German prisoners from Afrika Korps is interrogate them. Africa Korps was probably as professional an army as you would ever have in any army in any country. They were truly professional soldiers from top to bottom. A formidable opponent, you might say.

We did a lot of improvising. We had no idea of how to go about doing all of this. In talking to some of these people or interrogating them, I suddenly realized that I hadn't spoken German in several years. It really became frustrating at times not to be able to fluently speak my first language.

Little did we know that in the II Corps, which was Operation Torch really, that we were the guinea pigs for what was later established. In 1944 they formed an army group at Camp Ritchie in Maryland that, from those experiences that we had, gradually set up manuals and everything else to recruit people who had foreign languages, particularly German and Italian, possibly, or French, to set up a camp eventually to train these people in what we were doing.[5] We wrote the manual, so to speak.

One of my impressions of that region of North Africa was that all of the cities were surprisingly very modern. Beautiful highways, high-rise buildings all over the place. For some reason we had a chance to go to Meknes, a town in the desert that had a synagogue that looked like an old Berlin synagogue. Beautiful old ornaments and everything else. I think that a lot of the population were what they call Sephardic Jews that were originally from Spain and, of course, France. Commerce apparently built up all these cities over the years, from the 1870s into the early twentieth century. In December of 1942, we were taken out of these bivouac areas on what was called the "forty and eight." These were World War I freight cars, and they were called "forty and eight" because they held forty men or eight horses. They took us up into the mountains, the Berber Mountains. It was snowing—it's hard to believe this, but it was snowing—and then into the desert from there. That's where, in the Kasserine Pass and El Guettar and all these places, we not only met resistance, but we were absolutely clobbered. We were as green as grass. I mean, we'd never been in combat before. The Germans had an air force. They strafed us. They bombed us. We had lots and lots of casualties.

In North Africa we ended up in Bizerte, where we finally had the German surrender. Being on top of a mountain, you looked down into a valley with probably as many as eighty to one hundred thousand German prisoners. They were all rounded up into cages of sorts that they had there. That group was the original major prisoners of war. We also worked closely with the British Eighth Army, Montgomery, and that crowd over there. And I found out for the first time what a class system the English really had. We were always starving; we were always hungry. Never had enough food. Even C-rations sometimes didn't get to us at all. So I went to one of their camps—and I found that they had a special section for noncoms, a special section for the lower-class people and whatever—to beg them for a tin of biscuits that we had from them. They seemed to be better supplied than we were.

Our division became known as having stopped the Germans with concentrated artillery when they made a major thrust through the American lines. The guy that set up this concentration was the colonel in charge of all artillery for our division, who later became our chief of staff. His name was William Westmoreland.[6] We fought through a concentration of opposing tank forces that the German Panzer forces presented near the Kasserine Pass area.

I was, by the way, for two weeks, attached to French troops. They were called the Goumiers. They were Berber mountain troops, and they were natives. The first day I was there, they caught a sheep and they strangled it, put it on a tree limb, and, with their wonderful knives that they had, they slit the belly open a little bit and blew into the area to be able to open the outer skin of the wool around it. Then one guy built a little fire with some stones surrounding it. Another Goumier took the liver and the heart and everything like that. They had these long sticks that had sharp points and they would put this meat on there. Then they held it into the fire and turned and offered, "Here, eat it."

They were people that had these huge belts and these what looked like nightgowns, these striped nightgowns that were very warm. I mean heavy wool nightgowns. They wore mostly bands around their heads, and they all had huge beards. They were people that could go out, at night especially, into the German lines and cut off their ears. They would have ears all around their belts. Ears, when they could have slit their throat. They were fierce-looking guys. Once I was going in a jeep, and I saw this small formation that looked like a platoon of Goumiers with a French noncommissioned officer who had a swivel stick under his arm. They were supposed to be at attention. That meant their rifles had to be positioned correctly, and this guy goes up to one of them that apparently was a little bit out of line and he hit him with that swivel stick across the face. I began to think, you know, Why they don't rebel against these guys, the French? These were French natives. No, they didn't. That was apparently par for the course.

You talk about primitive living. We would set up tents near a wooded area and everybody would have dysentery—everybody. I mean you would hardly be able to get up and get going. At the end of the fighting, they took us near, outside of, Sidi Bel Abbès, where the French

Moroccan Goumier sharpening his bayonet, Italy, 1944. *Courtesy of National Archives and Records Administration.*

Foreign Legion was two miles away. We had to be setting up shelter halves in there, and most of us were just ill. If you went to the kitchen to get something to eat, your mess kit was covered with flies all over the place. After the fighting, our commanding general made us put full field packs on and run a mile. All we were wearing is boots and underwear, no tops. They pushed in order to keep our physical strength up.

Eventually they moved us to a town called Oran, which is near Algiers seaport on the Mediterranean. There we embarked on ships, small merchant ships, headed for Sicily. We were the first ones both in Africa as well as Sicily. I remember we landed after dark outside of Palermo harbor, and we were strafed again on the boats by Germans. The British had already landed on another part of the island. We unloaded near Palermo, and we had to walk with full gear about two miles to a railroad track. We were taken inland from there.

Sicily was really interesting. I recall an overnight in a jeep on top of a mountain in the interior of Sicily. I mean you felt like you were in New Guinea or someplace like that, far from any civilization. There was nothing else around. We had one of these huge aerials on this jeep. You'd wake up, and the guy turned on the radio and the Armed Forces [Radio] played Glenn Miller tunes in this godforsaken place. Your spirits were lifted all of a sudden. It was just great to have little things like this. It was just terrific. It was near a place called Troina in Sicily. I remember swimming in the Tyrrhenian Sea and thinking to myself, Here goes Odysseus. *The Odyssey.*

I saw my father for the first time in seven years in December 1943. He had remarried and escaped from Germany to England with help from friends in a major Lloyd's Underwriting Firm. My unit was one of two divisions that were supposed to go into Italy from Sicily in the late fall of 1943. All of a sudden they shipped us to England because we had combat experience. We were stationed in the south of England around Winchester to train newly arriving divisions that were going to eventually be used in the Normandy invasion. While I was in England I was sent to British Intelligence School in London. They were fabulous. They had done this for so many years, and they knew all the techniques and the specific things that you were looking for and how to interpret a map. We were there for almost two weeks. There were several different classes that you went to. I thought to myself, My God, this is like day and night from what we had to pick up by ourselves of what we wanted to know. It was an eye-opener because I learned so much more than what we were guinea pigs for in North Africa and Sicily.

While in England I would have furloughs every few weeks and took the train up to see my family and stayed with them. They were nervous wrecks during the Blitz because their apartment, or "flat" as they called it, was near what they call Hampstead Heath in London. That was the major concentration of antiaircraft guns around that area. In the middle of the night when those things went off, everybody took their ready-made bedding and went down to the "tube," the subway, and remained there for the rest of the night. I remember staying with them, and this was the first time in two years I had slept in a bed. I put a pillow over my head while the guns went off and turned around and went back to sleep. So it didn't bother me much.

When I was assigned to work with British Intelligence School for two weeks, I probably was the only American soldier ever that stayed with his family in London instead of being billeted in American facilities at that time. I was actually taking the bus every morning to work and back in the evening. So it was really a lot of fun.

After landing at Utah Beach, the significant breakthrough came at Saint-Lô, in France, the Normandy area. That was where the German concentrations were. It was the area that we needed to go through to start a large pincer movement in France. The fields of Normandy are surrounded by these hedges. It was hedgerow fighting. The breakthrough initiated with the Allies using fighter planes to start the bombardment. I was in a field where headquarters of our engineers' battalion was located one field over. They had two trucks filled with mines. One of our P-40s flew over. The P-40 carried 500-pound bombs under each wing strap. They had a tendency that if they banked too steeply, one of the bombs would roll off, and this happened and right into the engineers' field. It killed a large number of troops; this huge black cloud went up. This was only one hundred or two hundred yards away from my position at most. At the time, we thought that was a signal for the bombers that were supposed to follow. We knew that thirty-six hundred bombers would fly over and bomb the Saint-Lô area in front of us. It is well known that over four hundred American troops were killed, including General McNair, who was one of the top officials in the US Army. McNair happened to be an observer in the area at the time. He was among the dead there.[7]

They didn't bomb us, but we were a half mile or maybe three-quarters of a mile back from where they were bombing, lying on the side of the embankments, dug in, but not in a deep foxhole. I was lying on my stomach, and after a while I was black and blue this bombing was so intense and so huge. The thirty-six hundred bombers came in after the P-40s and Mustangs and everything else had done their work strafing or bombing. I saw these clusters, maybe, coming down right near me. It was a sight that you never would ever want to see again. I felt any day now could be the end. Imagine practically the whole of the British and American combination of air force in Europe was flying over there to soften up that line.

Then the breakthrough came, and we were able to make this big hook to the Falaise Gap and enclose several German armies that were still opposing us in the Normandy area. We captured two or three German armies that way.[8] It was probably a brilliant move. Most of us felt that General Bradley was the most brilliant tactician, but also we got to know him in North Africa and Sicily. He was kind of our guy, so to speak. General Manton Eddy was a real disciplinarian but also a very good tactician. Our division really was one of the experienced divisions. We cut off the entire Cotentin Peninsula. At the bottom of it was Cherbourg, and we captured the whole German Seventh Army there.

I would say that I was lucky, because there were many times I was with the aid stations. When we landed in Normandy, I had a field day with both wounded and nonwounded German prisoners. I have a commendation from the general for establishing a method where either an ambulance would take me to the aid stations or a jeep that I had available to me. I probably was the only soldier in the American army in combat that could go anywhere I wanted to. I met French Resistance fighters. There were townspeople in these villages in Normandy that I spoke to. Fortunately I knew enough French still that I was able to speak. Gradually, as you go along, you learned more of the language. In many ways I was everywhere.

Field interrogation basically means that, if you have a prisoner, the first things you ask are: "What outfit were you in?" "Where did you come from?" "What concentration, what outfits were in that area?" "Did you come by train?" "What specific area did you bivouac in?" You want to get basically the idea of what's in front of you right now. "Where are the concentration of troops?" "What outfits are they?" "Are they Panzer troops?" "Are they infantry?" "Are they artillery?" "Are there railroad guns here?" "Whatever did you see?" Then, you frisk his entire pockets looking for whatever he has, like a passport: where he was born, where he was raised, whatever. He may have family pictures. "Is that your wife?" "Is that your son?" "When were you decorated?" "Where?" "Where'd you come from?"

By the way, when we landed, among the first units that we found were conscripted Poles. They weren't even Germans. They were fighting for the Germans, and of course they were lucky and happy as hell to be American prisoners at this point. So that was easy. Then you come across somebody, especially in the more elite units, like the tankers, some Panzer units, and SS troops. They become very arrogant. They don't want to do anything. So a lot of the time Geneva Conventions go out the window. I remember one just before we got into the fighting of the Battle of the Bulge. We captured a guy like this that was really, "I'm not going to tell you anything." So we'd hand him a shovel. And I said, "You start digging." And I said, "You know what this is? This is going to be your grave, right here." I'd take a .45 and just play around with him while he's around there. On occasions I had a guy that was my first sergeant, about six foot three, huge guy, big guy. I said, "He wanted to get slapped a little bit." So you would. One of the things we learned with a lot of people was, "When we get through with you, we're sending you over to Russia." That was really the key. Whether men or women, civilians or military. I said, "We can send you over to Russian forces in no time at all." That's what made them talk, for the most part.

I didn't have a whole lot of trouble. There was one instance where I did something I was really ashamed of. We had a guy that came in on a stretcher who was a captain of a tank unit, an elite army unit. You talk about a guy that was arrogant. I mean, it wasn't simply "I'm not telling you anything." He talked back to you. I don't know. I was so mad that I just hauled off and slapped him. Here he was on a stretcher. He was apparently not just conscious, he was in pretty good shape actually. They'd brought him in. Some of the officers around me just looked the other way, but I felt, Jesus, what made me do something stupid like that?

Another instance that stands out occurred in the Ruhr area. We virtually had over thirty thousand soldiers give up. By that time, in the spring of 1945, you had men that were sixty years old, you had men who were twelve years old. The most pitiful-looking people in uniform. Well, they brought in a general to me, and we were in the schoolhouse at the time. The colonel of the medical battalion said to me, "I understand you're going to be interviewing a German general." He said, "I'm going to give you my jacket with the epaulets of colonel on there so that you look like a professional interviewer for this guy." Well, this guy, he seemed to be in his sixties, and you almost could feel pity for the guy. It was sort of like, Thank God, it's all over for me. There wasn't really a whole lot that I wanted out of him. I just wanted to know, "Were you in charge of these people?" Yes, he was. This large group that had given themselves up. He said, basically, "It's all over for us." I asked him some questions: Where he had been? Were there any staff people anywhere nearby that he knew of? Was there any additional fighting going on in there? Essentially, he just answered, but he was so listless in a sense that you felt like this isn't even really an interrogation. Now, the other thing is that you may have maps that you take from them. You ask them, "Who was here? There?" "Is there anything at all that I should know about of any value that you can tell?"

Papers were prepared from reports. I was always using a field telephone to call in what I had learned. Then G-2 would put all of this information that was fed to them from different areas into a memo, secret memo, that was going around that showed all the units that were opposing you, what towns were involved, where they were bivouacked, where they were here, did they have any air force left, did they have any special forces left, was there any kind of weapon that you had to look out for. It was in great detail. It was all spelled out so that you had a corps or an army that would consolidate all that information that was in front of them. It was probably one of the more important things that helped them make strategic moves at that time. When we were still in the bivouac area, around Thanksgiving as I remember, several days before the Battle of the Bulge started, we had somehow picked up a few German prisoners. Several of them mentioned to me that their major concentrations were around the city of Aachen and Cologne, and nobody seemed to pay any attention to it. Most seemed to say, This is nothing special. Well, there was this huge concentration there, probably over two hundred and fifty thousand troops and tanks that were in the breakthrough. I almost was caught because, when we moved, we were supposed to be moving north, and I was going south on this highway towards the town of Malmédy. Malmédy became infamous as the site where some American troops were captured and they were mowed down by SS troops in the snow.[9] Right near that area is when I realized I was going the wrong way. I heard shooting, just wild, going on by artillery and everything else. I said, "We've got to be in the wrong area." I was in a personnel carrier with six other guys and my driver. I said, "We better turn around. We went to the wrong direction." We hightailed it back to find our units. But those things did happen. Oh, we were very lucky because, if we had gone maybe another mile, we wouldn't be here. That's for sure. None of us would be.

People don't know how many times we starved. We didn't have food, or the little C-ration or K-ration that they had with us was gone in no time at all, and it was dreadful. Canned Spam and stuff like that, how sickening it was. In Sicily, outside of a town called Cefalù, we were bivouacked in a grape orchard. The grapes were to be made into Marsala wine. We were lying there in these ditches between rows and rows of grapes. We reached out from it and ate. After two days I didn't ever want to see any grapes again. Never in my life did I want to see any grapes again. We got so sick and tired of it. If a farmer or anybody brought something to eat or we found some eggs that could be fried or cooked, if it was anything unusual, it was just heaven. In Port Lyautey—keep in mind we landed on November 8—it was around Thanksgiving time when somehow our kitchen units got ahold of a great big sow. They killed it and built a pit. All day long they rotated that damn thing. And I remember at night somebody had gotten some bread in town, big round loaves of bread. We ate bread with nothing on it whatsoever, and they sliced this pig up. It was like going to the most famous French restaurant you ever could imagine. I mean, little things like this were just unusual. It's a lot of the little things I encountered and that stick in my memory.

There were a lot of little things that one could think are really not of any great importance but stand out in my memory. In one instance we were in a bivouac area, a farmer comes along with a wheel several feet wide. It was some goat cheese that he gave to us. I had a guy in central France that came late one afternoon. We had set up pup tents outside of this town, and this guy came along with a bottle of champagne that he had kept for about sixty or more years that he wanted to give to somebody, one of the liberators. Things like that.

Another that stands out comes from my time in England. My father would greet me at the train coming from Winchester into London and would say that Ani, my stepmother, was going to have a roast for me, and she had to pay with all kinds of points. She knew the butcher and did a little finagling to get some really good meat: "She's going to have a roast for you tonight." Just the greatest.

I was very lucky because it wasn't until we were in the Hürtgen Forest that I was wounded the first time. I was actually standing near some ambulances when all of a sudden I said to one guy, "God, something is stinging me!" Well, a piece of shrapnel sliced right into my calf. Fortunately, it was just a flesh wound, and I went to my old company, which was called the "clearing company." They gave me a tetanus shot, bandaged me, and said, "You're sticking around here for about a week. Don't you go anywhere." And I did.

The next time around we were on the east bank of the Rhine River. We had captured the Remagen Bridge. It was really called the Ludendorff Bridge after the famous World War I German General Ludendorff. You know, history tells you it was intact. They were ready to blow it. The guys there to blow it ran away, and they later on were shot by Hitler's personal command. They were all shot because they didn't stand their ground or they didn't do the job that they were supposed to do.

One interesting thing happened right on the banks of the river. There were small houses around there. We were looking for a place to stay. I went up to this house. An old guy, he must have been in his seventies, comes out, and he said, "I'm the only one here." He speaks perfect American English. I said, "What the hell?" He said he spent twenty years in the United States, but he moved back, and his whole family was gone. He lived there alone in this house. I said, "Well, we're taking it over." And he said, "I have some eggs here, some fresh eggs." So, you know, anything that you could get in the way of regular food or semblance of regular food was wonderful. So about four of us went upstairs, and he had a complete empty room with a huge plate-glass window overlooking the Rhine River. At the other end of the room was a dilapidated old couch. So we sit there on this couch, all of us, and just joking around, kidding around, whatever. One guy even had a bottle of wine that he swiped from somewhere.

The Germans, by this time, tried to demolish that bridge. I swear to this day that I saw, out of the corner of my eye, what almost looked like a huge fireball. It was followed by an enormous explosion. It lifted us from the couch, and this glass from this plate-glass window is all over our faces and body and all of it, not very deep, but sufficiently so that we all were bleeding. We went to the aid station to get us fixed up. That was the only two times I was hit.

In the mid-1930s, while I still lived in Berlin, I had heard of instances where prominent Jewish residents were taken away by the Gestapo in the middle of the night. Sometimes they were released after brief periods of detention. Others disappeared. I always felt that things looked so ominous to us all. What would happen to us? You just don't know what's in store for us. A number of families that I was close friends with moved with their entire families either to France or to England, or some of them actually even went to Argentina. For the last hundred years or so, Germans have been just enamored with South America for some reason, Argentina and Brazil especially. Not just a bunch of SS people that escaped there, but long before that. The ones that stayed in any European country, it was a given that they would not make it, that they would be captured. I didn't realize at the time how lucky I really was to be able to start a whole new life after moving in 1936. We had nothing to look forward to in any way, shape, or form. It was just a dead end for us. It was almost like being snared somewhere and you're in a maze and you can't get out. You felt sooner or later you would be taken away. If you were in an apartment building and you looked downstairs, particularly on weekends, you'd see thousands and thousands of Brownshirts marching. The SR and SS were always marching in these huge formations. Most folks have seen pictures of Nuremburg, where they had one hundred thousand uniformed people and Hitler speaking to them and this kind of thing. We all saw this, whether it was on the news or in pictures or actually in person. It was frightening because you felt this was a new force.

I loved being on my own in a way. I'd love to go off somewhere. I remember going to a wooded area outside of Berlin on my bike. I had some sandwiches with me. Lo and behold, on two sides of me were Germans in uniform practicing with their weapons in there. They were on maneuvers. This was in 1934 or 1935. I thought, What the hell is going on? But it had to be something that they were doing that was supposedly prohibited under the Versailles Treaty.[10] It was "verboten."

In the early 1940s, about the time I was entering the army, I heard about what came to be known much later as concentration camps. My father had written from England that he had received word that a number of cousins and my maternal grandmother had been sent to a detention camp in a town called Auschwitz, in Poland. Unfortunately no one ever heard from them again. I also remember, in 1942 in England, my father knew friends who owned shortwave radios which picked up daily clandestine French Resistance "Calais Calling" and, on occasions, they heard of mass killings in camps. It would not be until 1945 when we would finally become aware of the extent of the barbarities that were taking place.

Around April 11 and April 12, 1945, we were clearing pockets of resistance in the Ruhr industrial areas. Our latest assignment was to start a 150-mile motor march to the Harz-Nordhausen area. In this area remnants of the Eleventh SS Panzer Army were bottled up, refusing to surrender. German high command had also formed three new divisions. They too were among the holdouts. Two elite divisions began facing the 9th.

The Harz Mountains had few equals in national fortification. It was approximately twenty-two miles across and sixty-eight miles long, up to four thousand feet, excellent observation posts. Unquestionably the Hitler regime chose this area to become a highly industrialized enterprise. As I recall, the First Army planned to bypass the Harz Mountain Fortress then encircle the area. The reduction of this pocket constituted the last major obstacle facing the VII Corps.

As we were motoring, mostly in two-and-a-half-ton trucks, toward the town of Nordhausen, we came upon a railroad yard and saw, on flatcars, fins and other large components of V-2 rockets. We came upon there by accident, really. All of a sudden we noticed a railroad yard. I got out of the truck and said, "I want to climb on that flatcar to see how high these fins really are." Several other guys did the same thing. Then, we got back in the trucks and, lo and behold, here two minutes later, approximately a quarter of a mile away, we come upon a well-camouflaged entrance to a mountain tunnel with big netting around and large poles that looked like they're made like a piece of knitting stacked up outside. These were apparently part of the rocket. What part I still don't know to this point because everything was disassembled. We saw a narrow-gauge railway going right into this facility. We went in there first to take a look. Inside the tunnel were rows of highly placed electrical lights. We observed small-gauge railroad tracks, long steel tables, some benches, scattered chains, and other unidentified paraphernalia. The tunnel was all lit up. It looked like a factory that had been emptied out completely. There were no signs of human beings inside the tunnel.

Then you walked a little further, about four hundred to five hundred yards, and, lo and behold, you see all these people lying there on the ground. We started taking pictures. In a way, cruel as it may sound, we didn't have a bunch of individuals come asking for help. None of that happened because the few that were alive were virtually dead. The carnage and horror of Nordhausen had been uncovered earlier that day by tankers of the 3rd Armored Division and infantrymen of the 104th Division.

In the slave-labor camp the living and the dead were lying side by

Lager Nordhausen concentration camp, April 12, 1945. *Courtesy of National Archives and Records Administration.*

side. The living were too emaciated to move their limbs. The dead were unburied or half-buried. SS troops had stacked bodies in ditches. Yet we took photos with cameras we recently acquired while fighting on the Ruhr. We had uncovered a German AGFA plant with large inventories of new cameras, tripods, and lenses.[11] We walked around. There were no barracks; there were no facilities. If there were barracks, they had been bombed out. In the periphery of the camp there were any number of buildings that were completely bombed out. Just the steel structure was still standing here and there. Then, along with it, you were constantly feeling, I'm going to throw up because it's overwhelming stench. At the same time it was so quiet. It was just dead, this dead silence. It was like a cloud was overhanging everything. It was just eerie, a very eerie feeling of no sounds, highly unusual in that respect. Some of our medical officers did get involved in sorting out and seeing whether somebody was still alive or having the townspeople take out the dead, who were virtually skeletons. That's what they were, just skeletal remains of people that were put in these trenches alongside.

We learned that one group which could not walk had been chained in the mountain tunnel for three months without seeing daylight. I also spotted a bank of very large ovens on the premises. There was no doubt that camp personnel burned the dead in these ovens. On the grates you could see bones.

In due time we learned that Nordhausen had a long, drawn-out system of torture. One method was to crowd several hundred prisoners into a courtyard. There, on a raised platform, the condemned were hanged. Others were taken to the mountain tunnel, chained to work benches, and worked to death or beaten to death. They were there to assemble parts of the V-2 rockets. Almost all prisoners were simply starved to death. The prisoners of this notorious camp were French, Russians, Poles, Lithuanians, Romanians. I'm not certain that any Jews were at that camp.

We commandeered the mayor of nearby Nordhausen to round up able-bodied men to dig additional long trenches to bury the skeletal bodies. I also remember that several townspeople exclaimed that they knew nothing about the slave-labor camp. This infuriated us even more at the time. Almost everywhere you would ask people in these communities whether they knew that places like this existed. This was especially true where there were some very unusual things that were going on. Particularly with a camp like Nordhausen, where the town is less than two miles away, I mean, within walking distance. They claim, "We never knew this place existed." This was just a plain defense mechanism to say, "We're not involved in this. We didn't know anything about it." You found that in the German army a whole lot. There was almost like a trait on the part of the Germans whether in the service, in the army, or in civilian life: "We're not involved in this." I thought, No, you were just wonderful people that just obeyed the guy at the top.

By this time I had been in combat for three years through eight major campaigns. The kind of things that you see: people blowing up in front of you. The vision again of a P-40 that dropped the bomb unintentionally right near our division headquarters in France always stayed with me. A soldier right in front of me, just a few feet away, a guy that I knew was in the MPs, his whole face was gone all of a sudden. Right in front of me. He kept walking. When you're in shock somehow, bodies keep moving. You see that. I saw people who, when the bridge over the Rhine collapsed, had whole girders fall on them. I saw soldiers lose their arms. You see all this stuff, so many different kinds of devastation. Bombings, whether it's just buildings or whatever. I remember being in a field in France and hearing a railroad gun going off. You don't know whether it's hit in your area or not. In some ways you get numb, but at the same time you're constantly on guard. You never know whether from day to day you're going to be hit or not hit or whether you're still alive.

It is hard to explain: Nordhausen slave-labor camp was a very traumatic experience. In another way, however, seeing the camp was in some sense familiar. It was a terrible shock, but in a way we were attuned to it. I'm not saying you'd become blasé about any of it, not at all.

Many of us in our outfits became attuned to the enemy's way of thinking and the way they reacted. Our guys, in a way, were much more sophisticated than I realized that they were. Initially I thought I was very different from the rest of our guys who were Americans. I had been brought up in a different country that not only threw me out but was intent on killing all of us. I assumed they would feel different. They didn't. They felt pretty much the same as we did. Whether it is what happens in combat or it was a general feeling about what the Nazis were doing to us, we were really defending our country and our way of life. I think they felt as strongly as I did for the most part. There may be a few people who to them it was a day-to-day way of life and it really didn't matter. We had our share of guys who were Virginia farmers or Pennsylvania farm people, and we had people that were in the fire department of some little town in upstate New York. Everybody from all walks of life just mingled together. There were people who were truck drivers in civilian life, or mechanics. You had truly a mixture of everything.

The war was a major watershed in my life, and the life of fellow soldiers obviously. In 1945, during the occupation, we started to form an association that would be perpetuated after the war.[12] Starting in 1946 we had annual reunions in major cities, the first being in Washington. We met in New York, Philadelphia, and Columbus, Ohio. Gradually, we moved out into other parts of the country. Our meeting this August 2012 in Pittsburg will be our sixty-seventh reunion, and the veterans will turn over the whole operation of the association to the sons and daughters. They already have formed an auxiliary several years ago. In the late 1940s and early 1950s, the association formed chapters in different parts of the country. It took until 1992 for us to form a Texas Greater Southwest Chapter. At our first meetings in Belton, Texas, we had over seventy veterans there and their wives. I've been president and treasurer of that group. Our last meeting was in April 2012 because there were only three of us left. There were a lot of widows, some sons and daughters. Most attendees came from Dallas, Fort Worth,

Arlington, Houston, Austin, and Waco. I decided to close the chapter. We had been meeting twice a year. Lo and behold, at the end of the meeting I said, "We're closing this meeting." Everybody raised their hand and said, "We'd like to continue this as a friendship group." So I am currently planning for a November meeting there again to continue it on.

When I think about my experience at Nordhausen, it's just impossible for me to understand that there are people around, and lots of them apparently, who will say it never happened. It doesn't have to come from Iran or anything. It's right here in the United States. It's just amazing to me. With the photos, the direct accounts, the fact that there are people alive who've been in the camps. It is so tragic to me what some of the people I have met in my life have gone through. Virtually all of them lost one or more family members, close family members. Some of them, a whole lot of family members. How anybody could possibly even say this never even happened, it's amazing to me.

For a short time after returning from the war, Herbert Stern worked for an uncle in Cincinnati, and then he hired on with a scrap-metal company. As part of that work he was assigned to take over a defunct office in Texas City, Texas, in the early 1950s. He worked with that company for forty years helping grow the enterprise into the largest scrap-metal brokerage company in the United States. Stern was retired by the company in 1982 at the age of sixty-two. A few years later he began a second career, working in acquisitions, mergers, and industrial recruiting in the oil- and gas-pipe business. He had a highly successful career in that industry, working in the Middle East, England, and the United States before his second retirement at the age of eighty-eight.

Herb Stern's interview was part of the Texas Liberators of World War II Concentration Camps Oral History Project, funded by a grant from the Texas Holocaust and Genocide Commission. Copies of all materials were also deposited in the Library of Congress and the four Texas Holocaust museums—Houston, El Paso, Dallas, and San Antonio. See Herbert U. Stern, *Oral Memoirs of Herbert U. Stern,* an interview conducted by Stephen Sloan, with videography by Robert DeBoard, May 31, 2012, in Houston, Texas. BU Digital Collections.

Notes

1. In April 1933 German law began limiting the number of Jewish students in schools.

2. Camp Lee, built on a training camp from World War I, was home to a Medical Replacement Training Center during its early period of operation in World War II.

3. Louis Hubert Lyautey, Morocco's first French resident general, established the settlement in 1912.

4. G-2 designates the intelligence staff of a US Army unit. G-1 is personnel, G-3 is operations, and G-4 is supply.

5. The Military Intelligence Training Center began operations at Camp Ritchie in June 1942 and was run by the Military Intelligence Service of the War Department.

6. William Westmoreland later became a four-star army general and commanded US military operations in the Vietnam War.

7. Army Gen. Lesley James McNair was killed by friendly fire on July 25, 1944.

8. Many argue that the Battle of the Falaise Pocket, August 12–21, was the decisive engagement of the Battle of Normandy.

9. German SS troops murdered eighty-four American prisoners of war near Malmedy, Belgium, in December 1944.

10. Outlined in Part V of the Treaty of Versailles, the peace agreement that formally ended World War I.

11. Aktien-Gesellschaft für Anilin-Fabrikation, a major German producer of cameras, film, and photographic chemicals.

12. The 82nd Airborne Division Association.

THERE IN THE THICK OF IT 1943–1944

In November 1942, when the Allies were winning the Second Battle of El Alamein, Winston Churchill gave his prognosis of the war to a luncheon crowd in London, remarking: "This is not the end. It is not even the beginning of the end. But it is, perhaps, the end of the beginning." At the close of 1942, the length and outcome of the war were uncertain, but the Allies had a great deal to be optimistic about: Rommel was cornered in Tunisia, the Germans were surrounded at Stalingrad, and the Japanese had been pushed to the far western end of Guadalcanal.

EUROPE

Victories in North Africa following Operation Torch provided the Allies with staging areas that supported the subsequent Italian Campaign and operations elsewhere in Europe. The decision to focus on Italy after securing North Africa was made in January 1943, when political and military leaders, including Churchill, convened at the Casablanca Conference to determine the Allies' next step in the European Theater. Americans felt a cross-channel invasion of Europe was the logical choice, but the British argued for what would become the plan behind the Italian Campaign: an invasion of Sicily and then of mainland Italy to push the Germans up the boot, toward their homeland. The latter plan emerged the winner, and an invasion of Western Europe was put on hold.

On May 9, 1943, German and Italian forces in North Africa surrendered to the British. Later that month the Allies began bombing Sicily, Sardinia, and the Italian mainland. On July 10 they invaded Sicily, and on September 3, the British having advanced to the toe of Italy, the Axis country agreed to an armistice. Within a week, Allied forces landed on the west coast at Salerno and on the heel of the boot in Taranto. With heavy rains and snow often severely impeding Allied movements, driving the Germans out of Italy would cost thousands of civilian and military lives and take the rest of the war in Europe.

THE WITNESSES

FRED "RED" HARRIS was serving his fourth term in the Texas House of Representatives when the Japanese attacked Pearl Harbor. He soon after volunteered for the navy, entering as a lieutenant junior grade. His first assignment was aboard the USS *Croatan,* a Bogue-class escort carrier, launched in 1943, that patrolled for German U-boats in the Atlantic Ocean. The *Croatan* was part of a larger task group that ferried supplies and troops from the East Coast of the United States to Casablanca, French Morocco. Harris served as the *Croatan*'s flight deck officer.

OSCAR NORBERT DUCONGÉ became a member of the all-black 92nd Infantry Division in 1942. A college graduate, he went to Officer Candidate School and worked in the finance department. He continued in that position when his regiment was transferred overseas to Italy in the late summer of 1944. His company was in charge of preparing payrolls for enlisted men in the regiments assigned to them. Later, DuCongé volunteered for combat duty and was on the front lines of the Allied advance up the boot of Italy.

THE PACIFIC

By 1943 the United States had established a military presence in the South Pacific with bases at Nouméa, New Caledonia, and in the New Hebrides. Next, in their first large-scale offensive against Japan, they secured Guadalcanal. Then, beginning with Operation Cartwheel, in the latter part of 1943, and continuing through early 1945, the Allies in the Pacific implemented island-hopping (taking an island and then its neighbor) and leapfrogging (capturing strategic islands but bypassing Japanese strongholds and cutting off their supply line). These two methods reduced the time required, made the most of limited resources, and cost fewer lives. Under the command of Adm. Chester Nimitz and Gen. Douglas MacArthur, Allied forces battled their way to the Philippines (to which, in 1942, MacArthur had vowed to return) and toward Japan.

Taking these islands—most of which the world had never heard of—from the Japanese came at a steep price, with thousands of lives lost on both sides. Japanese soldiers defended their territory passionately, and Allied troops often faced last-ditch suicidal missions in the form of banzai charges and kamikaze attacks. Despite their efforts, however, the Japanese were unable to stop the advance of their enemies. In early 1945, Allied troops reached

Iwo Jima and Okinawa, and to the south forces were liberating the Philippines. The Allies were ready for the next phase of the war against the Empire.

THE WITNESSES

After eleven months as flight deck officer on the USS *Croatan* in the Atlantic, FRED "RED" HARRIS was reassigned to help assemble the crew of the new USS *Franklin,* an Essex-class aircraft carrier. There he again acted as flight deck officer. The *Franklin* set sail in early 1944 and served in the Pacific, where the ship suffered a kamikaze attack in October 1944 and a bombing in March 1945. The latter set off a succession of explosions that turned the ship into a floating inferno. Harris, who witnessed both events, stayed with the *Franklin* until it hobbled into Brooklyn Navy Yard in late April 1945.

In February 1943, radioman HOMER MARTIN boarded the USS *Hopkins,* a flagship high-speed minesweeper deployed in the South Pacific to detect and incapacitate underwater mines prior to invasions. When not sweeping, the ship often was on convoy duty, in which it worked to detect submarines and fight off enemy planes. Aboard the *Hopkins,* Martin took Morse code, and to keep spirits high he played records for the crew through the ship's speaker system. He stayed with the *Hopkins* through the end of the war, when the ship swept the entrance to Tokyo Bay for the surrender ceremonies.

FRANCES HARDISTY, a graduate of North Texas State Teachers College, joined the Women's Auxiliary Corps in 1943. After serving stateside for several months, she requested overseas duty and was stationed as a company commander in Hollandia, New Guinea, which the Allies had secured in the spring of 1944. She and her fellow Wacs worked in office and communication capacities, alongside men, until the war in the Pacific ended.

Cotton farmer EDDIE WEGNER shipped out in early 1943 to Hawaii, where he worked briefly on a beaching crew helping to bring seaplanes ashore. Afterward he received orders that took him to the New Hebrides, where, for a year and a half, he served as an aviation machinist's mate and naval air gunner. He also towed targets, carried mail, transported military leaders, and patrolled for submarines. His last assignment was on Guam.

FRED "RED" HARRIS

Fred Harris was born February 28, 1910, in the Oak Cliff neighborhood near Dallas, Texas. His father was a traveling salesman and opened several dry goods stores; his mother wrote poetry. In his youth Harris developed lifelong interests in athletics and music, participating in many sports and playing drums with local dance bands such as Herman Waldman's Orchestra. Harris graduated from Oak Cliff High School in 1927 and enrolled in Baylor University, where he had an athletic scholarship and worked a myriad of jobs to pay for room and board. While at Baylor, Harris lettered in football, basketball, baseball, and track, was named an all-conference end, and won all-conference honors in baseball. He left Baylor Law School to play professional baseball with the St. Louis Browns but returned and completed his law degree in 1932. After college Harris opened a law practice in Dallas and served four terms in the Texas House of Representatives. On October 16, 1935, he married Gussie Merle Hubert in Austin, Texas, in a church across the street from the capitol. Harris was appointed commissioner of District 4 on the Dallas County Commissioners Court in 1941.

ON THE MORNING OF DECEMBER 7 I WAS DUCK HUNTING with the captain of the Hella Temple Shrine Patrol, of which I was a member. He was a member of a fish and gun club just outside of Dallas, a little lake. It was pretty bad weather, and when we came in, the radio was blaring in the clubhouse. I knew something terrible had happened, but it was the next day before we understood what Pearl Harbor went through. And films and stuff started drifting back real quick. I was in my thirties. I had two small children—girls—and my wife. I wasn't anywhere close to being drafted under any circumstances, but this thing began to turn over in my mind.

A fellow named Thomas James Hamilton, a coach for the navy, designed a program known as the Hamilton Program. Within a very short period of time, he had practically every well-known coach in the United States in this program.[1] They had a recruiting office for naval air under the Hamilton Program in Dallas, Texas, and I was pretty active around. I missed very few games. I was always down to watch Baylor, and we saw all the games when we were in Austin. I would officiate every once in a while at high school games. I saw this program forming and talked it over with Mrs. Harris. I said, "I don't believe I can sit here and not be a portion of something." She says, "I think we can get by." So I joined the navy.

I had been county commissioner just six months when my resignation was turned in. Fortunately Mrs. Harris was appointed to carry out the remainder of my term, which would have been on through December of '42, and that helped a lot. Mrs. Harris is a brilliant woman. I knew she could handle it, and I knew there were enough of my friends there that could advise her. She was the first woman county commissioner in Texas, as far as I know.

The navy sent me to Quonset Point, Rhode Island, about five miles from Providence. It was about the latter part of September. I got up there, and it was pretty cold. There was nothing in the world, just barracks, and everybody was in a woolen blue shirt and a pair of blue navy trousers. We didn't wear our uniforms at all. We did wear officers' caps. All of the men who were at Quonset Point were officers. I went in as a lieutenant junior grade, the smallest that they had, and then they had them on up to full lieutenants there. There must have been five hundred of us in a class. They wanted administrative men in various airfields. That didn't set too well with me. I wanted competition. I wanted to get out and wrestle Japs hand-to-hand, all that sort of silly thing.

What they had to do was condition us in ninety days. Oh Lord, I knew everything that John Paul Jones[2] did; it was silly like that. It was mostly conditioning me into a life of discipline, knowing that the orders came down and you finally ended up giving them, and you held the fellow below you responsible for carrying them out. That's a big order. That's pretty hard to change a fellow's life all of a sudden like that, to where some fellow above you tells you to do something and it's not yours to question.

Here we were, away from our families. We were regimented into a cot and a little footlocker, and we went to school. We learned navigation and a lot of other things that in most instances never did do us any good. I imagine, if you want to know the truth about it, without having calculus and stuff like that, it was a little short freshman course in the US Naval Academy. That's about what it amounted to. Those who had graduated from the Naval Academy referred to fellows out there as ninety-day wonders: they became an officer in ninety days.

It came time to graduate, and they put it all up on the boards, and everybody went around. It looked as if you were trying to check out on your grades in college. There it was: "Lieutenant J. G. Harris assigned to the USS *Croatan*, Tacoma shipbuilding yards, Tacoma, Washington." Well, everybody congratulating everybody about where they were going. Some of them got Hutchinson, Kansas, and they were tickled to death with that; they weren't going to get shot at. I was tickled to death we were going to get out there on the water and see all that big ocean. It was close to Christmastime, and they gave us all a short leave. I got to come home and visit with my family at Christmas, and then I was on my way to Tacoma, Washington.

The crew was being assembled there. The plans of the day and so forth were being drawn up, which is your general-order book. It's what you go by; it's your bible. It was all being put together there by various administrative officers assigned to the ship. I became a part of it.

That was the worst-looking ship I believe I ever saw. There were three or four of them in the dock there at the shipbuilding company. They were slapping them together. The *Croatan* was a carrier escort. It was humpbacked, and it was fine pushing airplanes from the aft end forward because you'd get to go downhill, then go up a little. But I want to tell you, if you got in that sway, it was a pretty hard push. It was a cargo ship. All they did was put a deck across it and make a hangar deck down below to fix up the planes that might have gotten damaged.[3]

I spent about ninety days in Tacoma before that ship got ready. We lived in Tacoma in homes, wherever we could find a room. We'd go out to the shipbuilding company every morning. We'd get up in the dark and catch a bus, and there we'd stay till about four thirty, five thirty in the afternoon and study that ship. I crawled from one end of that ship to the other. If I went through every porthole, every vent, I went through it a dozen times. I said, "I don't care where this thing leads to. What difference does it make?" About three years later I found out that was very important. But that was what we were doing, and we went to school again. We did this, and we did that, and we took tests. It just seemed so—there's a war going on! What were we doing? I couldn't understand that, and neither could a whole lot of other folks. We stayed there long enough that Mrs. Harris was able to catch a train and come up and spend two or three weeks with me before I went to sea.

The captain of that ship was a fellow named J. B. Lyon, a Naval Academy graduate. The air officer was a flyer that had been grounded. He'd gotten enough rank to be air officer; he was a full captain. An awful nice fellow. His name was E. E. Fickling. He and I hit it off pretty early, with the result that when we pulled out of Tacoma, I was flight deck officer. That meant I was in charge of the entire flight deck.

It was about in April or May that we got under way.[4] We took out and went down the West Coast and went on down through the Ditch, or the Panama Canal, for the first time. Didn't have any problems going through it because it's a small carrier. Went on around and went all the way up to New York, and that was our home base. We set out for Casablanca, and we were escorting either transports of men or supplies.[5]

In those days Germany had no carriers. They had the Luftwaffe, which was land-based entirely. They didn't have range enough to come from places like Spain, for example, out into the Atlantic Ocean and cause any damage. We didn't bother about an air attack at all from the German empire. But they had a million submarines, and they were just sinking tonnage that was unbelievable.[6] One of our jobs was to seek out these submarines, and if there was one submarine out there in the Atlantic, there must have been thousands. We ended up my tour of duty aboard her with several submarines painted on our stack.

The torpedo planes, instead of putting a torpedo in the belly of the plane, or the bomb bay, we'd put big depth charges, and we'd put maybe four depth charges where the "fish"[7] would go. Then as we sailed over this quiet water in the sun, a submarine looked like a big catfish laying down on the bottom. They'd come up at night, and all the guys would come out on deck and get fresh air. They would also charge their batteries. Then they'd go down again at daybreak and hunt their prey. You could see them from up there every once in a while and just drop those big depth charges on them. Pretty soon you'd see all that oil come up, and you knew you had them.

I was in charge of the entire flight deck. Under me I had a catapult officer who was well versed in catapult machinery. Then I had a couple of good chief petty officers under me that were in charge of the crew. My crew consisted of personnel who pushed planes, personnel who drove tractors which towed planes, and then I had, at the aft end of the deck, an officer who landed aircraft. He was known as the landing signal officer. I didn't exercise any amount of rank over these particular people because the secret of a carrier is teamwork.

I launched the planes myself. I couldn't get too many launchings because we didn't have enough wind in the Atlantic a lot of times. I just saw that everything was in readiness. It's pretty hard to fly out there because the sea is very quiet; it doesn't get rambunctious much most of the year. Well, if there's no wind over the deck, I can't put a plane in the air. It has to fly into the wind to get airborne. If there's no wind across the deck, all he can do is fall in that ocean, so I took him to the catapults. There was one on the starboard side and one on the port side, and we'd have to shoot them off. We could land planes. They

The USS *Croatan* under way in 1943 with Grumman TBF Avengers and F4F Wildcats on her flight deck. *Courtesy of US Navy.*

might come in a little hot without any wind. Planes land into the wind; the wind slows you down and stops you.

I had an office where I spotted little to-scale plastic airplanes on a makeshift deck. I could tell just how I'd have to place those airplanes while we were landing because we only had two little elevators on this ship. It was so much smaller than the one I finally ended up sailing on.

We could carry a squadron of maybe nine bombers, nine torpedo planes, nine fighter planes. Then we got to doing away with the bombers because we couldn't do any good with those at all. We ended up just carrying a torpedo bomber for bombing rather than for torpedoing because we weren't trying to sink any shipping. Germany didn't have any ships in the Atlantic. We were carrying little Grumman Wildcats, stub-wing fighter planes. They remind me of a Farmall tractor. They probably had more armament than any plane the navy ever flew. They were just tough.

Now, we had to get supplies to Casablanca. It's a long ways over there, and the way we had to go was longer because we went out of New York all the way down the East Coast, past Cape Hatteras, missed Cuba, way on down to Belém, Brazil, at the mouth of the Amazon. Then we would angle over, and that was the shortest route to Casablanca. We'd miss the Azores a little bit. We had heard there were some German planes at the Azores.

For the most part it was Casablanca back to New York. Casablanca maybe to Norfolk, Virginia. We'd go into New York and get a whole deck load of obsolete planes. We'd take them over and give them to the French in Casablanca. If that happened, then we were escorted by a sister ship. Or we might escort a sister ship who had the planes on it. We would normally escort little task groups. They didn't get too big.

Eleven months I was aboard the *Croatan.* We'd gotten to where we knew Casablanca pretty well. There were some naval officers who were stationed over there permanently, and they had commandeered a big home and had servants and everything. We'd head out for their house. I think it was the old embassy. It was real nice. They had good food, good drink, and we enjoyed seeing them. We'd bring them some golf balls or tennis balls or something from the States which they couldn't get hold of or didn't have. They were living the life of Riley.[8] We'd stay at Casablanca maybe a couple of nights before we'd turn around and come back.

We also made one trip to Murmansk, Russia.[9] That's the coldest spot in the world. We took out from New York and went on up through Nova Scotia and over in there. It was cold! Oh man, it was awful! We were just sitting ducks except for our own firepower, which was nothing. We weren't too well manned, gunnery-speaking, because we didn't ever have anything to shoot at. We didn't stay but just a couple of nights, and it was warmer aboard ship than it was ashore. I didn't go but once, and I turned around and came back. The vodka over there, it tasted like white Karo syrup, and it was about that thick. I never was much of a syrup man, so I just stayed aboard ship—froze to death.

While at Casablanca in late 1943, Harris learned he had been transferred stateside to help train the crew of the new USS Franklin. *He caught a series of planes to Hensley Field near Dallas and spent a week's leave with his family before reporting to Newport, Rhode Island.*

The executive officer who was in charge of everything there was Commander D. L. Day. He was United States Navy, a graduate of Annapolis. The air officer, which would be in charge of all operations with regard to air and practically everything on the ship because we were a floating airport, was Commander Joe Taylor. Taylor was also a graduate of the United States Naval Academy. He was recipient of two Navy Crosses, which is very unusual. I did most of my reporting to him.

We were up there in Newport for quite a while, maybe a couple of months. It was in the winter of '43, always in the winter, and it was pretty cold up there again. I called Mrs. Harris and asked her to come up and live with me and bring the children, and she did. We lived in a little two-room house outside of Newport, Rhode Island. But it was bitter cold up there. Mrs. Harris would do the washing, and it'd freeze on the line just as hard as boards.

My responsibilities aboard the *Franklin*, compared to aboard the *Croatan*, were about five times greater. I knew right off the reel that I had a tremendous amount of planes; I could carry about ninety. The largest number we had carried on the *Croatan* was probably twenty-five. I was going to carry three full squadrons plus maybe one or two or three or four down on the hangar deck that would be standbys or they're working on one. They were always working on a plane that was either shot up a little bit or had some sort of a fuel leak or anything mechanical that takes place in machinery. They kept those down on the hangar deck, which was the second deck, and it was enclosed. But mine were all up there because they were ready to fly.

I had about two hundred and fifty men under me. On the *Croatan*, we might have had fifty in the flight deck crew. I would have the responsibility of all these men. I was responsible for their actions, for everything. The secret of a carrier is efficiency. Speed and teamwork had to be absolutely split-second, and we drilled, drilled, and drilled to attain that.

Also I had the responsibility of the squadrons. I was not a flying officer. By that I mean I did not have wings. But I had the responsibility of launching all planes. Very seldom did we send planes off by catapult because when we got to the Pacific, we didn't run into the same things that I told you about in the Atlantic. The Pacific is a violent sea. It's always got some wind out there. Planes get airborne pretty quick.

We were in Rhode Island a little over a month. By that time I'd met all the officers and I'd gotten in good friends with the air officer, Joe Taylor. Came time to ship the crew down to Norfolk, Virginia, where the ship was being built by Newport News Shipbuilding [and Drydock] Company. We went down and reported January 29, 1944, ready to board her. We entered Norfolk Navy Yard for commissioning January 31, 1944.

Now, Captain James Shoemaker had been the captain of the Norfolk Naval Air Station. That's about the swankiest air station I've ever been on in my life. The administrative buildings are built like the old Southern mansions, and the officers' club was out of this world. You'd think you were going into Tara.[10]

That was the day of the big-name band, and they were all subject to draft all of a sudden. Well, Captain Shoemaker sent a petty officer up there to New York, and there he contacted a fellow named Saxie Dowell. Saxie played saxophone in one of these big-name bands. He was also quite a composer and made lots of records. Shoemaker told Saxie,

"Get together the best orchestra you can find. I want you to get them all enlisted in the navy, and we'll take them down to the Norfolk Naval Air Station. All they'll have to do down there is play for this function, this social function, or at the officers' club on various nights when they have dances." It was a big naval air station.

Well, Saxie saw that was about the best thing that he could get out of this war, and he went to work. It's hard for me to tell you what he put together. It's unbelievable. He formed a band of some fifteen, maybe eighteen absolutely finished musicians in the big-band business and brought them all down to the Norfolk Naval Air Station.

About the time they all got settled down there and things were just utopia, the navy made Captain Shoemaker the commanding officer of the *Franklin* and sent him to sea. It certainly didn't please him too well to have to leave that haven that he was in command of. He picked his band up and put them on board ship. You never saw a more dejected group of musicians or people in your life than when they drug aboard that ship for the first time, but they became a very integral part of that ship. They'd get on the hangar deck, for example, later, as we would be taking on stores from barges or from other vessels or taking on ammunition or taking on fuel, even fueling at sea, and give concerts. It just did everything in the world for the morale of that ship.

The first flight quarters that we got in was about a month after commissioning, in February of 1944. That was when Commander Taylor flew aboard and landed his plane, got out, they took it down, and then the rest of the squadron started coming aboard. I think we were in Chesapeake Bay, somewhere up in there.

We had to learn to maneuver because we were in certain zigzag courses[11] at all times. And we learned to work with other ships because we knew that when we got out there we would be in a task group made up of several warships and we'd be in the middle because we were the floating airfield. We had to be protected. The next line of ships closest to us would probably be the battleships and then the cruisers outside of them and then the destroyers, or tin cans, way out, way forward and aft of us, following in the wakes. We were a pretty formidable group when you got in a task group.

When we finished our work out there in the Chesapeake Bay area, we had to then have a shakedown. There's where we were going to find out what we could do, what we had learned, what we had retained, whether or not we were efficient, whether or not we could work as a team, whether or not people had to be transferred. It was probably in March, somewhere in there. We always have a shakedown cruise down around Trinidad. There's a gulf down there called the Gulf of Paria, and it's about sixty miles long. It's a cute little gulf, and the prevailing winds down there were always perfect for flying conditions.

Well, Captain Shoemaker thought flight ought to belong to a navy aviator. That's natural. And there was a naval aviator aboard the ship that belonged to the ship's company, not to the squadron. He'd been assigned to the ship, but the duties that they had originally assigned him hadn't worked out too good, so they thought maybe they'd try him out as flight deck officer. They could always find something for a reserve officer to do, even though I'd had eleven months at sea.

So the first day of the shakedown, the first four planes that we launched, he launched them, and every one of them went in the water. I don't recall losing any pilots, but we lost four very high-priced airplanes, and one of those planes was full of photographic equipment, of which we had the best. Lord knows what that was worth in dollars and cents. When you got in the navy, so many things happened that made a conservative taxpayer just sick at his stomach.

Well, we had to find out what was happening. Was it the lack of coordination of the flight deck officer? Was there something wrong with the planes? Could every plane on the ship be fouled up some way? That didn't make sense. Yet we found out that there was one or two things that needed changed in the carburetor which would make the plane take off a little faster.

But still this boy didn't have the coordination, the rhythm to put those ships in the air. That's about what it was. It was a rhythmic motion. I wound these planes as tight as I could. The pilot sat on his brakes with all of his weight, and he revved up just as high as that engine would rev, and if it sounded all right to me, I let him go. He took his feet off of those brakes, and he was rolling. Now, a ship pitches. I don't care how big it is, it'll pitch just a little with the swell—and there we get back to rhythm again—to where I could send that plane down the deck as its nose was going slightly down in the water. And when it got almost to the end of the flight deck, the nose'd come out of the water and help throw him right on off. I launched about nine thousand planes off the deck of the USS *Franklin*, and I never dropped a one in the water. I've had them wash their wheels off.

Joe Taylor, the air officer, knew that I knew my business, and Joe made the suggestion: "Got a man here that's had eleven months in combat in the Atlantic at sea on a carrier. I don't care how small it is; it's all done the same way. That's what he was sent here for by the navy department. Let's try him," even though the other fellow outranked me a little bit. He was relieved of that responsibility, and I would launch my planes.

We came back from our shakedown to Norfolk Navy Yard, and in May we were on our way. We went on down to Cristóbal, and it was there that we started through the Panama Canal. The 20-millimeter guns out on the skin of the ship, we had to take those off because we were as wide as the canal locks were. We scraped a lot of times while those electric donkeys pulled us through.

In the Pacific aboard the *Franklin* we went to general quarters, which is battle condition, one hour before sunrise every day. Every day! And we stayed at general quarters for approximately an hour and a half. The best time for an attack on any kind of vessel at sea, by aircraft, is right at sunrise or right at sunset. The idea is to fly into you with the sun as a background. Thataway they're pretty hard to see, so you were most vulnerable at that particular time.

We flew nearly every day. It'd just be breaking dawn when I'd generally send off the first fighter. You could well see the flames coming out of his exhaust of his engines. Then it was time to recover planes, according to how far their mission was. If we should happen to have an accident, I generally was the closest man to him and cut him out of his chute with a knife because I didn't know whether he was wounded. I didn't know whether or not he had gotten hurt when he landed and maybe hit the barrier and veered off and hit the island structure and tore his plane up. The longer we flew the better we got at recovering planes.

I'll admit that when we first started out, there were an awful lot of wave-offs. A wave-off by the landing signal officer says that your wings aren't level, you're too high or you're too low, or all of a sudden something's happened on the deck and it's going to be awful crowded if you try to get on there. You should go around again. You can't imagine how small that deck is even though it was the length of three football fields. When you get up in that air and start looking down, that flight deck just doesn't seem as long as this table.

There was never any goofing-off time, it seemed like, where you could get you a little nap. We had launchings all the time. We had patrols in the air all the time, around the clock, sometimes at night. You could steal a little time off from the deck every once in a while and slip down, work it out with one of your officers. You knew about what time these boys were due back off of patrol. Go down to your quarters and steal fifteen or twenty minutes sleep real quick. We also had our own lounge, and it was really nice. We had a big stereo in there and worlds of fine records. We had a good library. But after you got out to sea and got really in troubled waters, you didn't have much time to lay around and read books. Every minute that you had to yourself, you were generally sleeping because you never got enough sleep.

Similar to my time on the *Croatan*, I was always busy at night because I would repair to my office. It didn't have a desk, but I did have a place to work. And therein I had a Plexiglas, drawn-to-scale flight deck. And I had just worlds of little toy airplanes made out of celluloid, and they were all drawn to scale, also whether they be bombers or torpedo planes or fighters. And I would simulate my deck for the next morning. Find out what the plan of the day was the next day. I'd have it early. Unless something drastic happened during the night to change all plans—and that happened quite frequently sometimes, and it caused nothing but chaos, I can assure you. But if it didn't happen, I would have set this plan up. I may have seventy-five planes. We tried to keep a few aboard in case we came under attack while our strike force was in the air someplace else, many hundred miles away.

Spotting your deck was quite a job because I didn't know exactly where all these planes were located down on the hangar deck, and I'd have to shift them around and move them around. It was just like moving chessmen: pull a plane out here; put another one in its place. We had tractors, and we had tow bars. We had welded big iron rings to the oleo struts of the respective planes. That's the shock absorbers where the wheels are on the deck. And we'd put these tow bars in, put them to a Fordson tractor, and pull them all over the deck. Those kids got where they could swing those planes around like they would a hay baler. We had the three elevators: one forward, one aft, and one over on the port side, and it was just sticking out over the ship. We'd have to bring planes up and take planes down.

When we would bring planes in, maybe the pilot would say, "I've got an oil leak someplace." Well, maybe that plane was the first one that hit the deck. The first one that hit the deck had to be spotted way up on the forward part of the deck. You might have to take out twenty planes to get that one to an elevator to take it down. All of that takes time, and yet it didn't take near as much time after these kids got used to it. They got where they were able to operate as a team, and they got along fast.

We also had firefighters on the flight deck. They didn't do a thing except man their stations because a fire at sea is the most dangerous thing that can happen. All old-time sailors are afraid of fire.

Our day ended anywhere from eight thirty till midnight. You learned to get along on a lot less sleep than you had. You learned to drink a lot of coffee and just live on it down in the wardroom. And the further we got out into the Pacific, the longer I had to work, the more hot meals I missed because my chickens were late on a lot of occasions. They were shot up. They were slowed up. We'd think maybe they were gone, and then all of a sudden we'd pick them up on the radar. We couldn't break radio silence.

After going through the Panama Canal we got to Pearl Harbor. We didn't know exactly where we were going after that. You have to go to Pearl because that was the frontier.[12] We stayed generally just long enough to resupply; maybe two days, three. Most part, I could go ashore after I got all my supplies aboard. Be sure that I had maybe a full complement of anything that was necessary to fix a plane with. That was under the V2 officers; that's the hangar deck officers. He was the maintenance man, kept those planes flying. He would have a plane in the air the next morning if at all possible, if he had to work all night. Those kids were great. I can't describe them.

At Pearl Harbor we couldn't just be tied up anywhere; we were too big. There were worlds of officers there. I had some very fine friends there, and they all lived in a house. They were all under this Hamilton Program. We would talk about the war and this, that, and the other, and they always had the niceties of life that other people didn't have. They had good food, too. They had a couple of Filipinos to wait on them and to work for them. We were so close and our bullhorn was so loud and our ship was so big that I could sit there on their porch, perhaps having a cold beer with them, and I could hear over that bullhorn: "Lieutenant Harris, report to the flight deck." Well, that ship was so big that I'd have time to get clear over to that ship and report to the flight deck. If I didn't get up there for fifteen minutes, that was perfectly all right. So I didn't have any problem. I just always had a ball at Pearl Harbor. I was there about four times, maybe three. We wouldn't stay too long there.

We joined Task Group 58.2 in June and went to the Bonin Islands. That's Iwo Jima, Haha Jima, and Chichi Jima. They're volcanic islands and look like solid rock: jagged, pretty good-sized. There were a million Japs on them, an awful lot of caves, and the armament was terrific. They were pretty close to Japan. We were sent to soften them up if we possibly could because we had an invasion coming.[13] We couldn't ever understand why in the world anybody would want to take Iwo Jima. Wasn't anything there.

We'd already taken Eniwetok Island out there.[14] Wasn't anything to it except a few shot-up palm trees and a beach. We used to go ashore there at Eniwetok as a recreation. Two cans of hot beer, that was the ration. It was just like you had on a pair of swimming trunks and walked up and down a sand beach. That was all there was to do. Now I will say this, that for the lack of something to do and just to blow off steam, I've seen one ship fight another out there, just fight like dogs, and then all wave good-bye to each other and get in their respective dinghies and go back to their ships. But I didn't get in with those eighteen-year-old boys. No. I'd get me a little shade.

We called it the milk run going towards the Bonins, and the fliers used to say that if you could fly through the flak that you'd run into in those three islands, you had your master's degree in flying because they threw it up pretty good. We didn't lose too many ships[15] in all of that time. We'd strike at them every day, maybe twice a day. Just keep them busy and keep them guessing what was happening.

They knew who we were, and we had Tokyo Rose[16] tuned in all the time. I always liked to listen to her because she had all the latest records, and when we were out there at sea and doing a lot of fighting, we didn't have that band playing all the time. She'd talk a little while; we just laughed at it. I've heard her report that we were sunk on a certain day and all this. Now, it's true on that particular day we might have been under an attack, but we weren't sunk and didn't even have any hits on that particular occasion. She was terribly inaccurate about things like that, and so you finally decided she was inaccurate about all of it. The best thing she did was, she did pick out good records, and the boys liked to listen to her.

At all times when we were at flight quarters, our guns were fully manned. Then we would pick up or get word from the bridge that there were bogeys, or enemy aircraft, bearing at a certain longitude and latitude approximately fifty miles away, something like that. We'd swing the guns in that direction and start trying to spot them, and we'd soon spot them. We'd open up on them, and generally we'd drive them away. They wouldn't get in too close. That happens all the time. I've been under attack at sundown and maybe somebody on a destroyer went to sleep.

I remember one afternoon out there in the Pacific, here came about six enemy planes, and they were already over the destroyer screen, which made it very difficult for us to try to shoot at them because we'd be raking the destroyers. They were coming right in, and I saw one of them drop a torpedo. I saw it take off, coming right straight amidship. I figured it was about time for it to hit. I just fell on the deck up there because I knew that it would probably jar you a little. Never did go off! It was a dud, evidently. But you think of an awful lot of things while that thing is coming at you, and things you haven't thought about in a whole long time, either.

I've had planes that were shot up pretty badly just before they got to us, and maybe the Jap was dead. The plane still flies itself, but he was probably in some sort of a dive. I've had him skip across the flight deck like you, as a kid, would take a flat rock many times and throw it at a lake and watch it jump across the lake. That's the way he did and went off on the other side and went in the ocean. I've had that happen a time or two. And when that happened, it generally took a boy with him who couldn't get out of the way or just happened to be in the path of the plane.[17]

Those are all sad things, but you learn to shake them off the best you can and go ahead about your business because you don't have time for a whole lot of sentiment out there. Things happen too quick. You had a whole lot of boys out there; your emotions had to be under control at all times. You might want to go down below to your bunk and to your little room. You might have wanted to go down there and let it out, and I'm sure some of us did, and I have. But I finally got up and went about my business as if nothing had happened. We were building up to what was to come, unfortunately, later on.

In July 1944, we covered the landings at Guam.[18] We gave air coverage all the time, soften up. The best way in the world to invade an island is to bomb that enemy. You've seen in westerns where some guy says, "I'm going over here; now cover me," which means just fire at random there where the fellow can't stick his head around the corner and fire back. Well, if you drop enough bombs on those fellows, they don't have time to kill all your boys wading ashore. We're not the only carrier out there, so you can just visualize the pounding we were giving those islands like Guam. Cruisers were getting to limber up their rifles, battleships were limbering up theirs, and everybody was having what they called their fun.

Funny things happen under trying circumstances. Money didn't mean much out there. You couldn't spend it anywhere. A whole lot of these boys in the squadron weren't married, and they'd take their pay. There was a great big standpipe in Guam. I presume it was a waterwork or something. And the pounding that island took is unbelievable. There couldn't be anything left on that island—except that standpipe and it still stood. There was about a five-hundred-dollar pot down in the ready room of that squadron for the fellow who knocked down the standpipe. The last time I heard of Guam it was still standing. Nobody ever did knock it down.

I had listened to so many tales. Pilots come back and they shot down two or three enemy planes. Of course the photographic machines that went along could generally verify all of that. But, "I got him. He's mine." I'd heard so much of that. So one day I walked up on the bridge and I asked Captain Shoemaker, I said, "Captain, I'd like permission to go ashore." He looked at me like I was crazy. I said, "With your permission, I'd like to check out on a 20-millimeter machine gun and crawl in the back seat of Commander Kibbe's[19] dive bomber. I'd like to go over and see Guam. I've been bombing it here for what seems like a month. I just want to see how bad it's torn up." And he thought that was the funniest thing that he ever—can you imagine a guy who was real secure on top of the flight deck wanting to get over there and get shot at! But he said, "Permission granted." So I went down and I had this petty officer show me how to pull the trigger of that machine gun, what to do to it if it got jammed—as if I would have done anything at all—and I spun my seat around and off we went off that flight deck.

We flew around Guam, didn't see a thing down there. Finally we saw two or three tiny trucks moving around. Kibbe said, "We'll just go down and get them." So I went down backwards. It's quite a sensation, but it's not near the sensation until he gets ready to nose up, and then all of a sudden it looks like you're going right on out that cockpit. We were in a two-seated dive bomber. I let a burst out of my guns so I could go back and tell them that I knocked out a truck or two. I didn't see a thing, it happened so fast. But I actually flew off that carrier, and that's why I tell you that deck looks awful small when you get back to that ship and start coming aboard.

Later in '44 we were over in the Palau islands, and we were beginning at that time to try to get back the Philippines. We were flying a whole lot of sorties over there, and we were having trouble with the army. They were quite gun-happy. We had several boys come back and stated that the army wasn't too good on plane recognition and would shoot at anything that flies, and that we actually had some army boys shoot down some navy pilots. Fortunately, none of them were killed. They crashed in the sea and were picked up.

We went on into the Second Battle of the Philippine Sea, later known as Battle of Leyte Gulf.[20] That was quite a sea battle. We'd been looking for the Japanese fleet for years. Couldn't find them! They just got away from us all the time. That was the day that we thought we had found the Jap fleet. We launched early in the morning. Everything was thrown in the air from the three or four carriers, and very shortly we broke radio silence and they stated that they had several ships afire on up the way. In an hour or so we passed several burning clear to the waterline. We had caused quite a bit of damage.

That was not the Jap fleet. It was a dummy fleet. And it was put there in that strategic position to where we could find it while the main fleet slipped through some straits down there and attacked a bunch of our smaller carriers. We followed them down those straits a little while, and we sank a couple of their big cruisers. But they got away again.

In October we received directives that the Japanese had what was known as a kamikaze fleet. It was a bunch of screwballs that had dedicated themselves to the emperor to die, and he had blessed them all. They were fanatics, and they were to dive their planes into the ship, if necessary. I'll never forget reading the directive — we had to read them all that came through — and I thought, That's the silliest thing I ever heard of.

Well, afternoon of October 30, one of those fellows peeled off at about twenty thousand feet above us, and here he came! We were off of Samar. It was still a pretty good piece from Manila, but we weren't too far off of it. And evidently he came from over in that area and had attained that height where it was pretty hard radar-wise to get hold of him up there. Here he came out of that sun, and he just kept coming. We kept the fire at him, and he kept taking it. In a minute he went through three decks. He had a couple bombs with him, one under each wing. He just went right on through that flight deck and on through the hangar deck. The tail of the plane was sticking up through that steel hangar deck. Of course, he was dead. He may have been dead before he hit the ship. He hit just about the aft elevator.[21]

Well, he did his job! We had no runway. We were out of business all of a sudden as an airport. We lost fifty-six boys, and we burned for several hours. We knew there was no use to try to fix the flight deck; that was gone because the elevator was buckled. Our planes in the air were recovered by other ships in the task group.

We went to Ulithi for assessment. We were there several days before the decision was made to send us back to the States to be repaired. The aft elevator was absolutely gone, and that's a part of our operations. We had to have it where we could get those planes down to the second deck and back up to the first deck in a minimum amount of time. We also received what decorations that were dished out for the disaster of October 30, 1944. I received the Bronze Star and a Purple Heart from Admiral Nimitz.

While at Ulithi, Captain Shoemaker was relieved. He'd done a good job with the short time that the *Franklin* had been alive. He was to go to greener pastures, and greener pastures was shore duty. He was relieved by a Captain Leslie E. Gehres, a real taskmaster. In the first place, he was a mustang, a man that came up through the ranks. He was not a United States Naval Academy graduate. He came up from a seaman in the navy air force. He was quite a pilot. He flew in their Blue Angels, the acrobatic team.[22] They've got to be the best. They sent him up to

Alaska, and he was flying up in there and had made captain. That was the hellhole of the world, so to speak. You're guarding Russia; you're guarding Japan.

I've had a lot of boys come aboard ship, and the first thing they'd ask me when I went up to the cockpit after they landed: "Who's captain?" "Captain Gehres." "Oh my Lord! I flew under him in the Aleutians. He'll kill you." In the worst weather in the world, he'd make them go out on patrol up there, and an airplane can't take all that ice. It just won't fly when it gets heavy. He had quite a reputation, let's put it that way. He brought the *Franklin* back to Bremerton, Washington.

Bremerton is right across Puget Sound from Seattle, and it was there that we received a short leave. Survivors' leave generally is a thirty-day leave, but they didn't know how long it was going to take to fix us up. They pulled everybody off of practically everything they were doing and swarmed aboard our ship with priorities to get her done because we didn't know how close we actually were to trying to wind this war up out there.

I got two weeks and went to Dallas and visited my family and was able to be with them at Christmas. We were at Bremerton Navy Yard about two months, a month of that probably being taken up with complete leave for the entire crew.

The USS Franklin *left Bremerton February 1, 1945, picked up Air Group Five at Naval Air Station Alameda in California, and then headed back out into the Pacific toward the war zone, making stops in Pearl Harbor and Ulithi.*

We kept steaming north towards Okinawa. On March 18 we were not too far off Okinawa and found through our photographic equipment some shipping being built on Mainland Japan. We're still looking for that main Japanese fleet.

We must have gone to general quarters six or seven times that night. It just seemed like the minute we'd get back in bed that gong would ring again, and here we'd go. Well, it's not easy going through a big carrier that's loaded down with airplanes on the hangar deck and it's pitch dark, even though you've been going that same route for lo these many months.

I remember on our first voyage with Air Group Thirteen, they had a flight surgeon and he'd been going to general quarters for two or three months the same way. One morning, going to flight quarters—it's still dark—instead of turning to the left, he turned to the right and just stepped off a hundred and fifty feet down in the Pacific Ocean. So it's a little dangerous sometimes. Fortunately, we picked him up with a destroyer a little later.

After about the seventh time I just stayed up. In the morning, we go back to general quarters. I started launching. We were striking where we had seen these photographs of the shipping being built. Other carriers in the force had their orders, and planes were in the air everywhere.

I'd gotten through all of the fighters that I intended to send off. We were in fine shape, and I was about into my sixth bomber. They had to have a little more run, and they were always behind the fighters. The TBFs, or the torpedo planes, being the heaviest plane, carrying three men — one in the tail turret, one in the bubble-up, and the pilot — and generally a torpedo, a "fish," they had to have a lot of run. They were on the aft end of the deck.

Everything was turning up, very noisy, and all of a sudden there was an explosion. This airplane had come in — it was a Judy; that's a certain type of Japanese plane — and he had come in right straight over the front of the flight deck — forward. The bomber I had just sent off, he flew right over him, like he was coming aboard backwards. His first bomb was a five-hundred-pound bomb, struck forward just a little bit aft of the forward elevator. That concussion blew me aft in the air about ten feet.

About the time I hit on my hands and knees, the second bomb he dropped was just forward of the aft elevator.[23] In other words, he just skip-bombed us, and I was blown about ten feet back. I ended up just about a foot from where I started. My breeches were torn pretty badly, and again I picked up shrapnel. My arms and knees were skinned up awful bad. Didn't pay any attention to it because all hell had broken loose. Those planes that were left on the flight deck — and there were quite a few — began blowing up.

On the aft end of that flight deck, those torpedo planes were carrying a bomb — a rocket — known as Tiny Tim. We'd never flown a Tiny Tim before. We'd heard about them, and it was to be a rocket to end all rockets. Tremendous size! I didn't know how much run I was going to have to give those things, so I gave them as much as I could give them. I just had them right on the aft end. When they started swishing and going off, like one big, huge Roman candle, they cleared everything out of the way right up that flight deck. It took planes and men and everything else with it. This rocket had received so much attention in the navy department that they had sent photographers from Hollywood and flown them out to the ship to make a sequence known as "Tiny Tim." It was to carry the whole story of Tiny Tim all the way through, and this was to be the first launching of Tiny Tim, that morning.

The fact that the photographers were there is the reason that all of this disaster is recorded on film, and most all of the movies or TV shows that you see today where carriers are blowing up or on fire, that's the *Franklin*. They just happened to be there, and they just happened to have their cameras loaded to take Tiny Tim going off the deck. But they didn't ever get to take Tiny Tim going off the deck because it didn't go off the way they were supposed to get it. There was a ship blowing up.

I couldn't breathe. I was looking for a life jacket because I didn't launch with a life jacket. It was too cumbersome, impaired my efficiency. There was this boy, one of my kids, he was dead and I took it off of him. I was trying to get through the smoke. The captain was trying to turn the vessel into the wind so it'd take the smoke away because electrical fires, there's nothing in the world that smells worse. Imagine a whole city of electrical appliances on fire at one time, and it was just choking. You couldn't get your breath. And the billows of black smoke, you didn't know where you were.[24]

You were getting bounced around with other explosions. Kids dead all over the deck. The oleo struts of the airplanes, full of that oleo strut juice, just slick and slimy all over the deck. By that time the ship had a terrible list. I saw a lot of boys get caught in this oily stuff—mixed with blood, too—and they'd start sliding just as if they were on ice and go clear on and over the side of the ship.

We were looking for anything to fight the fire with, just anything. Everything was blown up. We didn't have any water. We didn't have any hose—maybe something that might be comparable to a garden hose, and I'll assure you that won't put out much fire. Flames were a hundred and fifty feet in the air, maybe higher. We were burning all over. Fire was rolling out off of the lower decks into the sea. That was all aviation gasoline on fire, octane gasoline. The rifles fore and aft of the island structure, the five-inch guns, fire coming out of them. The kids inside of the gun mounts were cooked, couldn't get out. There was screaming everywhere.

Everything going off, guns and ammunition, and we didn't have any water to dampen, wash down, our ammunition. We couldn't flood, and that's one reason we didn't know where the next explosion was coming from.[25] I got me a couple or three or four guys, and we went into these gun mounts up forward. Everybody was dead, and we began picking up those hot shells and passing them one hand to the other and throwing them over the side. I don't know how many we handled in the four mounts, maybe five hundred shells. Our hands were raw. They were burnt.

The USS *Franklin* following a Japanese air attack on March 19, 1945, with the USS *Santa Fe,* at left, offering assistance. *Courtesy of National Archives and Records Administration.*

I tried to go down on the hangar deck. It was a funeral pyre. It was just solid with fire. Everybody at their battle stations was trapped. There was a crew that was eating. They were still eating when we found them. Those in the hospital were just laying there in the bed. The concussion had killed them dead. Those who had worked all night on the hangar deck and slept in the day: all in their bunks, dead. All concussioned. We found all those later. We lost about eight hundred boys.[26]

The first thing that came alongside was a little destroyer, the USS *Miller.* We had a breeches buoy rigged,[27] and I remember putting Admiral Davison[28] in the breeches buoy. I don't know, you do some funny things at times. I wasn't ever going to see anybody again. This was it. Things like this couldn't happen and you survive. I put this little fat admiral in this breeches buoy, and I just gave him a big, good kick, and down he went clear to that other deck on the *Miller* much faster than the breeches buoy generally carries you. But that couldn't bother me because what could he do to me? I wasn't going to be there much longer. They pulled out with the flag[29] as quick as they could.

And along came the USS *Santa Fe*, a cruiser commanded by a captain name of Harold Fitz. He came right alongside, and some of his crew used their fire-fighting equipment to allow them to get as close as they could without catching the *Santa Fe* afire. There were two or three breeches buoys lines strung over there as quick as they could. That was to take off the wounded that were in stretchers if you could find any. We put about three or four planks maybe two feet wide together, put a rope around them in several places. A fellow held the rope up on the

Franklin, and another fellow held the rope down on the *Santa Fe.* A fellow stood in the middle and held the rope so that those that were already blinded could go down holding onto that rope, walking. Then we started moving our wounded over to the *Santa Fe.* I don't know how many times I was aboard the *Santa Fe*, leading people over there.

We burned four or five days, something like that. We just had to let it burn out. Passageways were flooded. I finally got down below. All of the terrible things that happened to us in pre-commissioning days, all the silly things of reading blueprints, I don't know how many lives that saved, of being able to know where you were in that torn-up ship because you had had to study that thing so long back there, crawl through ventilators at the shipyard and stuff that just was absolutely asinine, except if you could have found a ventilator, brother, you'd have been glad to get in it real quick and know where it came out.

We continued to do whatever we could and bury our dead. We didn't have any ceremonies. We didn't have anything left to do anything with at all. We picked them up and threw the body over the side. Most instances, it was charred beyond recognition. It was very gruesome.

Seamen were wearing officers' coats. Officers were wearing sailors' caps. We didn't have any water. Didn't have any galleys for the men to eat. Our galley, the officers' mess, was intact, so we brought all of the enlisted men down there. They acted just like they were an officer; they sat with us. We didn't want much to eat.

We had no engines, we had no boilers, and we drifted within fifty-two miles of the Japanese shoreline. We had to get out of there. The USS *Pittsburgh* — it's a heavy cruiser — let us know that they'd try to tow us. So we went up on the forecastle[30] deck, and we took a torch and cut off those two fifteen-ton anchors. That left nothing but the chain, and they got a big, heavy line over to us — the kind that you tie your ships up to at the dock — big ships — hawser line. We made that line secure to the chain. Then we let them know that we were ready, and they began towing us at two knots. That's not very fast when everybody's shooting at you and you're blowing up.

The *Pittsburgh* had played out quite a bit of line to be safe from the fire, but they were pulling a ship that originally had weighed thirty thousand tons, and they were in danger of attack. So everybody huddled around us like mother ducks and gave us all the protection they could. We had several near misses the rest of the day, but I don't recall ever getting hit again. They towed us maybe about twenty-four hours. They hadn't gotten us very far away, but by that time we had fixed one boiler and there was a possibility that we could get some steam out of another. We were still listing bad. We were still on fire in some places. As soon as we got those boilers fixed the captain says, "Let's get out of here!" We could go about fifteen knots, and that's a whole lot better than two or three or four. We signaled them, told them that we could get under our own way much faster than they could tow us. That suited them fine because their ship was in danger too.

We didn't realize that that was the Okinawa push. The Okinawa push actually kept, maybe, some of those clowns off of us because they were busy protecting their own shores. We started back to Ulithi and then went on to Pearl. We had a couple of destroyers that went with us. They didn't have much firepower. The *Santa Fe* was still close by, but the *Santa Fe* was full of wounded. They were laying all over the deck, and they didn't have a place to put them. Filled up the hospital as quick as they could, and that didn't take long on a ship.

It's all just a bad dream from there. We kept working. I never worked so hard in my life. Oh! We cussed Captain Gehres because of being such a taskmaster, but he was taking our mind off a whole lot of things. Everybody learned to use a blowtorch, cut away stuff that was hanging—all over, debris everywhere. Steel. Throw it over the side, push it over the side; every bit we could get, trying to get all the ballast we could.

Most of my division was dead. The flight deck burned all to pieces, nothing but debris and holes. The second hangar deck was blown all to pieces. We had to cut it all off and throw it over. Not much of those boys were alive. Some of the orchestra even got killed. But I ended up in a watch down on the sixth deck way under the waterline. It was kind of a damage-control watch. I put in four hours on and four hours off all the way back. It was just work, work, work. We all took on jobs that we never had done before.

When we got back to Pearl, it was quite a sight. We were all drawn up on the flight deck. We were a sad-looking sight, no uniforms. There were three or four instruments left and three or four or five musicians. Saxie was alive, and when we came into Pearl, Saxie had his band up on the forward part of the flight deck playing "The Old Gray Mare Ain't What She Used to Be." We were a sad-looking sight. That ship, it scared people.

We stayed for a few days. We were anxious to get on out of there, and they didn't want us in Pearl. They wanted that berth open for a fighting ship. We weren't a fighting ship anymore; we were a ghost ship. They wouldn't take us on the West Coast because, there again, everything was to stay open to fix up a fighting ship. We had to end the war pretty quick. We started from Pearl and went through the Panama Canal. We were still listing pretty badly, but we had got a lot of weight off of it. We had no trouble going through this time. It was just a bunch of big holes. When we got over to the east side, we started up to Brooklyn Navy Yard.

As we went into the navy yard and were winding our way around to the berth they were going to put us in, we passed right by the *Franklin D. Roosevelt*, which was absolutely the latest thing in carriers.[31] There was their entire crew drawn up at attention. One of my kids—they were all mine—sang out right as we passed them, "You'll be sorry!" It just kind of broke the tension.

At any rate, we arrived in Brooklyn the latter part of April 1945. We got the Presidential Unit Citation, and there were several citations. I left the ship before the citations were passed out. I received the Navy Cross and the Silver Star and another Purple Heart. They sent everybody to hotels in New York, but I wanted to see my wife and kids. I caught a plane out of New York and flew home.

When Harris returned home, he traveled all over the state speaking about his experiences aboard the Franklin *in a war bond drive. He spent the last weeks of the war at Melbourne Naval Air Station in Florida as aide to Capt. D. L. Day, the first executive officer on the USS* Franklin. *When Harris mustered out, he was promoted to lieutenant commander. Soon after, he and his wife welcomed their third daughter and Harris returned to his political career, serving two terms in the Texas Senate and running an unsuccessful campaign for lieutenant governor in 1950. Later, Harris and his family moved to a ranch in Hamilton County, where he entered the cattle and Angora goat business and opened law offices in Hico and Hamilton. Harris returned to the Texas House of Representatives in 1951 when Gov. Allan Shivers called and urged him to run in a special election. After the session the Harrises moved to northern New Mexico to escape the severe 1950s drought, but they returned to Texas in 1960 when Harris accepted a job offer with the Oak Cliff Chamber of Commerce and returned to practicing law. Three years later he was appointed judge of the Dallas County Court at Law No. 3, and served through 1975. During his time on the bench, Harris discovered a talent and love for oil painting and put on several one-man western art shows in the following years. Upon his retirement in 1976, Harris and his wife moved to Waco, where he served as the first chairman of the Waco Taxpayers Association.*

Judge "Red" Harris's life history was collected in twelve interviews as part of the Institute's longstanding Texas Judicial Systems Project. In interviews six, seven, and eight he shared memories of his service in the navy from 1942 through 1945. Fred "Red" Harris, *Oral Memoirs of Fred*

"Red" Harris, a series of interviews conducted by Thomas L. Charlton, September 7, 1977, through December 5, 1977, in Waco, Texas, BU Digital Collections.

Notes

1. In 1942, Lt. Cmdr. Thomas Hamilton, former head football coach for the Naval Academy, created the training regimen for five Navy Aeronautic V-5 Preflight Schools in the United States. Football was the focus, and recruits were required to play it daily as a form of physical fitness. The V-5 program trained more than 80,000 men during the war and stressed creativity and initiative in drills. The NCAA did not regulate the V-5 football teams but allowed them to compete against college teams, and many credit V-5 with saving college football during World War II. After the war many football coaches, at both high school and college levels, implemented V-5 techniques in their own training programs. Kurt Edward Kemper, *College Football and American Culture in the Cold War Era* (Chicago: University of Illinois Press, 2009), 11–12.

2. US naval hero who fought in the American Revolution.

3. The USS *Croatan* was a former mercantile hull that the Seattle-Tacoma Shipbuilding Company converted into a Bogue-class escort carrier. Boyd Childress, "Aircraft Carriers, US" in *World War II in Europe: An Encyclopedia, Volume 1*, ed. David T. Zabecki (New York: Garland, 1999), 800.

4. The USS *Croatan* was commissioned on April 28, 1943.

5. The *Croatan* sailed out of Hampton Roads, Virginia, on August 6, 1943, for her first operational cruise, providing cover for Convoy UGS-14. The ship docked at Casablanca for the first time on August 26 in need of fuel pump, catapult, and radar repairs. William T. Y'Blood, *Hunter-Killer: US Escort Carriers in the Battle of the Atlantic* (Annapolis, MD: Naval Institute Press, 1983), 95–96.

6. During World War II, German U-boats sank 2,840 merchant ships—14,333,082 gross register tonnage—and 149 warships. Eberhard Möller and Werner Brack, *The Encyclopedia of U-Boats: From 1904 to the Present Day*, trans. Andrea Battson and Roger Chesneau (Mechanicsburg, PA: Stackpole Books, 2004), 10.

7. Torpedoes.

8. A carefree existence.

9. Starting in August 1941, the Allies delivered supplies via Arctic convoys—often called the Murmansk run—to the Russians, to help them keep the Germans at bay. The Germans were well aware of the convoys, and some of the heaviest fighting in the Battle of the Atlantic took place in these frigid waters. David Fairbank White, *Bitter Ocean: The Battle of the Atlantic, 1939–1945* (New York: Simon & Schuster, 2006), 206.

10. The fictional plantation home of Scarlet O'Hara in *Gone with the Wind*, the 1936 historical novel by Margaret Mitchell.

11. To protect against enemy submarines.

12. Hawaii was only a US territory during World War II but had been home to the US naval station at Pearl Harbor since 1899. Because of its strategic location in the middle of the Pacific Ocean, Hawaii became critical to the Allied victory in the Pacific during WWII. Ships frequently stopped at Pearl Harbor for repairs, fuel, and supplies.

13. American ships and planes bombed Iwo Jima during the nine months leading up to the American landings on February 19, 1945.

14. The Battle of Eniwetok was fought February 17–23, 1944.

15. Planes.

16. The name given by Allies in the South Pacific to any of the females who broadcast Japanese propaganda in English over the airwaves.

17. In one such event, near Taiwan on October 13, 1944, one *Franklin* crewmember died and ten were wounded. This is considered a kamikaze attack even though it happened six days before Japan began organizing its formal naval kamikaze units. Robin L. Rielly, *Kamikaze Attacks of World War II: A Complete History of Japanese Suicide Strikes on American Ships, by Aircraft and Other Means* (Jefferson, NC: McFarland, 2010), 114–15, 317, 318.

18. The Battle of Guam took place July 21–August 10, 1944.

19. Richard L. Kibbe.

20. Fought October 23–26, 1944.

21. Kamikaze pilots often aimed for elevators on aircraft carriers, to cause as much operational damage as possible. Joseph A. Springer, *Inferno: The Epic Life and Death Struggle of the USS* Franklin *in World War II* (St. Paul, MN: Zenith Press, 2007), 157.

22. Gehres had flown with the Nine High Hats, the forerunner to the Blue Angels. Springer, *Inferno*, 169.

23. From the get-go, confusion existed as to what type of Japanese plane bombed the *Franklin* and whether it dropped one or two bombs on the carrier. For a detailed look at these matters, see Springer, *Inferno*, 325–30.

24. In an oral history interview, Bob Frank remembered that on the morning of March 19 he stood at his post behind Harris on *Franklin*'s flight deck. A V2 Division officer, Frank was listening to the engine of each plane as it got ready for takeoff to determine if it had enough horsepower to get airborne. Frank recalled that in the chaos that ensued when the bombing occurred, some of the pilots fled their airplanes without turning off the engines, and in the blinding smoke men were running into the propellers. Frank shut off as many engines as he could before the fire reached the flight deck. Springer, *Inferno*, 199, 203.

25. In the event of a fire, a ship's crew will often flood the gunpowder magazines in an effort to prevent explosions.

26. Official reports from the March 19, 1945, attack cite 798 killed and at least 487 wounded. Springer, *Inferno*, 317.

27. Similar to a zip line, a breeches buoy is a rope apparatus that connects two ships and is used to transfer people from one vessel to another, usually during rescue operations. Each person is placed in a personal flotation device with an attached leg harness and then moved along the rope.

28. Ralph E. Davison.

29. Davison's admiral flag, which the *Franklin* had been flying.

30. The front section of the upper deck on a ship.

31. The USS *Franklin D. Roosevelt* was launched on April 29, 1945.

OSCAR NORBERT DUCONGÉ

Oscar DuCongé was born on April 19, 1909, in Pass Christian, Mississippi, the ninth of fourteen children, and grew up in New Orleans, Louisiana. Both of his grandfathers had come to the United States as a result of the Haitian Revolution. DuCongé's father was a journeyman barber; his mother, a housewife and music teacher. One of his older brothers, taught by their mother, was the manager of Louis Armstrong's first European tour. At a young age DuCongé began learning the barber trade, and in high school and college he delivered packages for a drugstore. DuCongé graduated from Xavier High School in New Orleans, attended a semester at City College of New York, and then completed his bachelor's degree at Xavier University in New Orleans in 1931, with a major in sociology and minor in philosophy. During high school and college he participated in football, baseball, and track. After college he worked in New Orleans both for Unity Life Insurance Company and for the Federal Emergency Relief Agency as a home visitor and an adult-literacy educator. He married Mary Jacques on January 2, 1937.

I GOT IN AS A SOLDIER IN WORLD WAR II pretty nearly accidentally. As an adult teacher I was given the assignment of registering people for Selective Service. I was the registrar, and I registered myself. I turned in all my cards and other paraphernalia to the draft board, and three years later I had not heard from the draft board. It was in 1942 then, and I was very worried because I got to thinking by myself, Well, maybe they might think I'm not registered and I might get in serious trouble.

So I began to check up on my registration. I went to the draft board one day; they couldn't find any record. I went another day; they couldn't find any record. The third day, they found the record, and three days later I had "Greetings from the President." I had no idea they would take me because I was already by this time thirty-three years old or maybe thirty-two, and I was very fat, too. I didn't think I was in any shape to go in the army. I was no taller then than I am now, which is just about five five and a half, and I weighed about 210 pounds. As a matter of fact, before I was actually inducted into the army, the doctors held me at the camp to have me redo a physical because there was some question as to whether or not I could be accepted into the army. They put me to bed and made me to rest for twenty-four hours and did the examination all over again and then certified me for limited duty.

When I was inducted into the army, it was about June 1, 1942. I was sent, like a great number of other recruits, to Fort McClellan, Alabama. We were racially segregated. Basic training at that time was thirteen weeks, and somehow or another I managed to get through basic training without losing too much fat. I really didn't have any difficulty with but one phase of my basic training, and that was getting over the wall. The running of the obstacle course, with that one exception, I could do very easily, and the games we played as part of training exercises I was able to adapt to pretty easily. I was a kind of agile fat man, and I surprised quite a few of the younger guys and some of the skinny guys too because most of them figured that I wouldn't be able to do it.

Most of the men who went through basic training with me were shipped off to various places, but I was retained because I was supposed to go to Officer Candidate School. But school after school refused me, principally because of my condition, and then some of the schools that I could have attended I didn't want to. For instance, I had an opportunity to go to a tank school, and I wouldn't under any circumstances consider going to infantry school. I wanted to go to school at Fort Harrison, Indiana, which is the Army School of Finance,[1] but I couldn't get in. So I remained around Fort McClellan, Alabama, for another thirteen weeks, completely unassigned, with no duties or anything else. Looking back on that period, I realize that I had quite a good thing.

But after the second thirteen-week period, I was assigned to the 92nd Infantry Division, to the finance department. Of course the army was completely and totally segregated at that time. That was, in a sense, the way you expected it to be. A large number of the officers during training, even the very junior officers, were white, but the troops were all black. Subsequently, when I was assigned to the 92nd Infantry Division, then the officers in the 92nd Division were principally black with the exception of the higher-grade officers, who were white.

The 92nd Division was actually a carryover from the black soldier divisions of the 1870s and 1880s.[2] The insignia was the black buffalo, and the headquarters were Fort Huachuca, Arizona. Before the division could be assembled, they had the units training at Fort McClellan, Alabama; Camp Atterbury, Indiana; north of Little Rock, Arkansas; and Fort Huachuca. After a period of approximately six months, the entire division was assembled at Fort Huachuca, after which we began preparations for overseas duty.

We had no esprit de corps.[3] This is one of the sad things about it. I think they had the idea of a reinstitution of this type of esprit de corps that might have been found, but it didn't carry down to the rank and file through the various officer chains. Now, of course in my particular section, in the finance section, there were nineteen of us. All of us were college graduates or better, and most of us had an appreciation of what happened from our personal knowledge of history in regard to the division.

I was not very clear as to the purpose of the 92nd Division except that we had the feeling that it was an attempt to integrate black soldiers as fighters without effecting a meaningful racial integration. The orders to integrate the military services came from President Truman after World War II was over, and we began the process of integration as a result.[4]

Incidentally, I attribute the integration order of President Truman as with equal importance to the Civil Rights Act passed by President Johnson because, in my opinion, this integration of the armed services acted as a catalyst for the rest of the country. White young men began accepting black young men in a way that they had not previously accepted. They began to know about each other. Now, of course there was quite a bit of friction, but nevertheless the total result was positive, despite occasional conflicts, occasional riots, and so forth and so on.

Since I was in finance, I was attached to Headquarters Company, and the people in Headquarters Company were very carefully selected. They were practically all educated people. The talk in Headquarters Company of course was entirely different from the talk in the combat company. We in Headquarters Company were extremely anxious to make a tremendous showing, because we were going to show what black soldiers could do. I don't know if this was carried down all the way to the ordinary private with the rifle, because I think the ordinary private with the rifle in the 92nd Division was just like the ordinary private anywheres else. He wanted to get this thing over with and get back home. As far as idealisms and the ideology and philosophy and all these kinds of things, these were not his concerns. He wanted to eat as well as he could and sleep as comfortably as he could and then get back home as soon as he could, and this was all. Fight if he had to but would prefer not to fight. I think, if I read it right, this was the total consideration of the division.

But in the Headquarters Company, we smart alecks probably had a different attitude. We were kind of show-offs. We were going to say, Lookie here. We're just as good as anybody else, and we can prove it. We can fight as well as anybody—although we ourselves were not the ones to do the fighting. Understand what I mean. We were pretty much together in spirit because the cadre for Headquarters Company and all its branches—G1, G2, G3—they were all carefully selected. We had everything in these companies—I mean at the enlisted man's rank—from college graduates to PhDs, and so we really thought we were hotshots.

As long as I was in finance, I was in charge of enlisted pay. The highest rank that I received—grade, rather—they don't call it rank in regard to enlisted men—was that of what they called a tech three, or staff sergeant.[5] But I was in charge of enlisted pay. I prepared the payrolls—that is, the people under me. We had about twelve. We had no privates in finance. We had the two-stripers, the three-stripers, and the four-stripe,[6] like myself. We received the payroll from the companies; we prepared what they called a change list because the army at that time paid off every company. They had exactly the number of five-dollar bills, exactly the proper number of ten-dollar bills, one-dollar bills, half-dollars, quarters, dimes, pennies, and nickels so that a company commander, when he received his payroll, he had exact change for every man in the company. They were paid in hard cash. And this was a tremendous job, and all of this had to be ready by the twenty-third of the month.

We really had about from the tenth to the twenty-third to get this together, because then we had to get the money from the nearest Federal Reserve Bank. We went and got this cash in armored cars with machine guns back and forward and this kind of thing, and then got back into the finance office and did the physical separation of the money so that by the thirtieth of the month the payrolls for all the companies were ready. And then of course it was a question of the company commander coming in and grabbing his bag of money and going back to his company. Then we had a supplemental payroll, which we had to get ready for the fifth. Those guys who for one reason or another were red-lined,[7] as we used to call it, who were not paid on the first, who were left off the payroll because they were on furlough or AWOL or something else. We had a much smaller payroll to make up for the fifth, which we called a supplemental.

Between the fifth and the tenth we really didn't have much to do, and then it was a question of ducking out on drills or anything else that was unpleasant. But the rest of the time it was pure office work. When I was at Fort Huachuca, I went to work at eight o'clock in the morning and got off at four thirty, just as if I was in an office in civilian life.

We went overseas before the Battle of the Bulge, in August or September of 1944. It took the division that long to really get ready. The first regiment was assigned to Africa. The second one joined up with

Men in the 92nd Infantry Division use a mortar against the enemy in Massa, Italy, in November 1944. *Courtesy of National Archives and Records Administration.*

the first down in the bottom of Italy, around the heel where all this big fighting was: Monte Cassino and Salerno and so forth. The rest of the regiment, the other two regiments, and the rest of headquarters joined after Rome was taken.[8]

The division went by regiments to Italy rather than as a division. I think this has something to do with strategy and logistics. But a very strange thing happened to us. When headquarters landed in Livorno, Italy, there was a black colonel from Chicago, and I think his name was Gates. When we landed, Axis Sally[9] said over the radio, "Colonel Gates, how is everything on the South Side of Chicago?" And of course this amazed us because everything we had been doing was so secret. It was highly secretive. As an example, instead of going directly to the port of embarkation on the East Coast, somewhere not too far from Atlantic City, the train went all kinds of ways so that anybody looking would not know what was happening. And the very night we landed, Axis Sally asked Colonel Gates how was things on the South Side of Chicago.

We had one or two black regiments assigned to us from time to time. One time we had the 366th Infantry Regiment assigned to us, and we had the 372nd Infantry Regiment attached to us. Then we also had a regiment of the Nisei—they are Japanese Americans[10]—who were attached to us. Our finance office had to pay all of these regiments. In regard to the 366th, probably our most illustrious person from that regiment is Senator Edward Brooke.[11] He was with the 366th with us. Now, we've had some other people. Of the black generals we've had, three of them were company commanders in the 92nd Division at the time of World War II.

When I went to Italy we lived in a hotel. The army had commandeered a number of office buildings and hotels and things of this kind. And where we had the finance office, it was a hotel and we lived upstairs. The government had made arrangements with the Italian government, and we paid the troops in Italian lira. But most soldiers didn't really draw a whole lot of money in Italy, because most of the soldiers were saving their money through what we used to call Class E allotments and Class F allotments[12] and war bonds and different other things. Soldiers really didn't have much opportunity to spend the money, so the amount of cash, even though it was in lira, was not very great proportionately. It amounted to, some months, a couple of million dollars, but it still was not great in proportion to what we'd been disbursing in the States. It was only as large as it was because of these attached units. These various units—the 372nd, the 366th, the Nisei—they were attached to us for specific duties. For instance, a reconnaissance unit was attached.

Compared to a place like the United States, Italy is very small, and when headquarters was set up in Viareggio, we remained in Viareggio until the great push began when the Germans were really not able to fight at all. And then when we began capturing them in droves, they began surrendering by the hundreds and thousands. Then it was a race, really. We were just racing to try to keep up with the advancing units. But practically all of the time the Headquarters Company was in Viareggio, which was about thirty kilometers from Pisa on the Mediterranean coast,[13] up the boot. So the headquarters was pretty stable.

One of the things that happened to me, I got into difficulty with an officer and I cussed him out. I had a lot of friends, schoolmates, and, in some cases, relatives among the officers. A very good friend of mine, Dr. Flournoy Coles, he told me that I was going to get court-martialed and I'd better do something about it. So I applied for combat duty. They laughed at first, but I was pretty sincere. I had two reasons for doing so.

One, I was saying to myself, It's a shame I'm way over here and don't know anything about what's going on. I was working with figures and paper and really didn't have a feel for what was going on except for the shelling occasionally, which was not touching us directly. We could hear it, but it was almost as if I wasn't in the war. That was one reason. Another reason: I got into trouble with this very senior-grade officer.

So when my friend told me I'd better do something about it and we got to figuring out what to do, he said, "Why don't you apply for a transfer and ask for my regiment? If you get in my regiment, I can handle it." I asked for a transfer, but I missed his regiment. Nevertheless, I had an experience as a combat soldier that I wouldn't take anything for, although now I wouldn't do it again. I was sent to the 365th Infantry Regiment, and at that time the fighting was still going on. We would go up on the line at night so that the movement of the troops would be disguised as much as possible.

We simply began a process of attempting to drive the Germans back towards I guess you might call it Austria. There was another fork of British soldiers on our right who were trying to drive them into Tito's land, Yugoslavia. But we were just going up the boot. We were probably inland about a hundred miles from the Mediterranean coast.[14] Whenever they counterattacked, they counterattacked in order to gain additional time. At this point they were fighting for time and for territory so that they could probably solve their problems of logistics, transport, and so forth.

I really didn't hear any talk about the 92nd being great night fighters. There's not a tremendous amount of fighting done at night, at least in the sector in which I was. You had a lot of very disagreeable things to do at night, like patrols. You had outposts to man, where you'd stay there all night long in one or two positions and then in daylight retreat back to another position. But as far as night fighting is concerned, there was very little of it. At least very little I saw, and I was up on the line.

You'd be surprised how small the perimeter is that a soldier is involved with in battle. He sees the same people, a limited part of a company, after he goes up on the line. He doesn't even see the whole company anymore until the company is pulled back. He is probably with a squad, and the squad lives as a complete entity. Supplies come up to the squad and things of this kind rather than masses of men together, and your vision of what's going on is extremely limited.

I had some funny experiences—real funny. Some sad, some tragic. And I don't know whether it's a conscious process or not, but I don't think of the tragic much. I think of some of the funniest things.

I remember once we attacked, and the Germans counterattacked. And they were counterattacking in a stronger force than we were, and we got the order to pull back. It wasn't a retreat, but it was a pullback. So when we began pulling back, there was a guy—I'll never forget—his name was Marlin from Florida. I've never seen or heard of him since. But in pulling back he started running, and he got shot right in the butt. It was the funniest thing to the whole bunch of us, that here's a guy, he got a Purple Heart for getting shot in the butt. It was really funny, and I can think of it now and laugh to myself because I witnessed it. It actually happened.

There were a tremendous number of things. There was a couple of very, very sad things. We were in a farmhouse, and we were, in the daytime, about four hundred yards from the Germans. We could see them, and they could see us. But everything was peace and quiet. That night some smart aleck got the bright idea of lobbing a mortar shell over there at the Jerries.[15] It would have been not so bad if they'd have lobbed a mortar shell back. But evidently they telephoned or radioed, and we got one of those eighty-eights[16] right into the farmhouse. We left thirteen people buried in there. There was no way of ever getting them out.

I remember one time I was going up at night to an outpost. It was really a lookout post. And I was probably twenty feet from the outpost when an eighty-eight fell right in — right in — the outpost. There were four people in there, and they were killed immediately. I was no more than twenty seconds away because I was to relieve these people. These kinds of things are sad, but I don't think about them often.

One of the most awful things that ever happened to me was a daylight patrol. You've heard of the night patrols. Now these are bad. But the daylight patrol is much more awful than anything that you could possibly conceive about at night because in the daylight patrol the commanders send out a group of men, and they can be seen and they're fair game. The purpose is to continue going until you draw fire, and this makes it awful because you know that someone looking at you can pick you off at any time he gets ready. The only thing that prevents him from picking you off is because, for this reason or that reason, they don't want to disclose their position at the time. I was on a number of daylight patrols, which were very, very scary. And on one of them at least, quite a number of our people got shot up. But this was the purpose. When the enemy opened fire, then the people with the walkie-talkies and so forth could talk back — radio or telephone — and our planes could come over.

We had an experience, in February I think it was, of 1945, when we were in a very bad position, a cul-de-sac, and we were pinned down. We couldn't move, and the planes hadn't been able to fly for three or four days. We woke up one morning and had a bright, bright sunshine, and in about twenty minutes we heard the planes coming over. I guarantee you that was really some relief because we could not have extricated ourselves from there without the help of those planes. And

Members of the 92nd Infantry Division advance through the Po Valley in the final stretch of the Italian Campaign, in April 1945. *Courtesy of National Archives and Records Administration.*

when they came over, well then, talk about the red, white, and blue! These people that sing these songs about "My Country, 'Tis of Thee" and all the rest of it, I imagine it's almost impossible for them to realize and appreciate how good that red, white, and blue or "USA" on those planes—how good they looked.

Those Nisei, those Japanese Americans, they saved our butts one time because the Germans actually had us on the run when they came up and helped us out. They just reversed things. They were tremendous in combat. I don't want to get on my soapbox and everything, but that's one of the real injustices this country has done. The Japanese Americans' property was seized, and they were sent to these various camps and all these kinds of things. I don't really know if these people have ever been really paid, and their sons were simply tremendous.[17]

I remained in Italy the duration of the war in Europe, together with the company I was with at that time. We were redeployed to the States preparatory to going to the Pacific. While I was on leave—they gave everybody leave—we were told to report to the nearest camp. Now, what happened to me was, the Congress passed a law putting out, so to speak, all the draftees who were thirty-five or older. So I was notified while on furlough that I was to be discharged, and it was simply a question of going to the nearest camp to pick it up. I was discharged at Fort George G. Meade[18] because I was just about thirty-five to forty minutes out of Washington. The war was still going on in the Pacific, but evidently they must have had some ideas about when it was going to end.

My wife was working for the Red Cross in Washington, so I just went to Washington and I got a job. When I was in Alabama, she was in Alabama. When I moved to Fort Huachuca, Arizona, in the Arizona desert, I was able to get her a job with the American Red Cross through some friends of mine. When the division shipped out, she was transferred from Fort Huachuca to the Washington office. So when I returned to Meade, there she was in Washington. It was just a question of everything working out real fine for us. During the whole war we were separated only that time when I was in Italy, and she was in the process of making arrangements to come over there with the Red Cross. So it worked out real well for us.

We remained in Washington until January of 1946. I worked briefly at the Post Office Department, I worked briefly at the Commerce Department, but like most soldiers my plans were just not firm. The job at the Red Cross for my wife was going to terminate pretty soon, so we decided to go back to New Orleans. She decided to go back and get her degree, which had been interrupted, I think, somewhere around 1929 or thereabouts. I decided to go to school in social work in Atlanta, Georgia. So that's what happened. We went back to New Orleans. She enrolled in Xavier in New Orleans, and I enrolled at Atlanta University School of Social Work.

The benefits of the GI Bill and the benefits of some of the other bills where you can't measure the tangible—maybe there's no tangible worth. It's really intangible, but yet the impact is tremendous. Unless someone was to come along and say, "Well, I'm going to pay you some money to go to school," it would not have occurred to me to go. It was one of those things that you'd like to do. Just like for years and years I used to say, "I'm going to Hawaii," but it was a joke. It's no longer a joke. I can go if I want to. I'm not particular about going. But for years I was going to Hawaii and spend a week or ten days or something like that. It was kind of the expression of an impossible dream. So what? It's free. It doesn't cost anything to dream like this, so you dream. But you're not very serious about it. This is the way the higher education—that is, above the college level[19]—was to me. It was not going to happen, so forget it.

Despite the fact that I eventually wound up as a combat infantryman and I faced the enemy in what amounted to, at one time, face-to-face combat and all the rest of it, in looking back over the whole experience, I found that I had a lot of fun. I like to say that I had a ball in the service, and I just didn't have the impression when I left the service that I had been robbed like so many guys did. A lot of guys felt that they had been robbed of some of the best years or months of their lives and so forth and so on.

I think the whole thing was the opportunity to have a series of new experiences and to go places and do things that I had not been able to do prior to that time. As an example, I doubt if I would ever really have seen the country of Italy had I not been in the service, and I probably had a better view of the country than I could have ever hoped to get as a tourist. I was able to visit Rome and Milan and Florence and Pisa and, oh, all kinds of places. I've seen some of the sights. I've been to cathedrals and all kinds of things that I would not have had, in all probability, the opportunity to visit.

I had some laughs at the expense of the army. One of the big jokes to me was that a month or two before we went overseas, everywhere we went we had to have our gas masks. We had to carry them with us. And the very first order we received after the landing in Italy around Livorno was, Turn in all gas masks. That's the first order we received, and I had a lot of fun out of that. The army saying is, Hurry up and wait. To me, this had a kind of funniness about it because it was just so unreal. As far as I was concerned, I didn't mind waiting for the duration of the war. So I guess probably it was my own attitude coupled with the opportunity for new experiences.

On top of that, for the first time in my life I was able to save some money. I don't know how much this had to do with it, but I'm certain that this played an important part because when I was eventually discharged I had about five thousand dollars in 1945 dollars, which was quite a sum of money. I did make some wise investments with it because I put just about all that money in the continuation of my wife's education and my own education. So I think that part turned out very well.

On the GI Bill, DuCongé earned his master's degree in social work from Atlanta University in Atlanta, Georgia, and also took graduate courses at Xavier University in New Orleans and at the University of Pittsburgh in

Pennsylvania. He had just been hired by the Domestic Relations Court in Pittsburgh in 1948 when he received a job offer from the Veterans Administration Hospital in Waco, Texas. Having never lived in a small town, DuCongé experienced culture shock upon moving to Waco and found it difficult to follow conversations about cotton, cattle, and farming. In 1954 he accepted a job offer from the University of Florida in Gainesville, where a new psychiatric center was opening. But when he arrived in the office and they realized he was black, they rescinded the offer.

DuCongé soon after returned to Waco, entered into a partnership with Garry Radford to purchase the Doris Miller Memorial Park, and managed the business from 1956 until 1972. During this time he also ran a life insurance agency and helped revive the Waco Negro Chamber of Commerce. He returned to his social work roots at the Waco Economic Opportunities Advancement Corporation, serving as director of community programming from 1972 until 1976. In the 1970s, DuCongé also served three terms on the Waco City Council, was elected as the first black mayor of Waco, and served as president of Caritas and the St. John's Catholic Church Council. In 1975 the state and local Junior Bar Association awarded him the Liberty Bell Award. Oscar DuCongé and his wife raised one son.

Oscar DuCongé shared his life history in eleven recorded interviews for the Institute's local and regional project, titled the Waco and McLennan County Project. He described his experiences in the 92nd Infantry Division in the third and fourth interview sessions. Oscar Norbert DuCongé, *Oral Memoirs of Oscar Norbert DuCongé*, a series of interviews conducted by Thomas L. Charlton, February 20, 1975, through July 31, 1975, in Waco, Texas, BU Digital Collections.

Notes

1. The US Army Finance School was at Fort Benjamin Harrison in Lawrence, Indiana.

2. In 1867 on the western plains, Native Americans gave the name "buffalo soldiers" to black soldiers they encountered from the 9th and 10th Cavalry Regiments, who were wearing buffalo hides as overcoats. Hondon B. Hargrove, *Buffalo Soldiers in Italy: Black Americans in World War II* (Jefferson, NC: McFarland, 1985), 1–2.

3. The morale of a group.

4. On July 26, 1948, President Truman issued Executive Order 9981, which forbade racial and religious discrimination in the armed forces. Because the military and the American public were unsure whether

this meant the end of segregation in the armed forces, Truman held a press conference and said that that was the intent of the order. Robert Shogan, *Harry Truman and the Struggle for Racial Justice* (Lawrence: University Press of Kansas, 2013), 130–31.

5. A Technician Third Grade (abbreviated T/3) was equal to a staff sergeant in pay grade.

6. Number of stripes, indicating rank, on the uniform sleeve of a member of the military.

7. A red line drawn through a name, denying pay.

8. American troops took control of Rome on June 4, 1944.

9. The nickname American troops gave to women who broadcast European Axis propaganda in English over the airwaves.

10. In this account "Nisei" (which means "second generation") refers to children of Japanese immigrants who were born and educated in the United States.

11. In 1966 Brooke was the first African American elected to the US Senate by popular vote. He served as a senator from Massachusetts from 1967 through 1979.

12. These allotments allowed troops to send money back home to their families.

13. More specifically, the Tyrrhenian coast, which is on the western side of Italy. The Tyrrhenian Sea is part of the Mediterranean Sea.

14. Again, referring to the Tyrrhenian coast.

15. Slang for German soldiers.

16. A shell from a German 88 mm gun, a World War II antitank and antiaircraft weapon.

17. Starting in early 1942, some 110,000 Japanese Americans living on the West Coast were relocated to internment camps. Many received monetary reparations through the 1948 Evacuation Claims Act and the Civil Liberties Act of 1988. Brian Masaru Hayashi, *Democratizing the Enemy: The Japanese American Internment* (Princeton, NJ: Princeton University Press, 2004), 1–2.

18. In Anne Arundel County, Maryland.

19. Graduate school.

HOMER H. MARTIN JR.

Born in Waco, Texas, on January 25, 1925, Homer Martin grew up in a house built by his father, a carpenter who later worked as maintenance superintendent of Waco's Cameron Park. His mother, a housewife, had been brought up on a farm in Moody, Texas. The Martin home stood about six blocks from Baylor University, and in his youth Martin attended many of the Baylor football and basketball games and cheered for such well-known Baylor athletes as Jack Russell and "Bullet" Bill Patterson. When Martin had no money for tickets to the football games, he simply jumped the fence at the stadium. He was the youngest of five brothers—Jack, Roy, Glenn, Bill, and Homer—all of whom graduated from Waco High School. Three brothers, including Homer, served in World War II.

My brother Roy worked for the newspaper and WACO, the local radio station. In 1943 he joined the naval reserve and was in until 1946. He was married at the time and had a child. He would not have been drafted, but he felt compelled to join the navy, where he already had two brothers.

Bill was the next oldest brother. I'm six years younger than Bill. Bill joined the regular navy in 1939 and was on the USS *Enterprise*, an aircraft carrier, on December 7, 1941. All the carriers were out at sea during December 7, so they were not attacked. He was an aviation ordnance mate and a qualified gunner in a torpedo squadron on the *Enterprise*, Torpedo Squadron Six.

The first big battle that kind of was the turning point of the war, as far as the navy was concerned, was the Battle of Midway, when the Japanese fleet came down for the purpose of occupying Midway.[1] Navy personnel had broken the Japanese code and knew of the activities of the Japanese fleet, and they were met by a US task force, at that time consisting of the *Enterprise* and two other aircraft carriers. As soon as they were able to locate the Japanese fleet specifically, many of the planes took off from the carriers, including Squadron V-6, of which Bill was a member but not flying. That squadron got lost and became separated from its air cover, and all of the fourteen planes in the squadron were shot down. All of the men were lost. If my brother had been flying at the time, he would not have survived.

Because his squadron was destroyed, Bill was transferred to another squadron on the USS *Hornet*, another aircraft carrier, which was later sunk in the Battle of the Santa Cruz Islands.[2] Bill was not injured in the attack. They were sunk by Japanese planes and torpedoes. He always liked to say that he got off the carrier and boarded a destroyer without ever getting his feet wet and survived the war. He was never aboard ship again. He spent the rest of his navy career on various bases in the South Pacific, ultimately winding up in Norfolk, Virginia, and retired as a warrant officer from the navy.

On July 10, 1942, about thirty days after I graduated from Waco High School as a seventeen-year-old, I volunteered for the United States Naval Reserve. I attended boot camp in San Diego, California. Boot camp lasted approximately thirty days and was primarily for the purpose of outfitting the sailors and to get their inoculations. There were a series of inoculations you had to go through. Kind of to take up the time, you did a certain amount of marching out on the grinder,[3] and they taught you how to tie knots, and they taught you a little bit about semaphore,[4] but it was mostly a waste of time, as far as really training for the navy.

We were given a test to determine aptitude for various areas in the navy and asked where we would like to be in the navy, if we had a choice. I chose aviation machinist mate because my brother was that. A part of the way of testing your skills was to give you code, Morse code.[5] They would give you a letter, and then they would give you another, di-di-dah-dah-di-dit, stuff like that, and ask if it were the same or different. I must have passed that test okay because they sent me from San Diego to US Naval Radio School at the University of Colorado in Boulder, Colorado, where they taught us Morse code, taught us how to type. That lasted three months.

If we graduated, which I did, you graduated as a radioman third class, which was the first rank above seaman in the navy and could have been a problem for me, but it really wasn't because I happened to get aboard a ship that had a bunch of good, regular navy guys. These were guys who had been in the navy a long time, and promotions were few and far between in the regular navy before the war. You would think they would resent some nineteen-year-old kid coming aboard ranked as a radioman third class, but they did not. They were always nice to me. They were soon transferred and were replaced by navy reserve.

I didn't have any other basic training than the radio school because

Stars like Maureen O'Hara collected used typewriters for the armed forces after typewriter factories switched over to war production. *Courtesy of the Franklin D. Roosevelt Library and Museum.*

there really wasn't much else for a radioman to do aboard ship, other than stand his watches and take code. You had radio receivers in front of you and transmitters in case you needed to transmit. When we graduated from the radio school, they sent us to the navy base at Treasure Island, California, which was out in the bay. It was a naval station at that time.[6] It's used for different purposes now.

Midnight on New Year's Eve 1942, I went aboard the USS *Rochambeau*, which was a French liner converted to a troopship. That was the first time I was aboard a ship of any kind. We left at the base in San Francisco, went under the Golden Gate Bridge, and nearly everybody except the regular seamen—duty sailors aboard the ship—got seasick. I certainly did, and I remained seasick during rough waters for a good many months following that. Took me quite awhile to get used to the sea. But once I got accustomed to it, I never got seasick again, no matter how rough the water was. Some people just never got over seasickness, and they were transferred to shore duty. But otherwise, if I was standing watch and seasick, I would have a bucket between my legs. I would be at a typewriter. The watch was for four hours. I'd type Morse code, vomit when necessary in the bucket, and have the striker[7] take the bucket out and empty it.

The *Rochambeau* went to Nouméa, New Caledonia.[8] We disembarked in Nouméa, which was in the South Pacific and maybe a hundred miles or so south of Guadalcanal, the Solomon Island areas. I waited there for further assignment, and on February 1, 1943, I went aboard the USS *Hopkins.*

The *Hopkins*, although it was constructed in 1920, was considered to be a World War I destroyer. It was what they called a flat-top destroyer, which meant it was constructed with an absolute flat top, and then the structures that were on top were added after the lower part was constructed. In 1939 it was converted to a high-speed minesweeper. They considered it high speed because it could make from somewhere between twenty-five and thirty knots. Other minesweepers were wooden-hull minesweepers, much smaller and not near as fast. Nevertheless, the draft of the *Hopkins*, the depth that it sank into the sea, was only fourteen feet and was considered to be capable of rising above the anchored Japanese mines, and we were able to do that. We were never hit by a mine. We swept a number of them.

I might mention about how they sweep mines because that is kind of interesting. There were two long cables that came from the end, the stern. But from the end of the minesweeper, there were two long cables coming out from the end at an angle, and at the end of these cables were what they called a paravane. A paravane was just a huge scissor; think of it as scissors. The cables coming from the back of the minesweeper would contact the mine cable and carry the mine cable back to the paravanes, where the scissors, or the paravane, would cut it. The mine would come to the surface, where sharpshooters would puncture it and sink it.

We swept as a squadron. We were kind of in a V shape. There would be a lead ship followed by other minesweepers forming a fairly large area. The *Hopkins* was the leader of the squadron. We had the squadron commander aboard. He was called a commodore; he happened to be a commander. And it was called Mine Squadron, or MinRon, 2. Until the war was practically over we were always the squadron leader and usually the first ship in the formation. Since we were a squadron flagship, Admiral Kelly Turner, who was in charge of that operation, was aboard our ship. The *Hopkins* was his flagship as well as MinRon 2's flagship. Turner was also in charge of the initial Guadalcanal invasion.

The *Hopkins*, having been at sea on December 7, 1941, was involved in the invasion of Guadalcanal in early 1942. It was used for various reasons: supply ship, troopship, sweeping the area, and what have you. But it was also involved in the Battle of Savo Island, the first and one of the most disastrous naval battles that occurred in the bay between Guadalcanal and Tulagi.[9] The *Canberra*, the *Quincy*, the *Vincennes*, and the *Astoria*,[10] they were all sunk. But before the *Astoria* sunk, the *Hopkins* took the *Astoria* in tow and was trying to get it close to the beach to beach it and save the ship. But the *Astoria* had significant damage. There were fires aboard ship, and the fires were getting close to the ammunition. They told the *Hopkins* to get away from it because it would ultimately explode, and sure enough it did explode—the magazines—and was sunk.

I boarded the *Hopkins* on February 1, 1943. We immediately joined a convoy. The *Hopkins* was frequently on convoy duty when it was not actually sweeping mines for an invasion. It was convoy duty to the Solomons. The marines and the army had already eliminated the Japanese from Guadalcanal and the island of Tulagi, which was across the bay from Guadalcanal. The bay was called Ironbottom Sound.[11] We anchored in Tulagi. That was my first experience of being anchored in a battle area. There were problems with Japanese planes still during that time. That was our first anchorage.

The first battle after I got aboard was not much of a battle. The islands just east and north of the Solomons—and a part of the Solomons, actually—was the Russell Islands, and that was the first invasion that I was involved in. We were a troopship. We had a small contingent of army troops aboard, and we swept for the other ships to get in. No mines were present. We landed the troops, and then we commenced to serve as a patrol ship and a convoy ship and a supply ship.[12]

An interesting thing happened at the Russell Islands. The two smaller boats aboard a minesweeper were called motor whaleboats. They were just great big life-saving boats. We had a crew of a hundred and fifty enlisted men, plus eleven officers. We also had rubber life rafts and that sort of thing. But going back and forth and sometimes getting very close to the docks at the Russell Islands, some of the sailors spotted a Chris-Craft, a very high-speed, luxury-type boat that was uncommon in the navy at that time. They thought that they could go in at night and take it, and they did. They went in, they jumped off of the motor whaleboat, they swam to the Chris-Craft, and for about the year following that, until we got back to the United States for overhaul, when that Chris-Craft was taken away from us, the *Hopkins* had one of the best small boats in the navy. That was my first battle. It wasn't much of a battle.

Normally, as radiomen, we had four-hour shifts and twelve hours off. That could vary depending on how many radio operators we had aboard. Sometimes we were under complement; sometimes we were over. Sometimes your watches might last a little longer than that. Sometimes your time off could be more or less than twelve hours. But

USS *Hopkins* in Empress Augusta Bay during the Bougainville invasion, November 1, 1943. *Courtesy of National Archives and Records Administration.*

as radio operators, on watch we were taking code all the time. After you took code for a while, you got accustomed to where you could take your codes. You could type it on a typewriter in front of you. Your mind would become two-dimensional, and you could actually carry on conversations and listen to the radio or what have you. You could do other things, but you would always be typing code. And that was a constant on the watch: taking code, from beginning to end.

Messages would come in the form of a coded message addressed from some ship to another or from CINCPAC—Commander-in-Chief, Pacific—to various task forces. Messages from Pearl Harbor, CINCPAC, were constant. They were going on all the time, and that particular frequency was manned all the time, except when we were in port and were relieved from active duty while the ship was being overhauled for one reason or another. The ship did go back to the States twice while I was aboard, both times for overhaul: the first time to get better radar, the second time to get better guns. I got a leave both times to go back to Waco, as well as a short leave immediately after graduating from radio school.

The radio shack was a fairly small room. It had two shelves, one higher than the other. One would come out below the other. On the higher shelf would be the radio receivers and transmitters, and below would be a series of typewriters. I think there were positions for four, maybe five. There would always be at least two manned, sometimes more. Depended on where we were and what we were doing.

The radio shack also had the record player that was tied in to the ship's speaker system. We had an excellent collection of records, both pop records—Frank Sinatra, Bing Crosby, and the Andrews Sisters—and an excellent collection of classical music—symphonic, choral, what have you. As a young guy from the small city of Waco, being unacquainted with classical music really until I got aboard ship, I started listening to it and grew to love it. We played a lot of it, and it got to the point where when guys would hear a lot of classical music on the speaker system, they would say, Oh, Junior's got the watch.

Crewmen were known by their last name. I would normally have been called Martin aboard ship. But Lee Martin from Thibodaux, Louisiana, was in radio school with me at the University of Colorado. I didn't know him at the time. We both crossed with the *Rochambeau.* I still did not know him. He and I both went aboard the *Hopkins* at the same time. I didn't know him till we got aboard ship. He was a couple of years older than me. So we had two Martins in the radio gang, which was a source of confusion. The gang and then the entire crew began calling him Pop. Naturally, they then began calling me Junior. So for my almost three years aboard the USS *Hopkins*, I was known as Junior.

When you were off watch as the radio operator, there were various things to do. We had emergency generators that we had to keep upkeep on, and there was an emergency radio shack that had to be manned from time to time. If I were not actually on duty in the radio shack, my general quarters position was usually in the emergency radio shack. I'd be back there by myself. I never had to operate it as an emergency radio because the radio shack was never hit to the point that it was destroyed or the operation of it was diminished in any way. When off duty you were kind of on your own. There were other maintenance duties. You slept a lot. In the summertime it would be hot below—our crew quarters was below deck. We had bunks. We had lockers below the bunks. But it was hot down there in the South Pacific. Frequently we would be sleeping above deck, using our life jackets to sleep on.

The first time I crossed the equator, I was on the USS *Rochambeau.* As a passenger I did not have to go through the initiation ceremony. I did not have to go through the initiation ceremony until I was aboard the *Hopkins* and we were going back for overhaul back to the United States when we crossed the equator. It was called the Ancient Order of the Deep, this process of initiation. You entered into the Ancient Order of the Deep, and you were initiated by Neptune Rex and his queen and his baby. They were in charge. They were selected by the crew, and they were always crew members. I never heard of an officer being one of those members of the royalty. The baby was always the biggest guy they could find, and they would put something that appeared to be diapers on him. As a part of the initiation ceremony, you had to kiss the baby's navel.

The initiations were of various kinds. What I remember was having to run through a gauntlet of sailors forming two lines. You run through the middle, and they would have their belt, and they would whack you on the back, on the rump. There were such initiations as that. Once you were initiated, you were given a certificate. Strangely enough, my certificate is not the one that was given on the *Hopkins*. It was given on the *Rochambeau*, although I wasn't initiated on the *Rochambeau*.[13]

I mentioned the first battle. The navy referred to invasions as battles. The additional battles: June and July of 1943, we were in the invasion of New Georgia. In November 1943 we're in the invasion of Bougainville Island, which was a part of the Solomons, as were the New Georgia Islands. In June of '44 we were in the invasion of Saipan. And July 1944 we were involved in the invasion of Guam. In January '45, the invasion of Luzon, more specifically the northern end of the Philippine Islands, in the Lingayen Gulf Landing. In February 1945 we were involved in the invasion of Iwo Jima. In 1945, March, we were involved in the invasion of Okinawa. In August of 1945 we swept the entrance of Tokyo Bay for the other ships to enter for the surrender ceremonies.

To apply to all of those invasions, the primary duty of the *Hopkins* and the other ships of its squadron was as a minesweeper. We would sweep the area for the invasion crafts and ships to come in for the invasion. We would sweep for mines, and if there were any, they would be destroyed. That was our primary duty. But after sweeping for mines, we would nearly always serve as a supply ship. Sometimes we would serve as a ship to bombard for the invasion or patrol against Japanese airplanes coming in or patrol for Japanese ships coming in and interfering one way or the other with the invasion.

In between invasions we were usually involved in convoys. A convoy would be a group of ships, usually supply or transport ships. We would be out patrolling around them, using our sound gear to search for any Japanese submarines that might be in the area or as defense against any Japanese warplanes that might be involved.

In connection therewith, I might mention where we first encountered kamikaze, in January 1945. We were involved in the invasion of the Philippines in the Lingayen Gulf, and our squadron was actually in the gulf sweeping when hundreds of Japanese kamikaze planes started coming in. The *Hopkins*, if attacked while sweeping, would cut the cables and paravanes so that we could speed up and maneuver without being encumbered by minesweeping gear.

This was a very large gulf. There were capital ships behind us—battleships. The *California* was there, the *West Virginia* was there, and many other kinds of ships that ultimately served to bombard the beaches and areas that were to be invaded. The kamikaze sunk three ships in our squadron: the *Palmer*, the *Long*, and the *Hovey*.[14] The *Hopkins* served as a rescue vessel. We had men jump overboard and go to the rescue of a number of these survivors. A number of them we did not rescue. We had a doctor aboard, which was one good reason we were used as a rescue ship, and he treated the survivors. The *Hopkins* was not hit by a kamikaze during that particular invasion.

From Lingayen Gulf we went to the invasion of Okinawa, and we served again, initially to sweep, secondly as a patrol ship. And again the navy ships had big problems with Japanese kamikazes, suicide planes trying to hit your ship, and they did in fact hit the *Hopkins*. They came in low. I did not have the watch that day. I was in general quarters in the emergency radio shack, which was aft, which was at the back end of the USS *Hopkins*. I was standing outside the radio shack, and I could see the Jap plane coming in low, very visible. All guns that could aim at him were firing. I don't know whether the plane was hit or not. Probably was.

But it was coming in a bit too high and turned wing down. The top of the wing hit a gun position on the *Hopkins*—it was a three-inch gun position—killed a gunner and wounded two others.[15] That was the *Hopkins*'s only casualty of the whole war, where we lost a gunner. It was a young man. He happened to be a member of the regular navy. There were other times when there were kamikaze planes flying around us and were hitting other ships, which, of course, frightens you quite a bit, but that was the only time that the *Hopkins* was actually hit by a kamikaze. We shot down a number of planes in Lingayen Gulf and then again at Okinawa.

Going from Okinawa, we were getting close to the end of the war. We had the detonation of the two atom bombs in Japan, which effectively ended the war.[16] Because we had lost three ships in our squadron we became a member of another squadron heading for Japan. We were heading for the Sea of Japan when the ships turned around and headed back to Okinawa.

I don't have any specific recollection of the end of the war, strangely enough. Somebody asked how I felt when I realized the war was over. I surmised that I thought most of us just simply felt relieved, and it was not any great, joyous occasion. We knew that had the war not been ended by the atomic bombs that there would have been thousands, if not millions, of military killed and Japanese killed during that invasion of Japan because they were fierce fighters in defending their property and their homeland. It would have been bad, and those two bombs probably saved my life.

But I know how it would have happened. We would have received a radio message—which I could very well have received myself. I don't remember being on watch at that time, but I could have been. These messages were in code, and they had to go to a communications officer or other officers who would decode them. This particular message would have told us that the Japanese had agreed to the surrender.

We went back to Okinawa. Then we left Okinawa for the September surrender ceremonies, and this newly formed squadron swept the entrance to Tokyo Bay. I happened to read that we swept fifty mines. The mines, incidentally, were anchored to the bottom of the ocean and were suspended by a cable from this anchor in the bottom of the ocean. Mines had triggers that extended all around them, which, if struck by a ship, would cause the mine to explode. Since the *Hopkins* and other destroyer minesweepers had a draft of only fourteen feet, theoretically we were able to go above them, and we did.

Our officers had been advised by the Japanese where the mines were located, so we were sweeping areas that we knew the location of, and no doubt knew the depth of, the mines. We did not consider ourselves to be in any danger. I distinctly remember mines popping to the surface and being hit by sharpshooters firing rifles at them and sinking them. They didn't happen to hit the explosive devices, so they didn't explode. They just sank. We swept fifty mines and sunk them and went on into Tokyo Bay. I'm sure the *Hopkins* was one of the first into Tokyo Bay.

We anchored near the *Missouri*, where, on September 2, 1945, surrender ceremonies were entered into by General MacArthur and members of his staff and members of the Japanese military and civilian leaders. I know from the logs that were kept that we first anchored near the *Missouri*. I also know that we moved; they moved us. I do not know the date that that happened.

I do want to mention Bill Mills, my lifelong friend. He was a year and a half older than me. He was a freshman at Baylor University, born and raised in Center, Texas, before he went into the navy reserve. He went directly from entering the navy to the *Hopkins*, where I met him.

Meeting him was a bit unusual. I mentioned that we played classical music aboard. There were a hundred and fifty of us aboard ship. Bill hadn't been aboard that long, and I don't believe I recognized him. But I do remember the guy chipping paint, whistling one of the Hungarian rhapsodies, probably one of the Brahms Hungarian Rhapsodies, which was most unusual. Where did this guy come from?

We got to talking, and I learned that he was from Center, had lived in Waco a year, and had attended Baylor. I immediately arranged for him to become what they called a striker in the radio gang. He was supposed to learn code but never did, so he never became an actual radio operator, but he spent the rest of his time aboard ship as a striker. He and I became very good friends, lifelong friends. He was best man in our wedding, and I was best man in his.

We were all pretty good guys. I got the good conduct ribbon,[17] as I think they all did. We behaved ourselves. It was kind of interesting, though, that Bill, being a Baylor student, and I, being a Bible Belt Methodist at the time, did not drink. Sailors on shore leave drank. They drank a lot. Bill and I would go to shore with them. We would go into the bars with them. It was a lot of fun. We were having a great time. They would order their whiskey sours and what have you and their beer, and Bill and I would order sweet milk, to the hooting and hollering of all the other guys. So generally the crew and the officers were nice guys. We all got along well together, and some of them got tipsy at times but not all that bad, really.

After the surrender ceremonies we returned to Okinawa, and we were there a short while and received our orders to go to Norfolk, Virginia. We went from Okinawa to Pearl Harbor to San Diego, California, through the Panama Canal to Norfolk, Virginia. I left the *Hopkins* December 10, 1945. My brother Bill, who had joined the navy in 1939, happened to be stationed at Norfolk when our ship went there to be decommissioned. We did meet, and we went out to dinner a couple of times.

From there, just simply got on a bus to Norman, Oklahoma, University of Oklahoma, where I received my discharge. That was a discharge center. I received my honorable discharge and my good conduct ribbon and was sent home in December. I went aboard a bus immediately to Waco and was met by my mother and father and oldest brother, Jack. Roy and Bill were still in the navy, so they were not there to greet me. And then it was just a few weeks later after that that I met Carolyn.

I entered Baylor during that spring quarter of 1946. Carolyn and her sister were already there. Bill Mills, my good friend, had dated Carolyn's sister, Grace. We were at the First Baptist Church one night—I was still in uniform; Bill was, too—where I met Carolyn. Grace mentioned that she was a fiddle player and thought she should play for me, so a few days later I got into a practice hall with Carolyn. She played for me, and it went on from there, sixty some-odd years.

I was the first person in my family to graduate from Baylor. Actually, except for the war, it's quite possible that I would not have gone to college. I might have followed my brothers and just gone to work in Waco. But having been involved in the war and having the GI Bill waiting for me when I got out, there wasn't any question about going to college, and it was definitely going to be Baylor. I never ever considered another college for the undergraduate. I considered Baylor for master's degree but thought, Well, maybe I should go to a different school. Therefore, I went to the University of Texas for my MBA.

To supplement the fifty dollars a month Martin received under the GI Bill, he worked several places during college: at Standard Hat Works for his brother Bill; at Hamilton Brothers Furniture Store, owned by his uncle; and at the Waco Parks & Recreation Department. Homer and Carolyn Martin married on August 21, 1948, and both graduated from Baylor University the next year. In 1952, after completing a graduate degree at the University of Texas in Austin, Martin became a certified public accountant in Houston. In 1964 the couple moved to Colorado Springs. After he retired from Colorado Interstate Gas Corporation in 1983, the couple returned to Waco to be near family but moved back to Colorado Springs in 1994, where their children and grandchildren resided. Homer's brother Glenn was the father of actor and comedian Steve Martin.

Homer Martin was interviewed for the Institute's special project, World War II Veterans, at the suggestion of retired Waco physician Dr. Simon Bunn. Homer H. Martin Jr., *Oral Memoirs of Homer H. Martin Jr.*, an interview conducted by Sarah Swint-Martinez, April 21, 2010, in Colorado Springs, Colorado, BU Digital Collections.

Notes

1. It is a common misconception that the Battle of Midway (June 4–7, 1942) brought a halt to Japanese expansion and was the turning point in the Pacific. In reality, following Midway, Japanese troops advanced on Port Moresby in the Territory of Papua. It was the Guadalcanal campaign (August 7, 1942–February 9, 1943) that put Japanese forces on the defensive for the remainder of the war. Richard B. Frank, *Guadalcanal: The Definitive Account of the Landmark Battle* (1990; repr., New York: Penguin Books, 1992), 598–99.

2. The Battle of the Santa Cruz Islands, which took place on October 26, 1942, as part of the larger Guadalcanal operation, is one of the

lesser-known carrier battles of the Pacific War. Events at Santa Cruz dispel the myth that the US devastated Japan's carrier fleet in the Battle of Midway, since only four months after Midway, four Japanese carriers overthrew the efforts of two US carriers. Mark Stille, *Santa Cruz 1942: Carrier Duel in the South Pacific* (Long Island City, NY: Osprey, 2012), 5, 11.

3. A concrete training ground.

4. A system of signaling using two flags, one held in each hand.

5. One of the advantages of Morse code in a combat situation is that it can often be read through jamming tactics the enemy might employ. Furthermore, should a radio blackout be in effect, Morse code can be transmitted by other means, such as lights, flags, horns, mirrors—anything that can be detected by sight, sound, or touch. L. Peter Carron Jr., *Morse Code: The Essential Language* (1991; repr., Newington, CT: American Radio Relay League, 1996) 1-1 to 1-3.

6. Treasure Island, a man-made island, was constructed for the 1939–1940 Golden Gate International Exposition. Plans were in place for the city of San Francisco to use the island as an airport after the exposition, but it was turned over to the navy. Treasure Island served as a key naval base during the war and processed as many as 12,000 men a day to the Pacific. Paolo E. Coletta and K. Jack Bauer, eds., *United States Navy and Marine Corps Bases, Domestic* (Westport, CT: Greenwood Press, 1985), 600.

7. A junior enlisted member of the US Navy who has declared an occupational specialty but has not yet become a petty officer.

8. In early 1943, members of the US Navy Construction Battalion, or Seabees, were hard at work transforming Nouméa, New Caledonia, into a massive 20,000-man naval base. Its location in relation to the Solomon Islands, the war zone at that time, made it a crucial naval operating base and supply depot in the South Pacific. The marine corps also relied heavily on the site as a supply depot and staging area. Paolo E. Coletta and K. Jack Bauer, eds., *United States Navy and Marine Corps Bases, Overseas* (Westport, CT: Greenwood Press, 1985), 241–42.

9. The US Navy loss at the Battle of Savo Island (August 8–9, 1942) was so humiliating it warranted a special investigation. One captain involved in the battle took his own life after being interviewed. Frank, *Guadalcanal*, 83, 122.

10. HMAS *Canberra*, of the Royal Australian Navy, and USS *Quincy*, USS *Vincennes*, and USS *Astoria*, all of the US Navy, were heavy cruisers.

11. Allied sailors gave this name to Savo Sound because of the large number of vessels and aircraft sunk there during the Battle of Guadalcanal.

12. The Japanese never occupied the Russell Islands in an official capacity, but they did briefly populate them as they withdrew from Guadalcanal in Operation Ke, January 14–February 7, 1943. In mid-February US reconnaissance teams detected no enemy troops on the Russells, but the US decided to stake their claim on the islands nonetheless, out of fear that the Japanese would return. On February 17 the Japanese launched an unsuccessful air attack against the approaching US invasion convoy, and American troops landed on the Russells on February 21 as part of Operation Cleanslate. After securing the islands, US construction battalions began turning them into a large naval base with two vital airfields, and the islands also became a staging area and training center. David L. Snead, "Obscure but Important: The United States and the Russell Islands in World War II," *The Journal of America's Military Past*, Spring/Summer 2003: 5, 7, 9–11, http://digitalcommons.liberty.edu/cgi/viewcontent.cgi?article=1021&context=hist_fac_pubs.

13. Equator-crossing ceremonies, sometimes called Neptune Parties, are a tradition so old in navies across the globe that their origins are unclear. To read other personal accounts of these initiations during World War II, see Rex Alan Smith and Gerald A. Meehl, eds., *Pacific War Stories: In the Words of Those Who Survived* (New York: Abbeville Press, 2004), 234, 319, 332–33, 430.

14. US Navy destroyers.

15. This transpired on May 4, 1945. Robin L. Rielly, *Kamikaze Attacks of World War II: A Complete History of Japanese Suicide Strikes on American Ships, by Aircraft and Other Means* (Jefferson, NC: McFarland, 2010), 260, 323.

16. The US dropped bombs on Hiroshima and Nagasaki on August 6 and 9, 1945.

17. Navy Good Conduct Medal.

FRANCES A. HARDISTY

Frances Audrey Hardisty was born October 2, 1914, in Birdville, Texas. Her mother worked as a café cook, and her dad was a laborer for the county. She had four brothers and a sister. Throughout her years at Birdwell High School, Hardisty was active in track and field sports and won medals in high jump, discus, and javelin. She pursued her interest in athletics at North Texas State Teachers College in Denton from 1933 through 1937, earning both bachelor's and master's degrees in physical education. Hardisty was very active on campus, where she was a class favorite in 1935 and an active leader in the Physical Education Professional Club, the Women's Athletic Association, Green Jackets, Mary Ardens, Forum Council, and Delta Psi Kappa.[1] *She taught physical education and coached girls basketball in East Texas for one year, then held a job with the Works Progress Administration until 1942. In 1943, at the age of twenty-eight, she joined the Women's Army Corps.*

I WENT INTO THE SERVICE BECAUSE I JUST HAD an interest in serving my country, and I felt that was the way I could do it. I went to basic training at Daytona Beach, Florida, for four weeks, and they taught you everything from marching to military law. From there I went to Officer Candidate School in Des Moines, Iowa, in the dead of winter. It was cold. I spent six weeks in Officer Candidate School, and of course your training there was to be an officer. We had more and more training, military drilling, marching, and that sort of thing. You had military law again, more of it, and you had map reading. I very well remember it because I flunked that. We did not have any training with a firearm. They didn't do that back then, thank goodness.

The marches were very short, just around an area there in the stadium. I doubt they were even a mile, but we did it regularly. I enjoyed it; I liked it. I learned how to do what they call a "marine drill," and I just loved that. Marine drill is kind of more sophisticated drilling. You turn loose to do just about anything you want to, to march in your group. In my case I had a company, which consisted of about ninety to a hundred people, and I just used to love to get out and march them. You do some fancy maneuvering with your company.

Let me give you a little bit of an experience I had at OCS. We had a little bin that they put our mail in or any information they needed to get to us, down in the rec room. I came in from class one day, and I found this note to report to the hospital at one o'clock. So I went to my platoon officer and said, "What's this all about? I've had all my shots. I'm not sick." She said, "Well, forget it." It turned out they called from the dispensary and told me to be sure to make that appointment at one o'clock. So I tread over there. I had a class at one o'clock, and I kept telling them that I had to be in class.

When I get over there, this really smart-aleck sergeant at the desk said, "How many sailors did you go out with down in Daytona Beach, Florida?"[2] I said, "They weren't sailors. They were marines." I hadn't been out with anybody; I hadn't had time. He said, "Well, we have to give you an examination for gonorrhea." I said, "I haven't even been exposed." Well, he sends me back to the colonel, and I couldn't get anywhere with the colonel either. To make a long story short, I had that examination.[3]

I went back and I told my commanding officer about this, and then she got on the phone. We had a little shavetail lieutenant assigned to us at that time, and I learned later that he made a trip over to the hospital and he laid them low. He laid it on the line to him and told him, "You can tell by looking at that girl she wouldn't do anything wrong."

It was just before graduation, and what bothered me about it was that each platoon in your company rates or grades the others in the platoon on various and sundry things, and I was afraid this would get out. If it had, it would ruin me as far as passing OCS even though it wasn't true. The next day in formation the commanding officer called out about five of these and said to report to her after formation. My name wasn't on it. I thought they were getting paid. I hadn't been paid since I'd been in the service, in basic and Officer Candidate School. Funds were running low. The next day she called me and called out some more names to report to her office. She paid all the rest of them, gave them their check, and I didn't get one. I said, "Well, don't I get a check today?" She said, "I want to talk with you about that on a trip to the hospital. The commanding general wants you to come by his office and accept his personal apology for this trip." I said, "Well, I tell you what, you can accept his apologies for me. I understand, and you needn't bother." So I didn't go.

On the morning that we graduated, I was out mopping up the floor in front of the commanding officer's office. This little shavetail that had been going to the hospital was in there, and he said, "Say, come here a minute. I want to ask you something. Did that little trip to the hospital have anything to do with your flunking that map-reading course?" I said, “Well, it could have.” I hadn’t flunked it till I got back. I didn’t like map reading to begin with, but that could have affected it, I don’t know. But he was really taking care of me, which I appreciated.

Then, the next Saturday was when we got our insignia placed on. I was running a little late getting into formation. I was so disgusted I was going home. I was going AWOL. My platoon commander sent somebody up to get me: “Tell her to come on down here and get in formation where she belongs.” So I came out a little late, and I got in the back of the formation. They put the tall ones in front, and it slopes down. As soon as she had an opportunity to talk, my platoon commander said, “Come on up here and get in the block. Get in formation,” so I got on it. She knew what the problem was. She knew why I was late, because I had told them, “Anybody that can be that inefficient, I just don’t want any part of it. I’m leaving. I don’t want a scandal.”

So she came back again and told me to come up front and said, “I want you to be the platoon commander today.” I said, “Well, gee, I would appreciate that.” I was the platoon commander taking them from barracks over to where they were going for graduation, which was quite an honor, I thought.

After officer’s training, I was sent to Fort Oglethorpe, Georgia, in the capacity of training other officers down there. Then I got tired of this. You know, over and over you get in a group and you graduate them and get in another group and graduate them. So I told my battalion commander—she usually marched with us—and I said to her one day as we were marching along together, “How about you get me a company out in the field?” So in about two weeks I had my own company.

I was sent then to Camp Van Dorn, Mississippi, of all places. Walter Winchell dubbed Camp Van Dorn the “hellhole of the South.” They hadn’t completed it. It still had the tar paper. You lived in tar-paper shacks. It was a temporary thing; they hadn’t completed it. I stayed there about a year and a half, I guess, and I was responsible for this company of the WAC. They worked in different areas on the base. Some of them worked in quartermaster corps. A larger number of them worked in signal corps. They worked in all the offices, from the general’s office on down. It was interesting, but then I got itchy feet again, and I asked to go overseas.

I got sent overseas to, of all places, Dutch New Guinea. I was in Hollandia, New Guinea, Base G. That was an interesting experience. I had my own company over there, too. The Wacs worked in all the

Wacs at clerical duty in the finance office in Hollandia, Dutch New Guinea, in 1945. *Courtesy of US Department of Defense.*

different areas. They worked in quartermaster, they were clerk typists, they were secretaries. They worked in the signal corps, and they helped with some of the messages that were sent back and forth. There were a lot of them in signal corps. And then they worked from the general's office on down. They worked for the personnel officer, the general, and the colonel. They just worked all over the base really.

One of the problems, being over there, is homesickness. It was my duty to play mother to them, as well as being a company commander. The hardest thing I ever did when I was over there, I think, is to try to write a letter to one of my Wacs' parents. The Wac had died, and she was only twenty-three years old. She died of pernicious anemia, which is something that takes you real quick. In the army manuals they tell you how to write these different kinds of letters, and I got out my manual and looked it up in there. And I asked several of the men that had this same experience. They all agreed it was a hard thing to do. But I finally got it written. I got back a real nice letter from her parents. We buried her over there, which I thought was fairly strange, but it was during the war, and they couldn't do all the things they can when it's not wartime. So they buried her over there with the idea that the parents could have her body moved later, after the war was over. But it's real touchy in a situation like that. After the funeral they give the commanding officer the American flag, which would normally be given to the parents. I mailed it to them. But I think nearly every Wac in the company was real touchy because it was so sudden.

Our housing was temporary, but good. In Mississippi we had the tar-paper shacks, but they were real nice. Overseas we lived in tents. The corps of engineers were still working in the area when we landed there. One asked, "Do you want me to put you a sink in your tent?" I said, "Yeah, sure!" So you know what I had for a sink? A helmet. It was a helmet hanging down, and they put a water faucet in there, and the helmet would catch the water. Better than nothing. Our housing was the same as the men's.

We had many rows of tents. Interesting thing about it, too, is that the girls would decorate these tents. They grew bananas over there, and they would hang up a stalk of bananas outside the tent, or they'd plant some flowers. They were all real pretty. Once a week at least I had to make an inspection of the area, with the sergeant. I would go on this inspection tour, and she'd take notes if I found anything wrong with them. We would both become so interested in what these girls had planted outside their tents or had put up as different kinds of decorations around their tents. They were real attractive. And the only thing, one time I found that one of the girls — I guess she'd been out with a navy man — had a navy blanket on her bed. I didn't blame her; they were much prettier than army blankets, which were OD, olive drab green. The navy blanket was white with blue letters on it, "Navy." They were beautiful. I kept wanting to get one every time I was over there. Never did. But I had to "gig" hers, which is what they would call it.[4] I had to give a mark against her for her having this kind of blanket on her bed. I didn't really care myself, but I had to.

Our meals were just wonderful. I was lucky every place I went to have a good mess sergeant. We had our own mess. I had one of the best mess sergeants over there [in New Guinea]. The men were always wanting to come over and eat with us. The cook was a Wac, a Jewish girl, real, real talented. She wasn't young; she was about forty-four years old. I think at first the WAC cooks went to the same school the men did, but later on they had their own school. She was good.

One time the general had his secretary call me and said, "We'll be over for lunch today." This was in New Guinea. I said, "Thank you, sir, we'd be glad to have you." What else can you say to a general? I went and told the mess sergeant, and she said, "Oh good! He likes cherry pie. I'll fix him some cherry pie." Where she learned that, I have no idea, but she knew! And so he and his right-hand man came over and had lunch with us. While I had him in a good humor, I said — this was

Women's Army Corps tent camp in Hollandia, Dutch New Guinea, 1945. *Courtesy of US Department of Defense.*

just before Christmas, and we had to wear slacks over there because of the mosquitoes — and I said, "Sir," — and I thought to myself, While you're in a good mood I'll ask you this — "do you think you could permit the Wacs to wear their skirts and blouses on Christmas Day?" And he turned to the colonel and said, "What do you think about that?" He said, "I think it's a fine idea. Sure." So they let us wear our skirts on Christmas Day. The girls got a real bang out of getting a change.

Overseas our basic uniform was OD, olive drab, skirts and khaki shirts and OD jackets. The officers were allowed to wear what they called the pinks, which I still think is one of the prettiest uniforms there is. They were actually grey but had kind of a pinkish tint to them. We could wear those with our OD jackets and the khaki shirts. I always used to love to wear that. I even bought me an overcoat. We had to buy those things, you know, the officers did. We were not issued them, but the [enlisted] Wacs were issued their clothes. I used to think those pinks with the OD jacket were the prettiest things. We were made to wear slacks over there, as I said, because of the mosquitoes. When we were here in the States, we had a summer uniform that was a khaki skirt and a khaki shirt. The winter uniform was a OD black jacket and an OD skirt, except the officers, as I said, could wear the pinks. Way back there the undergarments were khaki. The underpants and bras, the slips were all khaki — ugly. They didn't show, though.

Over in New Guinea, they gave us Atabrine. It made you yellow. This was to prevent malaria from the mosquitoes, and we were always yellow as we could be. You just had to bide your time for that yellow to leave your skin when you got home. My mother said to me, "Boy, you're yellow!" I said, "Yeah, I'm yellow," but I didn't have any medical problems.

When I was in New Guinea, we had what they call the Sentani Lake. That was General MacArthur's headquarters, and we were not permitted to use that name of that lake in our letters back home because it would be censored. The road up to this lake was real mountainous, a real dangerous road. I wouldn't say I was in real danger, but I used to love being up that road in a jeep. We traveled by jeep over there. When I was over there, I had a jeep and a driver assigned to me. I was a captain.

I don't have any proof of this, and I probably shouldn't say it, but I think, like it is today sometimes, sex is a problem. You know, the men over there felt sorry for themselves if they didn't have wives around. On the other hand, over there, when dating an officer, you found yourself with a married man more often than not. And more often than not, this married man, the first thing he'd do would be to pull out his billfold and show you his wife's picture and his children's pictures. So there wasn't anything bad going on. I think there was more of that among the enlisted personnel than there was among the officers. Most of the ones I came in contact with that I ever dated were well disciplined.

We didn't suffer from being harassed like you do today. We didn't have that. We had nothing to be ashamed about. I never felt any discrimination myself. Some women did feel discriminated against because they didn't get promoted as often as they thought they should. But the army had so many promotions they could give. I never felt like that. I just tried to do my job and let other people worry about things like that. The male officers treated me pretty well. Our pay was the same as the men's. Even the enlisted women would get the same as the enlisted men, and the officers would, too. We went to the same hospitals as the men. I would guess there are more problems today because of women's lib. We didn't have that, see, back then. We stayed in our place, and the men stayed in theirs. I mean that's just the way it was.

Over in New Guinea, Hollandia, Base G, I had to transfer one Wac one time. I had two women who were accused of being lesbians, and I had one of my officers kind of make a stakeout one night, and she found them in bed together. So I just transferred one of them. It was the easy way out to break it up.[5]

What are my best memories of the war? I liked the camaraderie among the Wacs, and the men, also. Talking about the sex deal, one time we had a party the afternoon the war was ending. One of the men had a liquor store down on the bay there, the landing, and it was for the marines, and I went to the party with this young man. He said, "What are you going to do to celebrate for your Wacs?" I hadn't given any thought to it. "I guess we'll have a little beer up in the rec hall, and that'll be it." We had beer rationed to us. We were only supposed to get three bottles a day, no more than three bottles a day. He said, "You want me to send you up some beer?" I said, "Yeah, if you want to!" So he sent me up I don't know how many cases of beer—four hundred dollars' worth. Well, I paid for it, and I paid for it legitimately because I had what they called company funds. It states in the manual that you can buy refreshments for your troops, so I bought them some beer!

The next day, the inspector general's office representative came over, and he questioned me to no end about this beer. I said, "That beer is legal. I'll show you my papers here. I have it in writing. I have a receipt." And he said, "Well, I know you're telling the truth." But while he was there he said, "Have you ever been on the colonel's yacht?" And I said, "What yacht?" He said, "You mean you don't even know about it?" I said, "I certainly don't know about it, much less have been on it." Well, it seemed the colonel lived next to the general who had this yacht, and he took girls out on this yacht for various and sundry reasons. I didn't know anything about it; I'd never been on it, and I didn't care to. Well, so the inspector wrote up his report, and I got a copy of it. First thing you know, the general is involved in this, and I said, "I haven't done anything wrong." For me to have that much beer on hand, it did look kind of shaky, I guess. Four hundred dollars' worth! But anyway, the Wacs had a good time, and they brought their dates in to the rec hall. As long as they had a good time I didn't care what the rest of them thought, but I got called on the carpet for it.

I didn't really have any worst memories, I don't think. The death of the Wac would be one of the worst memories. I had a good time. I really did. I enjoyed it, and I had some wonderful experiences. I guess one of the oddest things was overseas, in New Guinea, I had this sergeant that worked for the colonel, and she didn't think that any rules or regulations in the company applied to her because she worked for the colonel. She's the one that called me to tell me that the general and the colonel were coming over for lunch. And I had this little spitfire PFC, private first class, and every once in a while this gal that worked for the colonel would be the cause of making me put up some regulations that the Wacs didn't really care for, and this little PFC was one of them. I had to put this notice up that no more men were allowed in the mess hall. We would let the men that worked for signal corps and drove the truck to take our Wacs back and forth come in at midnight and get a meal. They didn't have any at their own mess when they came in. She reported that, and so I had to post this restriction on the bulletin board. And this little PFC, that night at dinner—I think we had spaghetti—marched down alongside this gal, this sergeant, and just tilted her tray, and it went all over her uniform. She did it purposely.

And this gal came to me and said, "See what they've done to me?" I said, "They haven't done half of what you deserve." And, oh, she gave me some long story, I don't know what. I said, "You know, if you were in some men's outfit and you'd done to them what you've tried to do to these Wacs, they'd take you out up on the latrine and beat you half to death, and that's exactly what should be done to you. I'm not too eager to suggest that, but that's what I should do." Well, she gave me all these excuses. But I went over to talk to the colonel about this and about how she was carrying tales. Well, he came by one day in the jeep, and he said he wanted to take me over to see something. That was an excuse; he was going to talk to me, get me away from the company. He said, "I've been hearing all these reports about this sergeant. You want me to transfer her?" I said, "That'd be too good for her," but they did transfer her out. He said, "Anybody who'll ever carry tales in will carry them out." I said, "Well, that's true." She got her comeuppance.

My time overseas ended when the war in Japan was over, VJ Day. And that was the night that I got caught with that beer. The war was over, and I was ready to come home and seek other ventures. I was sent back from overseas, sent back to the States, and I ended up in San Antonio. Another girl and I were riding on the train along together, and we decided to re-enlist. So when we got to San Antonio, we did; we re-enlisted.

I spent the night in San Antonio, and about four of us went down to a real well-known hotel for dinner. We were steak hungry, so we all ordered steaks. The waiter came out and told us that they were out of steaks, they didn't have any. That was most unreasonable for that type of hotel. There was a couple sitting right across from us that heard this conversation, and this woman came over and said, "Did I hear them tell you girls that they didn't have any steaks?" And we said yes. She said, "You wait just a moment." She went back in the kitchen, got ahold of the maître d', and we had steaks and they paid for them. She didn't like the way they were treating us. But we got our steaks.

When I got back home, I wanted to unenlist. I wanted to get out while I could. If I'd stayed in, I would have probably been a major. The next promotion would have been pretty soon, but I didn't really care that much about it. So I chose to get out after I'd signed up, and I was ready to get out and seek other areas. Looking back, I do value my military experience very much. It taught me how to get along with people—all types of people—better. Every job I've ever had has been working with people. In the military you have a real cross-section of people, and I think it taught me how to get along with them. It didn't teach me, I just learned it, I'd say, because we had every type imaginable.

After Frances Hardisty returned to the States and mustered out of the service in 1946, she worked about two weeks for a housing project in Texarkana, Arkansas, and then about six weeks for the Austin, Texas, Parks and Recreation Department, as supervisor over a number of city playgrounds and swimming pools. In August 1946 she began a career with the Veterans Administration Hospital in Waco, Texas, as chief of recreation. Hardisty retired in 1971, after twenty-five years of service.

Frances A. Hardisty was interviewed by a Baylor University student for Women during War, a class oral history research project for history professor Patricia Ward Wallace. See Frances A. Hardisty, *Oral Memoirs of Frances A. Hardisty,* an interview conducted by Courtney Williams, November 19, 1994, in Waco, Texas, BU Digital Collections.

Notes

1. Details on Hardisty's early life and college years are available in Frances A. Hardisty, "Biographical Information," BU Digital Collections; North Texas State Teachers College, *The Yucca, Yearbook of North Texas State Teachers College* (Denton: North Texas State Teacher's College), 1934, 1935, 1936, 1937, University of North Texas Libraries, The Portal to Texas History, accessed October 15, 2013, http://texashistory.unt.edu/ark:/67531/metapth61004/; http://texashistory.unt.edu/ark:/67531/metapth61005/; http://texashistory.unt.edu/ark:/67531/metapth61006/; http://texashistory.unt.edu/ark:/67531/metapth61007/.

2. During 1943 and early 1944, opponents of women in military service conducted a "slander campaign" to spread rumors of promiscuity among Wacs. Particular attention fell on women in training at Daytona Beach, where soldiers and sailors from nearby military stations were frequent visitors and where Wacs were housed in leased hotels and rooming houses in the popular resort rather than on a military base. Mattie E. Treadwell, *The Women's Army Corps* (Washington, DC: Office of the Chief of Military History, Department of the Army, 1953), 77–78, 208–11.

3. The slander campaign blamed Wacs for the spread of venereal disease among male soldiers. Pelvic examinations on servicewomen became routine in several army posts in spite of the fact that the rate of venereal disease among them proved very low. Leisa D. Meyer, *Creating G.I. Jane: Sexuality and Power in the Women's Army Corps during World War II* (New York: Columbia University Press, 1996), 35, 58, 100–7.

4. A gig was a military demerit.

5. In transferring the suspected lesbian, Hardisty followed the WAC's "informal methods of control" regarding homosexual behavior. The object was to avoid harmful publicity that might inhibit recruitment and feed opposition to women in the military. Meyer, *Creating G.I. Jane*, 159.

EDWARD F. WEGNER

Edward Wegner was born into the Blackland Prairie cotton culture in Burton, Texas, on January 18, 1921. Both sets of grandparents had emigrated from Germany, and he and his sister, Lillian, grew up hearing stories about the old country and enjoying German dishes, songs, and traditions. German was spoken exclusively at home, and he and his sister learned English when they started school. At a young age the Wegners began learning to help out around the farm: chopping cotton and corn, feeding the animals, milking the cows, and working in the garden. Cotton was the family's main crop, and during the 1930s they fought against cotton root rot, to which the blackland soil was especially susceptible. When he was through with his chores, Wegner loved to hunt, trap, and fish in the countryside with his African American friend, Henry Gilmon. The two boys usually shared their trapping earnings: Gilmon took the meat, while Wegner wanted the pelts to sell. In school, Wegner enjoyed participating in basketball and baseball and competing in spelling in interscholastic meets. He graduated from Brenham High School in 1939.

AFTER GRADUATION I CAME BACK TO THE FARM. The next year or so the war clouds were beginning to form, and farming wasn't paying off a great deal. It was a good life but not a lot of cash income, especially for young people. You know, they like to have a little more money.

I saw this ad where the aircraft companies wanted people to get into sheet metal work. So I went to this school in Houston and learned the sheet metal trade. After I received my diploma or my certification there, I went to the area between Dallas and Fort Worth: Arlington–Grand Prairie area. There was Consolidated Aircraft and also North American Aviation.[1] So I went to both places and took the necessary tests to be employed there.

But I think a lot of people that were in the know were beginning to realize that war was right around the corner. I was twenty years old, and they weren't too eager to have anybody that age. I was never able to get on for this sheet metal work with those plants. It was a weekly affair to go up there and check on it, and I was pretty well convinced that they were not going to hire me. I went to the Dallas area briefly to work for a housing construction business. They were building all those new homes out in the prairie there. And other jobs, of course, were very meager, too. I went to work in the Walgreen drugstores to make ends meet. Eleven dollars a week wasn't too appealing.

I decided the navy might be a pretty good place to join up, so I went down to the recruiter in Dallas, Texas, and signed up for the US Naval Air Force, as I was hoping to be an aviation machinist mate, which is aviation mechanic, because I had had a good bit of mechanical experience with automobiles.

After I enlisted I went home for a very brief period of time and then came back to Dallas and shipped out to San Diego. They would ship them out in batches, whole batch at one time. It was a motley assortment of people that went from Dallas to San Diego on the train — from all walks of life. But they were all people about my age, around eighteen, nineteen, twenty, maybe some of them a little older. We had one guy — this was in the days of the zoot suit.[2] His name was Millican; he was a genuine zoot-suiter. He had a genuine zoot suit on, and he lost that in the process when he got to San Diego.

Everybody had his hair tonic and his shaving lotion and whatever and all of our civilian clothes, of which we were relieved pretty promptly once we got into the training center. One of the first things was a haircut. They would ask you how did you want it cut, and some people were fool enough to say, "Well, I'd like mine cut so-and-so way." They did exactly that: straight over the top from all sides. And then your shots and your physical examination, and then you went through the line and were issued your towels and clothes — underwear and your uniforms and everything. The navy had a clothing allowance. They didn't have a lot of issue. I think the army had more issue. After your initial clothing, you had so much clothing allowance every year, and you could buy more on your own. But if you took care of your clothes, there was no problem.

Another humorous thing was, you went through the line to the stenciling department, and the guys there were a couple of old salts. They would stencil all your clothes — and you without any clothes on — and then say, "Stoop over and we'll mark you, too." And you know where that was!

I don't recall that I had ever been out of the state of Texas before I enlisted in the navy. It was definitely a new experience. But when you're young, in most cases, if you're anything like near normal, you're quite adaptable. There's new and strange things, but you can take them in your stride. I doubt whether you could do that so easy as an older person, but I don't think anybody had much trouble adapting.

One thing that was very grueling was the drilling, the military order. They didn't have nearly as much as marines and army. We were very, very fortunate. About the time we drilled was about the beginning of May, and it was quite warm in San Diego at that time. They'd drill the fool out of you. We would knock off from drilling, go back to the barracks. Across the bay at the marine camp, they were still going—Hut! Hut!—long after the light was failing. Those boys, I mean they are really put through it, as far as training. But one thing about it, you have to have order in the military establishment. You just can't have that many men and let everybody have a mind of his own. It's kind of a brainwashing deal when you really get down to it.

You were formed into a company. You were company so-and-so, and that was your company name until you were out of training. Then you went on from there. In my case, I went to aviation machinist mate school. It was on North Island, which is just outside of San Diego.[3] At that time there was a ferry there; there was not a bridge. I went to North Island and was not immediately in classes. The class periods came as there was room to put them. So we worked KP[4] and latrine duty and that sort of thing for a number of weeks. That was quite a chore because we had big barracks, and it was a lot of cleaning. The officer in charge would come with his group once a week, and they wore white gloves. They had a habit of going around especially over the door and window frames. If there was any black on their white gloves, there was hell to pay.

The first time we had payday I got seven dollars, after they deducted for company pictures and this, that, and the other—plus insurance. You took out insurance if you wanted it. The base pay was twenty-one dollars[5] a month for apprentice seaman.[6] That's what I enlisted as. And when all was said and done and payday came, I had seven dollars, and I guess that was about average for everybody. That didn't last long in downtown San Diego. I don't think anybody was able to make a fool of himself for the duration on seven dollars. Seaman second class was an automatic rating. You got that automatically, without any energy on your part, unless you were completely at odds with everything—well, if you got an undesirable discharge or something like that.

I went in machinist mate school about July of 1942, sometime after boot camp. But our class did not finish in San Diego. They moved our school and most of the others, as far as I know, from San Diego to Norman, Oklahoma, because there was fear at that time that the Japanese were going to attack the West Coast. After aviation machinist mate school, when I graduated from that, they were wanting air gunners. At Lexington, Oklahoma, they had a naval air gunnery school.[7]

That took two or three months. It was around Christmas of '42 when I finished.

After training we went back to San Francisco, and we were going to ship out, but this took awhile. There were people coming and going, and we were stationed on Treasure Island, which was a disembarkation place. They needed people on shore patrol, so I was fortunate enough to get in on that: went downtown and lived on Market Street in San Francisco. It was real good duty because when you didn't have the actual duty, you were free to come and go, in and out the door, which was not the case at any camp or station. You were strictly on orders. It was only when you had leave that you could leave the premises. But that was not the case at Market Street. Also, we didn't have duty every day, which made it better yet. You could do a lot of sightseeing and what have you if you had the money for it.

But then some of the guys were going down to Railway Express.[8] There was just lots and lots of rail traffic for the war effort, and they were very shorthanded with the military draft and so forth. I talked to some people that had gone down there, were making them extra money at Railway Express. I went there and I worked about a week or so off and on down there, too. Then we shipped overseas.

I was fortunate. Matter of fact, let me say this: I think somebody must have been very much looking out after me because I was always one leap ahead of the hounds as far as the bad things were concerned. I don't know whether it was the timing of my enlistment or what it was, but we disembarked from San Francisco the first time on the *Matsonia*, which was the flagship of the Matson Lines and had been appropriated or signed over to the navy for use for troop transport. We had the extreme privilege of being five to a stateroom. That was something extraordinary because most of the troop transports was like a bunch of cattle herded together. You had no privacy whatsoever, just hundreds and thousands of men on one ship going over. That was not the case with us on the *Matsonia*. It was a very pleasant trip to Pearl Harbor.

We went to Pearl Harbor and disembarked, and I was put on the beaching crew. There again, as I just mentioned awhile ago, if I had been shipped right on into the combat zone, I don't know what kind of story I could be telling nowadays. I don't know where the rest of the bunch went right off, but I was put on the beaching crew for about two months, which meant that I stayed there at Oahu.

The navy had two types of seaplanes. They were either two-motor or four-motor—or two-engine, four-engine. The navy doesn't call them motors; they made that clear to us. We don't have motors in the navy; that's an engine. Anything with pistons in it is an engine; motors are

A beaching crew at Naval Air Station Banana River, Florida, helps to bring ashore a Martin PBM Mariner patrol bomber seaplane in March 1943. *Courtesy of National Archives and Records Administration.*

electric. And you had two types of planes. There's one type was amphibious. It had a retractable landing gear in the hull. They could land either on water or on land. But the biggest seaplanes were strictly seaplanes, and you had the landing gear with two big wheels on a central pivot that you had to float out to the plane. They would land on the bay, come taxiing in reasonably close to the ramp, where we pulled them out. And you had to take the beaching gear—one man each float, with each one of the beaching gears—out to the plane. Then a line with a hook was dropped by the guy inside; one of the flight attendants in the plane dropped a little cable with a hook down through the hole where the beaching gear socket was, and he would pull that beaching gear up with a small winch. It had kind of like a ball-and-socket that would lock in place. Then we pulled them up on a ramp with a small tractor.

I had no problem since I was a country boy and a pretty good swimmer in my days. But we had this one guy who apparently had never been swimming or anything much, and he happened to wind up on the beaching crew. One day he was caught by an ill tide as he was floating out with the other gear—I had one, and he had the other—and instead of going toward the plane, he was headed out for the open sea. He was yelling pretty loud. We retrieved him all right.

But we did have a problem; it was real nice. We had this little beach shack. We had a boatswain's mate in charge of us, and he liked his alcohol. He knew where the torpedo storage was. Torpedoes run on a steam turbine fueled with alcohol. They're heated by an alcohol burner. This was good old about a hundred and eighty proof, and he would retrieve a jug of that ever so often. He used the gallon Coke extract bottle—empty bottle—and would go down there to that torpedo storage and get some of that. We had a Coke machine right there in the beach shack.

It was real nice. We were right there on Ford Island. Ford Island is inside Pearl Harbor; that's the military base. Right just outside of our beaching shack was the *Utah*. It was an old ship; it was not a first-class battlewagon anymore. Even right before the war they used it for a gunnery ship or whatever. The *Oklahoma* was upside down on the other side. The *Arizona*, it sank straight down, and the mast was out. There was just lots and lots and lots of oil and grease on the shore. There was a regular crust of it all along the beaches from all those sunken ships.

It was almost like civilian life. There I was, halfway to the battle zone, on a beaching crew with regular liberty in Honolulu or anything that you might like. Well, that all took an end, and we got our orders that we were shipping out.

We went on an aircraft carrier and went down to Nouméa, New Caledonia, and that was a separation center. From there we were separated, and my group was sent up a little bit east of the Solomon Islands. At that time, early '43, it was the war zone.[9] There again, I was right next to the war zone, but I was not primarily in it. We served the war zone, but we weren't right there where the shooting was going on. Of course it didn't really matter a lot. We were in aviation. You flew over trackless miles and miles of ocean; anything could go wrong with a plane. The enemy didn't necessarily have to get you, and the sharks were always glad to eat you if you didn't have something to protect yourself.

But there's another ironical thing. We had different types of planes: SBDs, the old Douglas dive bomber. We had one old JRF outfit, which was a seaplane. It was used for reconnaissance. We had a number of TBFs, Grumman torpedo bombers. We also had PBYs[10] for patrol and hauling.

Now, they're two- and three-place aircraft: the pilot, the radioman, and the gunner. If you had an SBD, a dive bomber, it was the pilot only and one extra crewman, which would be the radioman, so that the aviation machinist mate was automatically cut out on that trip. So I served mostly on TBFs, or we had some Martin Marauders, the army

The Grumman TBF Avenger torpedo bomber on patrol on April 26, 1944. *Courtesy of Associated Press.*

called them — we called them a JM1 in the navy — which is your Martin two-engine, medium-size bomber.

The gunner's position on the TBF was in the turret. It had a turret in the back with .50-caliber guns. It's on the top of the plane. They had another gun, a little .30-caliber machine gun that was sort of a stinger gun, down underneath. I think, in an emergency, the radioman would man that one, but when there were three aboard, the machinist mate would man the turret, which had twin fifties in it — .50-caliber machine guns.

We just went along, whatever the job was. One of our jobs was going where the fleet was and where the business was going on and tow targets to sharpen the eyes of the gunners. That was one of our jobs. We carried mail. We hauled the brass around, such as Admiral Bull Halsey. He was a personal friend of our captain, who was P. K. Will. I've got a picture of the two of them standing there together on one of the tropical islands down there where we were. There were others, too, but I was not familiar with everybody. And we did a lot of sub patrol. That was one of our main jobs. But like I mentioned earlier, we were a combat outfit, but we were kind of a reserve combat outfit. Somebody was looking out for us.

We went from New Caledonia up to the eastern side of the Solomon Islands to the New Hebrides, which is on the outskirts of the Solomon theater, and that's where we operated out of: New Hebrides.[11] They call that Vanuatu now. The main Solomon fighting was going on late in '42, and I was there in the spring of '43. A lot of that had been secured, but there was still a lot of fighting going on in New Guinea — Rabaul and on up, all of the chains of the Solomons in there. That was more or less right there outside of Midway. That happened before I got out there. That's where we turned the Japs back for the first time. Up to that time, it had been strictly more or less their glory. But then the Solomon campaign was a very iffy thing, too. Not a lot of equipment was allocated as it should have been because we were also fighting Hitler on the other side.[12] The issue was quite often in doubt as to who would come out on top, and a lot of good people lost their lives down there.

From the New Hebrides I went back home. We were there about one and a half years all told. After so long they rotated the personnel wherever it was humanly practical. When you enlist, they promise you thirty days leave every year. Well, this was two and a half years from the time I had enlisted. Not all of that was overseas; almost two years was.

We came back to San Diego, and I went by bus on home and had that thirty-day leave. Even met a few pretty girls back home. After the thirty days, went back to San Diego and then found out that our company had been split into two groups. The group that I was to be with was at the lighter-than-air[13] base at Moffett Field, Sunnyvale, California, which is just out of San Francisco but close to San Jose.[14] I was there about two months, and then they wanted a small detachment at Point Montara, which was south of San Francisco. We only had two planes there, but a few of the pilots and I went out there, and I believe we had one other enlisted personnel there.

Then one day the personnel officer came and said, "We need some people to go to technical school." And this is one thing you want to remember; I would assume this would be true. You get the general qualifications tests every so often. If you do well on those, when there's anything in the making, you're usually asked, Would you do this, or would you do that? You've been recommended to do so-and-so. So the personnel officer came down there one day to Point Montara and said, "We need some advanced-trained people in hydraulics, instruments, and propellers. And this school, Naval Air Technical Training Center, is in Chicago, Illinois, on Eighty-seventh and Anthony."

I really wasn't too eager to go. I was quite happy where I was. But when something like that was presented to you, you usually gave it second thoughts before turning it down because it didn't go too well in your favor if you refused anything like that. So I went to Chicago and went through the hydraulic school there, and that's where I met my first wife, right there at the school. She was in the WAVES.[15] Her name was Ann Hoekstra. She was from Philadelphia, Pennsylvania. It was one of those whirlwind romances, and we were married before I got away from there the end of that year.

During the war a lot of things were fast. *Fast* was the word, but nobody really lost any sleep about it. I think everybody kind of had a sense of urgency. You never knew what the next day was going to bring for you. And of course when you're young you go madly in love and what have you. I married her there in Chicago before I left. We were married at the school by a navy chaplain.

I had to go back overseas, so I left her. She was going to come down to Burton a little later if she could get discharged, but she developed polio before the end of the war and never came home, never saw Burton. I was overseas on Guam when it all happened.

After we married I went back to Burton for just a very few days, then went back to San Francisco and shipped out for the second tour. The staging area then was Ulithi Atoll, a very small island in the Caroline Islands. It wasn't square, but it was not more than a mile any way you looked from shore to shore. It had a runway on it, and the runway was from one end of the island to the other. There were just ships, ships, ships of every sort there at Ulithi at the time.[16] I was still aviation machinist mate and gunner, and we were stationed there. We did more or less the same kind of work: sub patrol, mail, and target towing and that sort of thing. Guam[17] and Saipan[18] had already been secured by then. But plans were being made for Iwo Jima and Okinawa and some parts of the Philippines yet.

Again our outfit was split, and I was sent to a group at Guam. This is where I received the bad news. It was right at the end of the war. Iwo Jima had been taken.[19] Okinawa's in the process.[20] And then, of course, come the final touch with the atomic bombs.[21] It was right after that Ann died, on the twenty-second of August, 1945. So the bombs had been dropped, and we were still doing the same duty day in, day out. But everybody knew that the end was near. And then I got the bad news. I received emergency leave to go home back to the States. I got as far as San Francisco with army transport, and from there I had to take a plane on my own across country.

She came down with polio, and she was also pregnant. That's where my first son was from. Joe, my oldest son, was saved by Caesarean section a day before she died. She had high hopes. She wrote to my mother and dad and my sister how she was looking forward to coming to Texas. But then she developed some problems in her pregnancy, and then the next thing was the polio. This was sort of an epidemic at the time all over.[22]

It's amazing to me, sometimes, how circumstances are. I had three uncles that were veterans of World War I and World War II. One was my dad's oldest brother. He served in the intelligence service in World

War I and also World War II, and he was out in Biak,[23] close to the area where I was the first time. Then he was transferred to Washington, DC, at a desk job. And this was close to Sharon Hill, Pennsylvania, which is a suburb of Philadelphia, where my wife was from. He and my aunt were the only ones in the family that ever knew Ann and her people during the war, before she died. I went home from Chicago; I didn't get to Pennsylvania after we were married. But then, when I received the bad news, my father-in-law, whom I had never met, said that they would try to hold her in state till I could get home, which seemed impossible to me, with me being out there.

Another thing that seemed real impossible—you think about this. When I came from Guam, we stopped at the Hawaiian Islands. We were there only one night, and there was a big camp there for people in the same category as I was: trying to get back to the States. Hundreds of them, mind you. And here, I thought about this cable he had sent: "Will try to hold in state." How long could he hold her in state? I said, "Lord, will I ever get out of this place with all these people already waiting?" And miracle of miracles, I was out of there the next day. I don't know why. I don't know to this day why I was sent out of there, but I was and went back to the States.

Later, when I got to Pennsylvania for the funeral, she was in a mausoleum. There was some guy that was generous enough that had this mausoleum put there, but it hadn't been used. The local authorities would not consider keeping her in a funeral home, so they moved her out there, and that's where we had the funeral. Twenty years later I was talking to my uncle, and he told me he was instrumental in seeing that she was kept there because the county officials did not want to keep her, and they were fully within their rights. But it's strange when you think that someone from here at home who had been overseas could be there at the right moment to do that sort of thing.

Ann's death was quite a blow, it was. And, of course, there was a little bitty baby there, too. I saw the baby at the time of the funeral because they had him there at Mercy Fitzgerald Hospital in Darby, Pennsylvania. My mother-in-law there, whom I had, of course, never met before either, she was a very fine person. Actually, she was my wife's stepmother. Ann's mother had also died when she was very young—her real mother. Mrs. Hoekstra volunteered to keep the baby until I could get out of the service and make other arrangements. So she kept him for one year. In '46, in the summer, my sister Lillian and I went up and we got little Joe home, and my mother took care of Joe then.

I must say, with all due respect to my dear mother, she wrote some beautiful letters. She wrote very faithfully to me overseas and everywhere. I had some other people that did, too.

I went back to San Francisco after the funeral. I assumed that I'd probably have to go back overseas to where my outfit was. But since the atomic bomb had been dropped and the war was over, the surrender had been signed, we never got beyond Moffett Field again. I was supposed to have been discharged here in Texas, but my old buddy that was with me, we had purchased a car in partnership in California. And once we were out of the service, we wanted to live it up a little bit. We pulled a few strings with the yeoman of the company, who I knew for many years, and he did a little paper rearranging. We got out at Shoemaker, California, instead of down here on the Texas coast.

So then we took off with the car, spent some time in Los Angeles, went on. He had numerous relatives in western Oklahoma, around Fairview. We spent some time there, and then he had some more friends and relatives at Claremore, Oklahoma. We went there, and that's where he met the wife that he had after the war. But I got out at Shoemaker, California, rather than here in Texas, as I probably should have, on Columbus Day. I remember that one: twelfth of October, 1945.

We came home, and I came back to the farm. I guess it's in the blood. You've seen what the rest of the world is like, half of it anyway. I had numerous trades; I had experience. But for some reason I never got into those. I know there were many times, when I was a younger person, I was not too intrigued with the farm. It was a lot of hard work, and the pay was not too good back in the thirties. But what I believe was the predominant thing that made me decide is, I think each individual has in his own mind something that he would like to do beyond all others. In my case, I think it was a sense of independence. I had worked briefly for different organizations as a hired person, as an employee. But I'm the type of person that likes to be his own boss.

In 1947 a friend introduced Wegner to Verlie Hinze, who lived near Carmine, Texas. They married on February 22, 1948, and soon after moved with Joe into a house Wegner had relocated onto the family's land and was renovating. After marrying, Wegner took over operations of the family farm and faced the challenge of restoring the land, which had greatly deteriorated during the war in the hands of tenants who had leased and rented it. Wegner was among the first in Burton to use the tractors and other machinery that became a normal part of the farm landscape after the war, and in 1949, he and his wife produced their first cotton crop. In the 1960s Wegner began concentrating on construction and phasing out cotton farming. Edward and Verlie Wegner reared three sons, including Joe.

Edward Wegner's life history was recorded in seven interviews as part of a project on the cotton culture of Burton, Texas, contributing to the Institute's collection titled Family Life and Community History. In the fifth interview he recounted his service in the navy in World War II. Edward F. Wegner, *Oral Memoirs of Edward F. Wegner*, a series of interviews conducted by Dan K. Utley, January 22, 1992, through September 16, 1994, in Burton, Texas, BU Digital Collections.

Notes

1. Consolidated Vultee Aircraft Corporation and North American Aviation were among the largest airframe manufacturers in the United States during World War II. Bill Yenne, *The American Aircraft Factory in World War II* (St. Paul, MN: Zenith Press, 2006), 8.
2. A suit typically consisting of a thigh-length jacket with wide, padded shoulders and pants that were wide at the top and narrow at the bottom.
3. The facility was known as Naval Air Station San Diego until 1955, when it became Naval Air Station North Island. During WWII and the Korean War, the airfield was a leader in the region for training and support of naval aviation. Paolo E. Coletta and K. Jack Bauer, eds., *United States Navy and Marine Corps Bases, Domestic* (Westport, CT: Greenwood Press, 1985), 561.
4. Kitchen police or kitchen patrol.
5. Roughly $300 in 2014 dollars.
6. Seaman Apprentice and Seaman Second Class are the same ranking.
7. Purcell Naval Air Gunnery School, also known as Purcell Naval Air Gunners School. Purcell and Lexington are neighboring communities.
8. Railway Express Agency (REA), a massive US package- and parcel-delivery company, had an air and truck division. From 1929 to 1954, REA had an exclusive contract with the railroads to handle express and express-related services. V. S. Roseman, *Model Railroading's Guide to Railway Express: An Overview* (Denver, CO: Rocky Mountain Publishing, 1992), 4, 7–8.

9. The Guadalcanal campaign took place August 7, 1942–February 9, 1943.

10. A type of seaplane.

11. During World War II the United States built naval bases in the New Hebrides on the islands of Efate and Espiritu Santo.

12. In the summer of 1939, after six months of study, Joint Board strategists recommended the Europe First plan to President Roosevelt in the event that the United States became involved in the war overseas. The plan stated that the European Axis powers proved to be the bigger menace, and fighting them should be given priority over fighting in the Far East. Roosevelt, who was primarily concerned about Nazi Germany's threat to US interests in Europe and South America, signed off on the recommendation. John Costello, *The Pacific War* (New York: Rawson, Wade, 1981), 63–64.

13. Lighter-than-air (LTA) aircraft include balloons and airships. Heavier-than-air (HTA) aircraft include airplanes, helicopters, and gliders.

14. In January 1942, the US Navy based its first LTA squadron at Moffett Field with the mission to patrol the Pacific Coast for Japanese submarines. During the war, Moffett offered LTA training and also assembled airships. Starting in early 1944, LTA crews at the base took classes in which they learned to identify and report schools of fish, to help fishermen and the nation's food supply. Later that year Moffett became a joint LTA/HTA facility. Coletta and Bauer, *US Navy and Marine Corps Bases, Domestic*, 322.

15. Women Accepted for Volunteer Emergency Service.

16. The United States took possession of Ulithi Atoll's five main islands in September 1944 and converted the atoll into a fleet anchorage and air base with accommodations for seaplanes. The runway Wegner refers to, on Falalop Island, was part of a former Japanese airfield that the 51st Construction Battalion rebuilt and enlarged. Paolo E. Coletta and K. Jack Bauer, eds., *United States Navy and Marine Corps Bases, Overseas* (Westport, CT: Greenwood Press, 1985), 341.

17. The Second Battle of Guam, in which Americans took back the island, ended on August 10, 1944. Japan had wrested Guam out of US control in the days immediately following the attack on Pearl Harbor.

18. The United States secured Saipan on July 9, 1944.

19. The Battle of Iwo Jima was fought February 19 to March 26, 1945.

20. The Battle of Okinawa took place April 1 to June 22, 1945.

21. The United States bombed Hiroshima and Nagasaki on August 6 and 9, 1945.

22. The first US polio epidemics in the mid-twentieth century occurred in 1944. Numbers of reported cases had been increasing since 1941, but with the global conflict the March of Dimes had difficulty impressing the public about the threat of polio—until 1944. David M. Oshinsky, *Polio: An American Story* (New York: Oxford University Press, 2005), 69–72.

23. US naval-base facilities were located on the island of Biak near Dutch New Guinea.

THERE AT THE END 1944–1945

EUROPE

One day that stands out among many prominent dates in the collective memory of the American experience in World War II is June 6, 1944. After a month of heavy Allied bombing of the European continent, June 6 saw the arrival of the Allied Expeditionary Force in occupied France, the largest amphibious military operation in history. American General Dwight Eisenhower noted the significance of the action in his charge to the ranks just prior to launch: "The eyes of the world are upon you. The hopes and prayers of liberty-loving people everywhere march with you. In company with our brave Allies and brothers-in-arms on other Fronts, you will bring about the destruction of the German war machine, the elimination of Nazi tyranny over the oppressed peoples of Europe, and security for ourselves in a free world."

Dubbed "Operation Overlord," the effort began with the landing of 155,000 Allied troops on the beaches of Normandy. Despite initial resistance, the overwhelming force broke through the Atlantic Wall constructed by the occupying Germans since 1942. As the Allies advanced into the continent, Germany launched a series of attacks on England using the new V-1 flying bomb. In early July, moving slowly through agricultural hedges in western France, the Allies engaged the enemy in several huge individual firefights. Then, in mid-July, the Allies captured Saint-Lô and began to break out of French hedgerow country.

The invasion of southern France began with Operation Dragoon on August 15, 1944. The Allied capture of major southern ports, such as Toulon and Marseilles, and the subsequent drive northward, up the Rhone River valley to Lyon and Dijon, would help liberate most of France within only four weeks.

The Allies pushed into Belgium by early September, and American troops arrived at the Siegfried Line, the western wall of the German defense system, on September 13. Along this line, the fierce Battle of Hürtgen Forest—the longest series of encounters between US and German forces — would not be won until early 1945.

The major German offensive of December 1944 would be known by many names, but most veterans remember it as the Battle of the Bulge. In an attempt to reverse the Allies' dramatic gains since Normandy, the Germans launched this massive effort, made more grueling by the onset of winter. Following the conclusion of the battle in January, the Allies pressed their advantage, regaining lost territory by February 1945 before advancing deeper into enemy terrain.

On March 7, when German troops failed to dynamite the Ludendorff, or Remagen, Bridge over the Rhine River, American forces began to cross into Germany. By the end of March, Germany was under attack from all sides. On April 4 the Allies liberated Ohrdruf concentration camp and the western Allies began to grasp the full horror of Nazi cruelty. American forces liberated several more camps, including Buchenwald, Dachau, and Mauthausen before the end of the war.

On April 25, American troops, who had slowed their rapid advance, met the Soviet army at the River Elbe near Torgau, Germany. Then, on May 8, the western Allies celebrated the final victory over Germany.

THE WITNESSES

On June 6, 1944, when he was just nineteen, HERMAN "HANK" JOSEPHS stepped off his LST into one or two feet of water at Omaha Beach, Normandy. Josephs, a communications specialist, was seconded to the 29th Infantry Division just before the invasion. He fought his way across Europe and was slightly wounded during the Battle of the Bulge. After the battle he was transferred to the 2nd Infantry Division and took part in the drive from Frankfurt am Main into Bavaria. Outside the city of Munich, Josephs was ordered to go to a nearby town to investigate a prison camp there as part of an intelligence and reconnaissance unit. That site was Dachau concentration camp. Josephs celebrated the end of the war in Europe with Soviet forces in Czechoslovakia.

RUTH ST. CLAIRE MURPHY joined the Red Cross in January 1942, after she had completed her nurse training at St. Francis Hospital in Evanston, Illinois. She then entered the Army Nurse Corps and went to Europe with the 58th Field Hospital, landing at Omaha Beach, Normandy. The unit worked in tents and blown-out buildings throughout France, Belgium, Luxembourg, and Germany, receiving patients from collecting companies. The field hospital worked in harsh conditions to treat soldiers and provide evacuations to general hospitals that offered more extended care.

In January 1942, while a college freshman, BILL LOGUE joined the army reserves. The next year he qualified for the Army Specialized Training Program and entered the army engineering program at East Texas State College, in Commerce. In February 1944 Bill's unit was called to combat duty. Assigned to the 99th Division, Logue came into France in October 1944 and moved up into Belgium. When the Battle of the Bulge began on December 16 with an intense German offensive, it caught the Allies off guard. Logue, with thousands of others, was taken prisoner by the enemy and transported to a series of prison camps, where he was forced to work for the Germans. Logue was in a Nuremberg prison in April 1945 when the 45th Infantry, an Oklahoma-Texas division, liberated him.

In September 1944, after months of training in England, JOHN VALLS went into Le Havre, Normandy, and was assigned to the 52nd Armored Infantry Battalion in the 9th Armored Division as part of Patton's Third Army. The division was fully engaged by the Battle of the Bulge that December. With the continued march toward Germany, Valls was on the front line for the mass surrender of German soldiers. He also encountered Bergen-Belsen concentration camp while his unit was moving through northwestern Germany. On VE Day, Valls was at Rehau, Germany, near the border of what was then Czechoslovakia.

An army air pilot, HENRY JACKSON "JACK" FLANDERS JR. departed for Europe on board RMS *Queen Elizabeth* on January 31, 1945. After a short stint in England he joined the 1st Tactical Air Force, a part of the Ninth Air Force. His specific assignment was with the 314th Fighter Squadron, one of three squadrons in the 324th Fighter Group. The twenty-four new arrivals in the 314th were replacements for an earlier group of twenty-four pilots, of whom only three still survived when Flanders arrived. On March 3 he flew his first mission across the Rhine River. He would fly more than four dozen missions over the next two months leading up to VE Day.

THE PACIFIC

The amphibious landing on Leyte, an island in the eastern Philippines, on October 20, 1944, began a long struggle to wrest the chain of islands from Japanese control. American and Filipino forces moved from island to island, facing enemy opposition all the way. It would take until the end of June 1945 to compress the Japanese force into just small pockets of resistance on Mindanao and Luzon.

While the Philippines Campaign was in full operation, American naval vessels bombarded Iwo Jima, Tokyo, and Yokohama in January and February. The US Marine Corps launched an invasion of Iwo Jima on February 19, and the battle lasted until March 26. The conflict, one of the bloodiest in the Pacific Theater, was the first American attack on Japanese home territory. It was the only battle against Japan in which American forces sustained the larger number of casualties.

On April 1, 1945, Operation Iceberg, or the Battle of Okinawa, began. Supported by naval, amphibious, and tactical air forces, the operation was the largest amphibious assault of the Pacific War. The engagement was characterized by the intense ferocity of the fighting and the staggeringly high casualty rate, by far the largest in the war against Japan. A grinding battle, it lasted eighty-two days. Victory at Okinawa would be a signal achievement: the island was to be the staging location for an invasion of the Japanese mainland.

Less than a month after victory at Okinawa, the clandestine work of the Manhattan Project resulted in the first detonation of a nuclear weapon at the White Sands Proving Ground in New Mexico. Following the successful test, two bombs were developed for use against Japan. B-29 bombing raids had been staged into urban areas on the Japanese mainland since November 1944, but on August 6, 1945, the first nuclear weapon was detonated over Hiroshima. The second device was dropped on Nagasaki on August 9. On August 15 the Japanese surrendered.

THE WITNESSES

An established surgeon at the outbreak of hostilities, HANNIBAL "DOCTOR JOE" JAWORSKI volunteered to serve a few days after he heard the news of the attack on Pearl Harbor. Jaworski's initial assignment was at McCloskey General Hospital, a large army surgical hospital at Temple, Texas. At that facility Jaworski treated wounded soldiers flown back from the battlefield. In May 1945 he responded to the call from the surgeon general for help organizing new hospitals in the recently liberated Philippines. There he was assigned to reorganize the 4th General Hospital.

When JOHN F. "JACK" ONION JR. volunteered for active duty in 1944, at age nineteen, he was assigned to the Marine Corps. Shipped out to the Pacific Theater from Camp Pendleton, California, in December 1944, he was assigned to 2nd Division, 6th Marines, 2nd Battalion, Fox Company. His group participated in a diversionary landing on the southeastern side of Okinawa during the invasion of the Japanese stronghold. After the Japanese surrender in August 1945, Fox Company was part of the occupying force stationed in Nagasaki in September 1945.

HERMAN "HANK" JOSEPHS

Herman Josephs was born in San Antonio on November 17, 1925, the son of a Ukrainian mother and a Romanian father. Josephs's mother came from Russia in 1922 with her four siblings. His father, originally named Josepovich, immigrated to the United States from Bucharest, Romania. The elder Josephs worked in the dry goods business, plying his trade by following oil-field activity in Ingleside, Refugio, and Kilgore, Texas, before settling in Corpus Christi. Josephs's parents met at a synagogue picnic, fell in love, and were married soon thereafter. The family weathered the Great Depression well. Josephs was a good student, and his parents gave him a lot of independence, even permitting him to drive when he was only thirteen. At age sixteen he enrolled in the University of Texas at Austin, and he thoroughly enjoyed his collegiate experience. Joining a fraternity, Alpha Epsilon Pi, he reveled in the active Austin social scene.

I'D HAD TWO YEARS AT THE UNIVERSITY OF TEXAS at Austin by the time I was drafted at age eighteen. I was a student prince for a year and a half, until I was drafted into the service. The first thing I knew I was sent overseas after just three months in the military. I was not prepared for what faced me. All I knew was, "Thou shalt not kill." And they stuck a rifle in my hand and said, "Thou shall kill thy enemy." So we went to an unknown enemy, and we killed them.

Before being drafted, in February 1944, the war was a million miles away. It could have been on the moon. We didn't hear much about it. It wasn't in the paper much, and we really didn't care much. We had a very carefree life. I worked every Saturday for an army/navy store making a dollar an hour, which was a lot of money then. I made fifteen dollars over a weekend, working Saturday and Sunday, enough to pay for my cleaning bill and Coke date with my girlfriend. But those were the days, really glorious, carefree. I felt that it was so unfair to be drafted, to be taken away from my panacea, my lovely campus. I didn't care so much about the studies. My favorite course was geology, which I enjoyed very much because it taught me a whole bunch. I learned all about cumulonimbus and so on and so forth. But it's the best days, after all these years — my college education.

I was inducted at Fort Sam Houston, San Antonio, and I was sent to Camp Wolters, up near Weatherford, Texas. I went through six weeks of basic training there.[1] The heat at Weatherford was terrible. A lot of guys got heat prostration from carrying a thirty-pound pack on their back. They shot bullets over our heads as we went through barbed wire, and it was really rough on a lot of guys. A lot of guys were overweight, and they had a hard time making it. My introduction to the service was not very good. There were a lot of sand fleas, much heat, and not enough water. It was just desert. That's where we were.

We shipped over to Liverpool, England. We were training to invade Normandy. We didn't know it, but we were. And it was so cold there it would freeze your head off near Liverpool. Nottingham was where we were. The wind just whistled through those tents like there was nothing there. And there was a little stove in the center of the tent—it was an eight-man tent—and there was a charcoal fire going, but that didn't help much. Couldn't take a shower because the showers were outside, and it was cold, cold, cold, as only England can get cold. That's what I said then. Of course it was colder in Belgium.

From England we took off from Bournemouth after a couple of months of training there. On June 5, 1944, we boarded a ship and took off for the French coast, where we landed and invaded Normandy, Omaha Beach. I was on an LST, and there were Landing Ship Troops behind us and in front of us. Some of them were hit directly by the shells and they went under—never got a chance to get on the beach. But fortunately our landing ship was not hit. Some of the guys had convulsions. They were throwing up they were so nervous. But the sergeant said, "Let's go. Let's get ready, men." So we locked and loaded, and they let us off at about a foot or two of water, and we slogged up the beach. We followed the 2nd Ranger Battalion in. We were the first ones on the beach.

A sergeant friend of mine—a good friend of mine, he was the only Jewish fellow in my company—he got hit by bullets the moment we hit the beach. He said, "Don't worry, Tex. I'll get you up the beach. It's a walk in the park." It was the first time I'd heard that phrase. But he got shredded. A dozen bullets entered his body. He was dead. I lay down in back of him and heard the bullets thud into him. He lay there in a pool of blood. The blood. The froth of the waves was red from the blood of the soldiers who were trying to get on the beach.

When they stopped to reload, during the silence, I got up and took off for the hill, which was about fifty feet high, where the Germans and pillboxes were. There were sand traps, barbed wire, and land mines,

US Army troops wade ashore on Omaha Beach on the morning of June 6, 1944. *Courtesy of National Archives and Records Administration.*

so I was damn lucky to get up there. A company of engineers had put a bunch of TNT boxes in where the sand was the shallowest, and they blew it up to smithereens. We went through there into where the Germans were, and we killed them. Some of the Germans tried to escape. They came out of the pillbox, and we shot them. That was my first experience with shooting a German. We had fire-blowers and machine guns. You either kill or be killed. It was the quick or the dead. I told my guys to lie down so the snipers wouldn't hit them. Some of them got up, and some of them got killed.

We went through bushes and trees and things like that, and there were Germans behind, it seemed like, every bush. We shot them as we went. They were using fourteen-year-old boys. That's how far down the list that they had gotten. They were using boys to kill people.

We thought we were ready until we landed and ended up in Belgium, close to Aachen. That's where they hit us with the Battle of the Bulge. I woke up one morning and got out of my tent about daybreak and someone was shooting at us with two German tanks, big tanks. They were shooting at the trees above our heads, and the tree limbs just lopped off from the shells. That was the first we knew that there was the Battle of the Bulge. I got hit with a little piece of shrapnel in the chest. My major, the regimental commander, he got hit in the leg, and I had to half carry him, half drag him back to the OP (observation post). There was an aid station there, and we got him bandaged up, and my wound had healed up pretty quickly. It was so cold that my blood coagulated very quickly.

That was the worst winter that they'd had in fifty years. It didn't get above zero for a month. We were living in foxholes, which got to be pretty wet because it was raining and/or snowing and/or sleeting. It was really miserable. My toes got so cold from the wet and the cold that I got trench foot, which means frozen toes. At the time they wanted to cut my toes off. I said, "No, not this child." So they didn't. Even now, when it gets to be too cold, my feet bother me a little bit.

I had been working in communications, which helped headquarters keep in touch with the rifle companies. I was a switchboard operator and climbed telephone poles or trees to string wire. Well, at age eighteen I was pretty wiry, you'll pardon the expression, pretty good at climbing trees. Of course, the trouble with that was a sniper could get you up in a tree. My buddy Bob got hit by a sniper when he was up a tree, and I helped him down. The tree was icy, but I helped him down. He came back six weeks later. However, I went through the Battle of the Bulge pretty much unscathed.

We were at Malmédy, the name of the town in Belgium. We fought off the German guys in their tanks and their automobiles and fought them off with an overwhelming show of ammunition and desperation. It was either live or die. A lot of guys died defending our flag, but we defended it.

A favorite memory during that period was when I was given a two-day leave from our encampment in Belgium. I took a Red Ball truck[2] down to Paris, and I met a beautiful French girl. I went up to her and said, "I'm a lonely Texan in the service, away far from home and loved ones." Her name was Charmaine, and she replied, "I speak English." She spoke five languages. She was reading a book as I approached her, and we became good friends. Naturally I fell in love with her. It started raining when I began the trip back to my unit. It rained for two days and two nights, so I couldn't get back. When I finally returned to where we were encamped in Belgium, I said, "Sarge, I'm sorry I'm late, but it rained for two days and two nights." He asked, "What did you do?" I confessed, "Well, I met a beautiful girl." He liked that. He said, "Well, I ought to get you for AWOL [Away Without Leave], but I'll just take away your stripes." And he did. We were friends, but he was a grizzled old sergeant. He had five stripes, three above and two below; he was a first sergeant. Nice guy.

After the Bulge they'd broken us up so much that we were sent to a replacement depot, called a Repple Depple, and I was transferred

Dachau concentration camp front gate. "Work makes [you] free." *United States Holocaust Memorial Museum, courtesy of Norman Coulson.*

to the 2nd Infantry Division, the Indianhead Division. I remained a communications expert. With Patton's ferocity we fought our way into Frankfurt am Main and down through Aschaffenburg and on down to Bavaria. A beautiful country. It was very green. They grow a lot of trees there. Such beautiful highways. Autobahns are beautiful. You can go a hundred miles an hour. There's no speed limit.

We were atop the Bavarian mountains looking down at little villages, which gleamed in the sun. People were sweeping up the cobblestones. We were told to go down and check on a little town near München, Munich, called Dachau. We were on our way to Dachau to find out what was going on there. My assignment was in I and R (intelligence and reconnaissance). They sent us down there to check and see what was going on. They knew about concentration camps, but we didn't. So we were sent to investigate what was going on as far as concentration camps was concerned, and we found out quickly. It was a horrible experience. We had been through four battles already, and we thought we were immune from being shocked, but that was quite a shock. Blew my mind. Had no idea such a thing existed.[3]

The first thing we saw when we got to Dachau was a sign over the entrance which says "Arbeit Macht Frei" ("Work Will Make You Free"). We went through the gate and shot a few Germans on the way in. They were escaping. By that time I'd confiscated a tommy submachine gun, which is a powerful weapon, and I let them have it, all that I saw. To this day I still don't buy anything German, made in Germany. I hated them so badly. And I'm afraid they're going to do it again. I looked at the prisoners in their striped garb, so filthy and decimated. One of them moved, and I went over to him. He said, "Bist a Yid?" ("Are you Jewish?") I said, "Ich bin a Yid." ("I am Jewish.") And then I told him, "Alles geet. Alles geet." I speak a little Yiddish, which is pig-German. "Alles geet. Alles geet." ("All is good. All is good.") I opened my C-rations and fed him a little soup I made for him. He died two hours later in my arms. I asked him what his name was. He said, "Meine namen ist Herman." I responded, "My name is Herman, too." I had tears in my eyes, and I cry every time I think about it. This poor guy, he was about forty years old and maybe weighed fifty pounds. That is how much he had been maltreated.

It's a hell of a load for a young fellow to bear. I was only nineteen years old. I had no idea that there were so many people in prison: Pentecostal people, priests, politicians, especially Jews. Behind bars, behind barbed wire, and treated like animals, worse than animals. Their beds there were just hard boards they slept on. The prisoners were so tired when they got through working them that they just collapsed, I figured. We saw about three dozen barracks and a few automobiles and gas chambers. We knew what they were for. There were dead people lying in the gas chambers. They had a ravine there, and they had piled the bodies in the ravine and put lye on them. So it was rather horrible. How can one man be that way toward another man and call himself a human being? That's more of an animal than a human being. Yeah, we had been through a hell of a lot, and then we had to go through that. That's a hard load for a young fellow. I saw what war can do. It made me hate war. By then it was getting dark. We were ready to leave, so we took off for Munich and joined our fellows in Munich, what there was of them.

From there we went to Czechoslovakia, to Raczetzany near the Austrian border. We heard news of the surrender on May 8 there at Raczetzany, near Pilsen.[4] Good beer. It was hot, and I got drunk. I don't drink beer, but I drank a half a bottle and that shook me up. I don't drink to this day.

I was happy. Happy to be with my men and happy to join the Russians, who were comrades at the moment. We met the Russians and learned a few Russian words like "dobry vecher"—that's "good afternoon"—and "comrade." "Ya tebya lublu," "I love you." I learned that from my mother, who spoke Russian. We were very friendly. They had vodka to drink, and they loved to drink, the Russians. And there was Old Blood and Guts with his pearl-handled .45s, and he was saying, "Give me enough tanks, and I'll go to Moscow." He hated the Russians. They took over Czechoslovakia whether we liked it or not.

Patton was on stage all the time. He enjoyed it very much. Should have been an actor, because that's the way he was. He didn't even know he was fully himself, but he enjoyed being Charlemagne and Napoleon all rolled into one. He was one of the wealthiest generals in the service. He came from a very wealthy family. And he could afford anything. But he was a great leader. He sure helped out, I think. He loved to see his name in the paper: "Patton Does It Again."

It was great news that the Axis had crumbled and that peace was declared. I was homesick all the time. I never adapted to military life well. I did what I had to do, but I was happiest when I was sent to the cook's tent. He had D-bars, which were chocolate bars. I enjoyed chocolate a whole bunch and could get all I wanted to eat. Peeled potatoes—at least nobody was shooting at me. Sounds pretty interesting, but it wasn't.

Towards the end of the war they'd been chasing me all over, trying to tell me about my father being ill. We went by truck to Le Havre harbor and got on a ship and went back to Camp Myles Standish, now Fort Myles Standish, right outside of Boston. The Red Cross allowed us one phone call, so the first thing I did was call my sister. She said, "They buried Dad three days ago," which was bad news for me. I'd wanted to see him at least. I came home on sick leave and was let out of the service in October.

I didn't talk about my experiences in World War II for forty years. I just didn't mention it. It was too horrible to dredge up my memory. Once, after I was back in the States, my sister came home from a date and she came in the front door and I was inside and had been dreaming that the Germans were invading. I had a P38 cocked and ready as she walked through the door. I was about to shoot her. I was really "verklemmt." In Jewish that means I was disorganized. She says, "Stop, Hank! Don't!" It was dark. It was about one o'clock. I had been sleeping, and the Germans were after me.

I began to share my experiences in 2001 because I have four lovely kids, a boy and three girls that I adore, and I want them to know what their dad was like. Very few parents open up to their children, so I wrote an autobiography of myself. Put a couple of poems of myself that I wrote and among other things, my whole life, from inception practically, and sent each of them a copy so they would have a genuine assertation as to their father's having been here.

Upon his return to the States, Josephs took over his father's dry goods store in Corpus Christi and, with his mother, transformed the enterprise into a successful pawn shop, Economy Loan and Jewelry. His interest in the pawn business stemmed from an experience during the war. He recalled his sergeant lending GIs five dollars on their watches and their paying ten dollars to recover the watches when they got their paychecks two weeks later. Josephs liked the business model. He retired in 1986. A self-described romantic, he married Ruth Josephs on June 27, 1948, and they had four children.

The interview with Herman "Hank" Josephs was collected as part of the Texas Liberators of World War II Concentration Camps Oral History Project funded by a grant from the Texas Holocaust and Genocide Commission. Copies of all materials were also deposited in the Library of Congress and the four Texas Holocaust museums—Houston, El Paso, Dallas, and San Antonio. See Herman "Hank" Josephs, *Oral Memoirs of Herman "Hank" Josephs*, an interview conducted by Stephen Sloan, with videography by Robert DeBoard, October 32, 2011, in Corpus Christi, Texas. BU Digital Collections.

Notes

1. An army camp from 1925 to 1946, four miles northeast of Mineral Wells. At one point in World War II it was the nation's largest infantry replacement training center.
2. The Red Ball Express was a convoy that carried Allied supplies.
3. On April 29, 1945, American troops liberated Dachau, the first Nazi concentration camp created in Germany.
4. The Germans signed a surrender document on May 7 in the French city of Reims. Per the agreement, the cessation of fighting took effect at 11:01 p.m. on May 8, now remembered as Victory in Europe [VE] Day.

RUTH ST. CLAIRE MURPHY

Born in 1912, Ruth St. Claire Murphy grew up in an army family. Her father, James Patrick Murphy, began serving in the US Army during the period of the Mexican Revolution and served for thirty-two years, retiring as a colonel. The family lived throughout the United States and in Panama, never staying more than nine months in one place. Murphy attended schools in such diverse places as Pedro Miguel, Panama Canal Zone; Decatur, Illinois; and Columbus, Georgia. She graduated from high school in Fort Leavenworth, Kansas, and in 1935 earned her bachelor of fine arts degree from Milwaukee-Downer College, now Lawrence University, in Milwaukee, Wisconsin. After graduation Ruth spent some years as a freelance artist before entering nursing school at St. Francis Hospital, in Evanston, Illinois. She completed her training in 1941. In January 1942, remembering her father's dedication to military service, she enrolled in the American Red Cross Nursing Service and became certified for military service. Her father, then professor of military science and tactics at South Dakota State College, swore her in for service with the Army Nurse Corps.

When I went into the nursing service, I went in as a regular army nurse, not a reserve. I trained with the Sisters of St. Francis, and believe me, when one of those big old sisters came down the hall with a black habit and her rosary clanking, you came to attention. I was ready for the army. There were maybe sixty or sixty-five nurses in my particular class. For training, we had a certain length of period in the operating room, we had a length of period in pediatrics, we had some time in the medical service and the surgical service. This was a six-hundred bed hospital, so we had everything there.

I was first stationed at Fort Snelling, Minnesota. We had young men coming into the service, mostly, that we took care of, gave shots, did all those things. The quarters were all around a great big parade ground, and it was cold in Minneapolis and St. Paul, and the wind blew over the parade ground. We were given our first issue of clothing, and evidently Uncle Sam wasn't ready for us because he issued us clothes from World War I. I got a pair of high-topped white shoes with pointed toes. Of course we never wore them; we just threw them away. During that period we wore blue. We didn't wear the khaki until later. We looked like girls from the home for delinquent girls, and when we got the khaki, we looked much better.

We didn't have officer status then. We came in with an officer's title, like a second lieutenant, but we didn't have officer status. We only got ninety dollars a month at the beginning, until we became officers. When we had officer status, we got more money. I think we got a hundred and fifty.[1]

I was in two or three other stations in the meantime between Fort Snelling and going overseas. Because I had a bachelor's degree, I became a chief nurse early on, so I took chief nurse's training most of that time. I was stationed at Fort Custer, Michigan; Pomona, California; and Fort Eustis, Virginia.[2]

I went overseas in 1944. After we landed in England, we were on temporary duty with the 5th Field Hospital. We didn't have any duties then; we just were preparing to go over farther. Mostly we got clothing and all kinds of equipment and everything. And, oh, it was so cold in England, so cold!—and cold in France, too. Then we went to Camp C5, in Southampton, and went over to France on an LST.

We landed on Omaha Beach with the 58th Field Hospital—eighteen nurses, fifteen doctors, three dentists, three medical administrators, and a hundred and fifty men. The little sailors were so happy to see all these nurses that they made a lunch for us. They made cheese sandwiches that you couldn't get your mouth over because the hunks of cheese and bread were so big. And they showed us their washing machine that they had made that used a jeep motor to run the washing machine.

Sometimes we stayed only three days or a week or ten days [in one place]. We set up our hospital in tents, mostly, or in old blown-out buildings, and we received the patients from the collecting companies. We set up in burned-out or bombed-out buildings, a TB sanatorium, and a school. Then they decided that they needed more evacuation hospitals, and we became evacuation.[3] Those little field hospitals were planned to break up into three platoons, and they would have a pharmacy, an X-ray group, six nurses and three doctors, and about fifty men. We would be in different cities. In Germany once, we were in Landshut and Regensburg and Munich.

The patients came in by ambulances, and then we evacuated them by train and plane and ambulance to a general hospital, where they got more care. We did not run out to meet them like they did on *M*A*S*H*.[4] We stayed right on our wards and the operating room and

US Army nurses, France, 1944. *Courtesy of National Archives and Records Administration.*

waited for the patients to come in on stretchers. Sometimes we would have so many we could only slit their shirts and give them a hypo[5] or give them a shave or something like that, just something to boost their morale—feed them. In particular we had so many burn cases, and I don't know why that was because I'm not smart enough to know what happens with ammunition and everything. They would come with their heads just completely swathed in the bandages, and there would be just a little hole for their mouth and just slits so that they could see.[6]

The nurses would take our D-ration, which was an old heavy, heavy candy bar, and we'd take those and melt them and put some canned milk in so they could drink it up through their straws. We didn't have very many fancy things to work with in the field hospital. We had to use our IV tubing for straws; we didn't have any straws. We didn't have anything to prop them up on their stretchers, so we made those out of old boxes. I remember particularly one beautiful, great big sergeant, and he had both legs and one arm blown off, and I was trying to feed him. He says, "Oh no, Captain. Don't try to feed me. I have to learn how to feed myself." We were brokenhearted, but we had to stay detached.

During the Battle of the Bulge, there were little fellows, young men, that came in that had been home for Christmas just a few weeks before. The Battle of the Bulge lasted about a month after Christmas. I remember soldiers lying in their stretchers crying for their mothers. We had an old dog named Bastogne, and she had puppies. So when we'd send these kids back to the general hospitals, we'd put a puppy in with each one. We'd get the puppy sitting back there to keep them company on their way. There's nothing like a puppy to take care of things like that. The soldiers were very grateful and respectful and very nice to us. Some of them, particularly some of the boys from Brooklyn, the little tough guys, thought that we were there just as camp followers for the officers, but we had to straighten them out on that. I never had any problems with any of the men.

The best experience was putting the injured kids on planes, getting them all loaded up to go back. They'd say, "I've got a million-dollar wound."[7] They'd get on the planes, and they were headed back to Paris, to London, and then home. That was the best part. One day, in Trier, Germany, we loaded 1,300 kids. We admitted them and loaded them on planes that one day. We were tired folks. But we were so proud of ourselves. It was the most the Third Army ever admitted and evacuated.

The worst memory—well, I didn't enjoy the boys crying for their mothers, I'll tell you that. What else would be worse? Perhaps Christmas of '44. The chaplain and I were giving out gifts to the different little fellows, and we went over to the POW camp. We had fifty German POWs with us all the time. The German POWs were not injured; they were assigned with us.[8] We had two on each ward, and we used to call them Hans and Fritz because we never knew their names. They would come and stand at attention, slap their heels together, and salute, "Herr Kapitän!" We went over to the POW tent, and they had been told not to make the slightest noise because if they had signaled to the other Germans, they could have very easily taken the hospital. And there they were around their Christmas tree singing "Silent Night, Holy Night" in whispers because they couldn't sing, and that was sad. Christmas may have been the worst time, but because we were trying so hard to make a Christmas for the patients, we didn't have time to be homesick.

I never felt a sense of danger because they were very careful. When we came over we came over in a convoy, and we heard these depth charges being dropped. We were kind of shaky about it, and we asked the captain what it was, and he says, "Oh, they're just practicing. They're just dropping the depth charges," but, really, they weren't. Then, when we were in the edge of Belgium during the Battle of the Bulge, we were so close to the big guns that we could hear them just cracking. We were a little frightened then, but they insisted that they were just practicing. One of the little boys from Brooklyn—I don't know why there were so many little boys from Brooklyn—would raise up on his stretcher and he would say, "Hitler, recount your men."

We had such miserable clothes. We wore fatigues, and we had little combat boots and helmet liners. We went into one of the hospitals once to visit, about three of us, and one of the patients raised up and he says, "Man! Look at that sex-repellent clothing!" We couldn't have gotten along if it hadn't been for the humor of the American GI. They saw something amusing in everything. One day there were so many of the black boys coming in, and I said, "Sergeant, how come so many of your men are coming in today?" He says, "Captain, us black boys haven't got a chance out there in the snow."

I was the chief nurse for the 58th Field Hospital, with eighteen nurses under me. There were a couple of nurses that were surgical nurses, and they knew much more about setting up surgery than I did, so I just let them go at it. By the way, don't think for a minute that World War II was anything like *M*A*S*H* or *China Beach.* It just simply wasn't. It wasn't all of that goofing around. We didn't have time.

The morals that we had didn't lead to much hanky-panky. We had met all those doctors' wives before we left. Most of all our doctors were married, and there was friendliness and camaraderie but no hanky-panky. I don't know if I know what sexual harassment is. If somebody puts their arm around me, I don't mind. We had no problems at all with our particular doctors. They were just fine, dedicated men. We never had the least bit of trouble with them in any area. I never had any attraction to the patients, because you had to be detached. I had attractions to some of the officers, but we had a very strict code at that time. We didn't associate with the enlisted men, and it wasn't because they were less fine than we were or anything like that. It was a matter of discipline. They didn't figure that you could go out one night with somebody and then order them around the next day, which I think is perfectly true.

We always had to have separate quarters. That's why I wonder about women in the service now because we had everything separately. We had our latrines dug separately and everything. They used to have to build a new latrine every time we moved, you know, a tent. They put up a tent and then built the seats, and one time one of the jokers built a latrine with a great big hole and put "Chief Nurse" above it.

About the rations. When we were in the States, we had A-rations, and then there were B-rations, which was nothing fresh. C-ration was three cans: beans, stew, and hash. That was when we first landed in France. That's what we had all the time. And then there's a D-ration, and that's that candy bar that's so hard we used to have to just break

US Army nurses reach Germany, 1945. *Courtesy of National Archives and Records Administration.*

it almost with a rock. All of the children loved it. The French children would ask for it, you know. Once, we had a good snow, and one of the boys said, "Oh, I wish I had some ice cream." He says, "You know, I've made ice cream out of snow." So we melted one of those D-ration bars and went out and got snow and mixed it all together. He had some chocolate ice cream. Then there's a K-ration, and that was a little box that had "Breakfast," "Supper," or "Dinner" written on it. It had three little cigarettes in it each time. The first little box had fudge bars, and the box at supper had toilet paper. Can you imagine living for day after day on beans, hash, and stew? And you didn't heat it. We didn't have anything to heat it on. Of course, when we stopped long enough, they set up our own stoves and we had decent food.

As we traveled through the country in the ambulances and everything, the French people would wave occasionally, but they were not very friendly at all. I guess some of them felt that they did better under the German occupation than they were going to do under us because they really weren't friendly, except the little children weren't bad. They would run up to you with their little rosy cheeks and their little cold hands and take hold of your hand and stuff. In Luxembourg, oh, they were good to us. They took our clothes and did our laundry and brought us things to eat and everything.

We evacuated many American POWs along with the other patients because most of those boys went through hospitals after they came out of the camps. We had many from Camp C5 and Stalag IX-B, but the boys from the Luftwaffe stalags were much better off than the ones from the Wehrmacht stalag. They had had so little food.[9] They had made a recipe book of the things they ate, like cockroaches and things like that. Of course, I'm sure some of it was a little exaggerated, but often they had nothing but lentil soup. They lost tens of hundreds of pounds, and they were just skin and bones when they came out of these places. They were very sad.

I remember one particular boy who was a redheaded kid from Arkansas, and he came into the mess hall and he looked at the table and there was a pile of white bread on the table, and he just began to cry. He just couldn't stand it. He hadn't seen white bread for so long. Those kids, when we fed them, there wouldn't be a thing left on the table because they would pick everything up and put it in their pockets, never knowing when they were going to eat again. I don't think they were so much mistreated as they were just starved.

And we had some English boys. We had a whole group of Russians once. I don't know how we got them, but they were there for evacuation, too, and they lifted everything from us. They took bedpans. They took urinals. They took everything they could find.

George Patton came to visit our hospital, and we went through the most grueling preparation. Every tent peg was right in one spot and whitewashed, and the sheets on the cots were all turned a certain number. They were measured six inches, and everything was all ready for old George Patton. He came in with his shiny helmet and his pistols. He walked around and came to one place, and he said to this young lieutenant, "Lieutenant, what's the matter with you?" He says, "Jeep accident, sir." Patton says, "You g-d s-o-b. I get you through the war in one piece, and then you go and kill yourself in a jeep accident." And of course, that's what happened to Patton. He was killed in a jeep accident. Then he said to me, "Do you girls still want to wear those helmets and helmet liners?" I said, "No, we don't, General Patton." So he said, "Okay, I'll have a directive out in the morning that you don't have to wear them anymore." I think Patton was a man that you either hated or loved. There was no in-between.

While we were over there, we were allowed to take three- or four-day passes when we were close to something. We visited France, Germany, Switzerland, Luxembourg, and Rome. The tours were set up by the service for us. We stayed in nice hotels, and we had tickets to the opera, and everything was very fun. It was wonderful to get away from the field where we were. We put on our Class A uniforms and got all dressed up. We wore fatigues all the time, and you got so tired of wearing pants. That's why I never wear pants now. Switzerland was lovely. I enjoyed it so much, and Lugano, in the Italian part of Switzerland, was so nice. It seemed like a great country of the wide middle class. There didn't seem to be a lot of real wealthy people or a lot of very poor people in Switzerland, not like there were in Italy and France.

I was at Dachau [concentration camp]. A group went from the hospital to see it. It still hadn't been cleaned out. It had just been opened up.[10] There were piles and piles of bodies and bones. The odor from the crematorium was still of burning flesh, and there were still corpses hanging up on the hooks, and some alive yet in those—I don't know what they call them but looked like stalls in a barn or something, lying in there in those striped pajamas. It was very, very, very bad. It was right after it had been liberated. That's why I said if anybody ever tells me there wasn't a holocaust, I'll poke them in the nose.

On VE Day I was in Landshut, Germany. We were set up on an airfield there. The first thing we did was take off those helmet liners because they just pushed our hair down. We just looked like witches. First thing we did is we took those off and put on our overseas caps so our hair wouldn't look so terrible. The doctors all went out and got jerrycans that they used to carry oil and all that kind of stuff, and they filled them full of wine, and they had a little drink of wine. It was a big day.

I was thrilled when the war in Europe ended. The big thing was now we go home. That's what everybody thought. We must go home now. But after VE Day I became director of nurses in the Third Army, and I was stationed at Heidelberg, Germany. I used to go around and inspect all the different hospitals. I got to go to Würzburg and all the German cities around there where they had hospitals. We went to see how the patients reacted. Did they react well to you? Were they treated well so that they were friendly and open? The hospitals were always so good to inspectors. I know in our hospital, we always just wined and dined the inspectors.

In Heidelberg I went to the university and took sculpturing. Everybody wonders why everything I do is always art. I never do anything medical. I was in Paris after VE Day on R&R and studied at the Sorbonne. The lights were on in Paris while I was there. Oh, that was a beautiful thing to see! I was asked to stay over in Paris and work on the staff of the *Overseas Woman* magazine to write stories and articles about nurses in the field, but I turned it down because I was so loyal to my outfit.[11] You often wonder what would have happened to your life if you had taken up on those little turning points that you didn't. I might still be sitting in Paris!

I also visited Bad Wiessee in Bavaria, Germany, a beautiful place where we were when all the badness was all over. It was on Lake Tegernsee, and there were chalets and hotels all around this lake, and we had five sailboats and two motorboats at our disposal. We had an orchestra that came at night that played to us during our dinner hour. We had excursions and all that sort of thing around there. It was real living.

When I returned to the States, I went to Fitzsimons General Hospital, in Denver, Colorado. I was still in the service. We took care of a lot of the boys that were coming back. I was on the orthopedic ward and with all the kids that had osteomyelitis, things like that. While I was at Fitzsimons, I signed up for overseas, for Japan. They had a thing on the bulletin board. I didn't know if I was going to Yokohama or where I was going, but I went to Tokyo from there and was there fifteen months.

I resigned my commission in 1949 with the rank of captain. I have no psychological trauma, and physically I have no problems. I've got arthritis in my knees from kneeling around opening those cans of C-ration, but I'm not going to charge the government for it! I think the army's fine. I don't know if I'd do it again, but I certainly value my military experience. I am certainly glad that I did it.

Ruth St. Claire Murphy received the Bronze Star for meritorious service in the European Theater. Upon her return to the United States from Japan in 1949, Murphy took a short break from nursing men and worked in obstetrics at St. Olaf Hospital, in Austin, Minnesota. In 1950 she began a twenty-two-year nursing career with the Department of Veterans Affairs hospital in Hot Springs, South Dakota. After her retirement from the VA in 1972, she moved with her mother to Waco, Texas, where her sister and family lived. Murphy spent her retirement in Texas as a volunteer for the American Red Cross, continued to work as an artist, and became a published poet. In 1991 her family honored her love of art and theater by endowing the Ruth St. Claire Murphy Visual and Performing Arts Scholarship at McLennan Community College in Waco.[12]

Ruth St. Claire Murphy was interviewed by a Baylor University student for Women during War, a class oral history research project for history professor Patricia Ward Wallace. See Ruth St. Claire Murphy, *Oral Memoirs of Ruth St. Claire Murphy*, an interview conducted by Nathan Dale Howard, November 18, 1994, in Waco, Texas, BU Digital Collections.

Notes

1. Salaries for army nurse officers were 50 percent of a male officer's salary for the same rank until June 1944, when army nurse officer status rose temporarily from relative to regular, with full pay and benefits. The raise lasted only for the duration of the war plus six months. In 1947 army-nurse commissions finally became permanently equal with men's. Evelyn M. Monahan and Rosemary Neidel-Greenlee, *And If I Perish: Frontline U.S. Army Nurses in World War II* (New York: Alfred A. Knopf, 2003), 123–24, 436.

2. For a list of Murphy's assignments, see Ruth S. Murphy, "Biographical Information," BU Digital Collections.

3. The wounded advanced from field medic through a series of stations for aid, collecting, and clearing before reaching the field hospital, with its surgeons. Then, if they needed more complex treatment, they were moved to the evacuation hospital and, perhaps, from there to a general hospital. Albert E. Cowdrey, *Fighting for Life: American Military Medicine in World War II* (New York: The Free Press, 1994), 154–55.

4. A television series, broadcast from 1972 to 1983, depicting a fictional medical evacuation unit during the Korean War.

5. An injection with a hypodermic needle.

6. Tank crews were especially vulnerable to burns. When hit by enemy shells, Sherman tanks ignited instantly, causing second- and third-degree burns among tankers who survived. To preserve critical body fluids during transport from the front to the hospital, medics wrapped burn victims with compression bandages. Monahan and Neidel-Greenlee, *And If I Perish,* 419–20.

7. A "million-dollar wound" was serious enough to remove a soldier from combat but was not life-threatening. Cowdrey, *Fighting for Life,* 154.

8. Almost eighty thousand prisoners of war served Allied medical units "as everything from laborers to record keepers," often under the supervision of military nurses. Cowdrey, *Fighting for Life,* 108.

9. The nearest US field hospital was the first stop for American POWs recovered from German prisons. The Luftwaffe, or German air force, operated seven camps for Allied air corps POWs, and the Wehrmacht, or German army, operated a large network of transit and permanent camps for captured Allied ground troops. Stalags housed enlisted men

and noncommissioned officers, and Oflags housed officers. The lack of food at Stalag IX-B, near Bad Orb, was a sharp memory for prisoners who managed to survive. See Thomas Saylor, *Long Hard Road: American POWs during World War II* (St. Paul: Minnesota Historical Society Press, 2007), 40–41, 51–53, 121, 204, 214.

10. Dachau concentration camp was liberated on April 29, 1945.

11. Beginning on the evening of VE Day, May 8, 1945, lights illuminated the streets and displayed the famous monuments and fountains in the center of Paris after six years of enforced darkness. Allan B. Ecker and Howard Katzander, "It Was Sunny in Paris," *Yank, the Army Weekly,* May 1945, Victory Edition, 5–6, accessed June 20, 2014, http://www.oldmagazinearticles.com/VE-Day_in_Paris_France_pdf. Although it is unknown how long and what subjects Murphy studied at the famed Sorbonne, she was a lifelong lover of art and poetry. *Overseas Woman* was a monthly magazine published by the US Army European Theater of Operations Information and Education Division for military women serving abroad after the war.

12. "Ruth St. Claire Murphy," obituary, *Waco Tribune-Herald,* March 7, 1999. "Ruth St. Claire Murphy Scholarship Benefits Art, Theatre," *McLennan Highlander Quarterly,* Fall 2011, 3.

BILL LOGUE

Bill Logue was born in Waco in 1924, the youngest of six children. His father's experience in the 1930s as a public servant in local government — city councilman, county clerk, and mayor pro tem — roused Logue's interest in politics and public service and provided the inspiration for him to serve in student government in Waco High School. After graduating in May 1941, Logue entered the accounting program at Baylor University that fall. Two months after the attack on Pearl Harbor, he enlisted in the army reserves, which allowed him to stay at Baylor another year. The army was the only branch of service that would accept Bill because of his poor eyesight. In April 1943 he reported to Fort Wolters, in Mineral Wells, where he passed the test to qualify for the Army Specialized Training Program. After basic training at Camp Maxey, in Paris, Texas, he studied engineering in the army program at East Texas State College in Commerce. He was stationed there from September 1943 to February 1944, when the army reduced the ASTP and called Logue and his fellow students into combat duty.

When we got word that they were going to disband the program and we were going to be joining an infantry outfit, it really hit home with us. We went back to Camp Maxey, and we went into the 99th Division. There were thousands of us. This division had been activated out of Pennsylvania and Kentucky, and here we were, a bunch of smart-aleck college boys joining it, and we weren't particularly welcomed. The officers were already in place, the noncommissioned officers' positions, and so we came in as a bunch of privates.

There was some adjustment. It was a different group. I'm sure I was naïve to a certain extent; I had certainly led a protected life. There were just a lot of things about it that I did not enjoy. You have these first sergeants that give you just h-e-c-k, you know, very degrading. To be real honest with you, there wasn't a whole lot that I enjoyed about the army. Somebody asked me why I didn't go in the reserve. I said, "Man, I didn't have anything to reserve." I was in there because I did volunteer. It was my responsibility and duty, and I went and wouldn't have done anything but that. But as far as enjoying it or making it a career or even going in the reserve, I had no thoughts about that. Period.

I wanted to get home to my mama and my daddy, and I wanted to get back in Baylor and get back to the things and people that I loved, and that's what I did.

But we had some good guys. I became very close with a buck sergeant, Louis Orum, from Colorado. He was Catholic and I was Baptist, but we spent a lot of time together talking about those things that are important to you in life. We spent some time in the foxholes together, and he was later to be one that was captured. He had the stripes on there and had a little old mustache, and apparently our German capturers didn't like that. They took a rifle butt and knocked him to the ground.

We took our training, and I finally made PFC, along with all my other buddies there, and we got word that we were going to ship out in September. They didn't tell us when, where, or how. I got to make a trip home to my folks, and then they put us on a train to Boston to Camp Myles Standish. We hit there in September, and while I would be interested today in what the leaves looked like, I couldn't have cared less back then. The beauty of New England was not on my mind. One of the things I remember, they gave us free tickets to a Boston professional football game. Here I am, sitting up in that grandstand with my poor 20/200 vision, and there were all these 4-F 250- to 260-pound college players that were now pro players, and I didn't have too good a taste in my mouth. Here I was, the biggest coward in the infantry, and I was headed into combat, and those big bruisers were down there on the football field playing.

Be that as it may, we hit Boston and stayed there for three or four days, maybe a week, and then we were out of there on to Europe. We were on small ships, liberty ships.[1] We had a real scare about submarines on the way over. A number of Allied ships had been sunk by the German submarines, and so we were really concerned. I was fortunate enough to not pull duty in the food preparation, nor did I pull guard duty, but I was extremely seasick and didn't have much appetite. The thing that stands out in my memory was the scare that we had with the submarines.

We landed at Southampton in England, and we were there for two or three weeks. We had some training, and that's the first I ever heard of fish and chips. One of the friends that I had was a fellow named Bill Hixon, from Alexandria, Louisiana, a nice guy and the only fellow in our platoon and maybe in our company who had a college degree. He woke me up one night and brought me a glass of milk that he'd talked somebody out of. We had no milk over there then. Rations were very scarce. But old Bill Hixon, interesting enough and unfortunately, was

Infantrymen push through the dense Hürtgen Forest, December 1944. *Courtesy of National Archives and Records Administration.*

the first casualty on December 16, when the Germans hit us with everything they had. Bill Hixon was blown away by the artillery.

So we crossed the channel there, and then our eyes widened because of the shelling that the French coast had taken. Of course D-Day was back in June, so a good bit of time had elapsed. But we came on into France and moved on up into Belgium, and we relieved a division that had been up there for a good while. We were green. This would have been in October. They moved us up on the front. We were understaffed, and they spaced us, as the historians now say. Of course we were just sitting out there, sitting ducks. At that time all we had was some combat patrols. We had patrols, a little firing but not a whole lot. Wherever you moved, you'd dig a foxhole. As green as we were, to our right was a division that came in after we did. That was the 106th Division.

The Battle of the Bulge had more casualties—more killed, more wounded, more captured—than any other battle in American history.[2] The element of surprise was on the German side. We had weather. It was snowy. The ceiling prevented or certainly limited our reconnaissance, which was very poor. In his last thrust, Hitler moved up all the artillery. I don't know how many divisions he had up there. He hit us there where we were very vulnerable. Saturday morning, December 16, 1944, they laid down a terrific artillery barrage. It was a tremendous element of surprise. At five thirty that morning, the artillery came in there, and it was of great magnitude. The artillery that was laid down by the Germans was unprecedented. We had a baptism of fire very early, and that's when we suffered our first casualties.

I have joked some, but really I was not a hero. I was afraid and fearful. At that time, of course, I was a single man. I was twenty years old, and my family consisted of my mother, father, brothers, and sisters. That was my family. I put my trust and faith in the Lord and accepted him and believed in him and believed in the hereafter, and that's what gave me strength. I didn't want to die. I wanted to get home to be with my family.

When it hit, we scrambled for our rifles and looked to our platoon leaders, our lieutenants, for direction. They tried to regroup us, and we moved around there and moved through some minefields. That afternoon, as we got off, we walked right into the Germans. The BAR[3] is the heaviest piece of armament in a rifle platoon, and this fellow named Jorgenson, who was the biggest guy in our platoon, was the BAR man. The Germans had what was called a burp gun. It fired so fast, so many rounds per second, that the gunner couldn't keep it under control. It would go right up. So in trying to regroup and get our positions, following our leaders, we walked into that kind of situation, and that's where we suffered a lot of casualties. But Jorgenson was our BAR man, and some of the fellows were able to drag him out but he had several holes there in his head. A fellow named Knoblock, who I'd met at Camp Maxey, was the ammunition carrier. He was great big also, but he managed to avoid the gunfire. We lost a number in that encounter and it was an experience that day and that night.

Ultimately we got into a situation where we took up position in some buildings, and it was out of those buildings that we fought as the Germans came forward. It was Sunday night, about dusk, that they moved the Tiger tanks up and started blasting away at us, and it was then that our lieutenant said we had to surrender. He took his handkerchief and put it on the end of the bayonet on the end of his rifle, and that's when we became prisoners. In our building, there were probably twenty of us in all. I'm not sure how many of our whole group were killed or captured, but we suffered some heavy casualties.

We were in Hürtgen Forest, out not too far. What was going through my mind? Of course fear. I mean, what's going to happen to us? Since then I've read that if you were captured by SS troops, your chances of survival were slim and none. They killed you. I mean, that's recorded history. They killed at the slightest. We fared much better, even with the isolated incident about my friend Lou Orum's being knocked to the ground. But there wasn't any brutality towards me. The problem that we had was that our overshoes were taken, our overcoats were taken, of course—all our valuables, the things that we needed as far as the weather was concerned.[4] That was December 17, and we were still standing around, walking, trying to get on boxcars as they tried to get us back into Germany.

But, being honest with you, they were not prepared for us. There had been thousands that they'd captured. We waited for boxcars there on Christmas Day of 1944. I'll always remember. It was with a lot of mixed emotions. We were trying to sing Christmas carols, not knowing whether we were going to live or die. But then they herded us in the boxcars. It's with some sympathy, empathy, that I hear about people being mashed in boxcars, because that's the way they had us, and when you have problems, kidney problems or otherwise, and you're just a mass of humanity in those boxcars, you got problems. Those were the situations that we were under. Food was scarce, if any at all, for a couple of days or so. Your stomach shrank. When I say they weren't prepared for us, they weren't prepared for places to put us, they weren't prepared for food, and so a lot of problems resulted.[5]

But they did get us back. We crossed the Rhine River, walking, at Bonn, Germany. I can recall that very vividly. With our hands in the air we walked across the Rhine River at Bonn. We passed Bonn, and then we finally got to the first prisoner-of-war camp. I believe it was XIII-C. I think my prison tags are Stammlager XIII-C. It was there I was able to write a postcard to my folks. Of course you had a consuming thought: everything was about food. You got so hungry. It's hard to conceive now. Usually when you're around young men that age, they're talking football, talking about the fairer sex. If you can imagine, that was not number one in the minds of those men. Food becomes the most important thing.[6]

On Sunday we had church. We had our own service because, you see, in the thousands that they captured, they captured chaplains and officers and enlisted men. We had a church service, and the building where we met couldn't hold them all. I don't know how many weeks we stayed in that thing, but the longer we stayed there, the more comfortable the men got, and our attendance, as you understand, dropped off. That's life, isn't it? We call on the good Lord, but when we are up on the top of the mountain, we somehow forget him. When we get down to the bottom, we need him, we call on him, don't we? That's just true to life. As we became more secure in that position of being a prisoner there, the church attendance dropped.

We were working there. There were some violations of the Geneva Conventions. They were not supposed to work prisoners in anything

Confiscated German photo of American prisoners marching to prison camps in December 1944. *Courtesy of National Archives and Records Administration.*

related to the war. They assigned us to various places. I went to a number of places, a number of the stalags.[7] I was never in one of these stalags long enough where the thing was organized and people tried to escape. I did what they told me to do, and of course I'm alive today. I got moved around a number of times because of the fact that I had pulmonary problems. I think there towards the end they were moving us around because the Allied forces were getting closer.

Once we were in Bamberg, and we were working in a grain elevator. I don't know whether it was rye or whatever. We'd take those seeds and we'd put a little water with them and try to cook them to try to get something to eat because we just didn't have enough to eat, and the guards would come in. I learned very little German, but I learned this much. They'd come in and they'd say, "Nichts arbeiten, nichts essen!" That meant, "No work, no eat!" And we'd yell back, "Nichts essen, nichts arbeiten!" "No eat, no work!"

Then one of the places they had us out digging tree stumps, and this was a violation of the Geneva Conventions because we were clearing for landing strips. But be that as it may, who's going to raise that question? But I did get paid some marks that I kept. Of course all the hale and hearty people were off in the front for the Germans, but the old men were guards, and every one of them had a cousin in Boston or sister in Brooklyn or this kind of thing. A lot of them would speak English. If not fluently, they spoke it in broken language.

But the hunger that you go under! I've often said that some good can come out of every situation. It hurts me even now to waste any food on my plate. I just don't want to throw any away. But you get so hungry, and you forget pride and all that. But I still had a little pride. We were out once, and this guard was peeling an apple, and of course we just had nothing. He was peeling that apple, and I watched him peel that apple and throw those peelings on the ground. I really didn't want to let him see me get them, but when he got out of sight I picked up those apple peelings, and what a delight! Those peelings were the only fruit I had during that time. You thought about food, you talked about it, you dreamed about it, you wrote about it.

I'll say a good word for the Red Cross, because during that time when we got to established camps and so forth, it didn't happen often enough, but we got Red Cross packages. That was a real delight. There was some canned meat, and there was something sweet in there, whereas you'd been getting some old watery soup and some old black bread that looked like it had been made out of sawdust. Of course, here I am used to good white bread from Jones Fine Bread or Rainbo here in Waco. But be that as it may, when they finally gave us a bread ration, it was this black bread that, man, my poor old stomach just couldn't handle, and I gave away my bread ration. After a while we got so little that I developed a taste for anything that I could put my mouth onto. We were in this camp, and we took turns of going over to the so-called kitchen to get this old imitation coffee in these great big old pans. Of course, here I am with this terrible vision and poor night vision; I blame it on that. They sent me with another guy over to the kitchen to get this big old thing of hot imitation coffee. On the way back, I stepped into a hole and that stuff went on me. It didn't leave any scars but it affected, at least temporarily, my seeing. I had to keep my eyes closed for a while, and somebody stole my bread ration there where I was assigned to sleep. We could eat anything that we could find. One of my friends, an old boy named Oren Henderson, stole the guard's lunch one day. I didn't know what was going to happen. Another time when we were out on a work detail, he found an egg a hen had laid, and he ate that egg raw.

While we worked for them in this grain elevator, I developed pulmonary problems. The Germans were going to send me back to a hospital for Allied prisoners in Schweinfurt, Germany, which was the most heavily bombed city in Germany by the Allied forces. Ball bearings were manufactured in Schweinfurt, and they had gone underground to manufacture these ball bearings. Well, be that as it may, they were going to send me back there with this old guard. By that time I had an old French overcoat that said USA painted on the back. My glass frames had broken, and I had those things tied on with wire. We were going in a boxcar, and we get into the train yards out there and the switching station, and, doggone, the sirens go on for a daylight raid of the Allied forces. Well, now, back in Bamberg, where we worked for them, they wouldn't let us go in the bomb shelters, but here I was the only one with this old German guard. I'll always remember Schweinfurt, where, with a little apprehension, I was the only Allied prisoner in that shelter with all these civilians. They had been bombed and bombed and bombed and bombed. But no harm came, and I came on out.[8]

I eventually got to Nuremberg, and there we got word Franklin Roosevelt died.[9] Someway we heard by the grapevine. If you remember the old films, it was at Nuremberg that Hitler had his stadium where he had his youth rallies. We walked by that stadium as I went to the place where they were housing Allied prisoners.[10] Here I was, I had been a prisoner only four or five months, and I ended up in a place where there were British subjects. They had been captured at Dunkirk in 1939 and were South Africans, New Zealanders, Canadians, and all the British subjects who had been prisoners about five years.[11] So I was certainly a new kid on the block. I was the only American there. They were older and more experienced, and they had a lot of experiences they were sharing. I did more listening than I did anything else. I was one of the younger ones there. I had celebrated my twenty-first birthday in January 1945 in a prisoner-of-war camp somewhere—Ebelsbach, I think, or Hammelburg.

In April 1945 we heard the sound of the artillery as the American forces got closer. We just knew we were going to be liberated. We knew that the American forces were going to come through there some day, and they were going to liberate us. And they did. We never lost faith. I believe it was the 45th Division, a Texas-Oklahoma division, that actually liberated us.[12] Oh, that was a wonderful experience! When they came through, the guards, the old men, interestingly enough, put down their guns, picked up brooms, and started cleaning up. Somehow we got the keys to where the Red Cross parcels were stored and, man, we got into those things. I think it was in orderly fashion. I don't know who did it, but anyhow, I got to eat some. They told us they were going to move us out the next night, and they moved in some hospital conveyances with the cross on the top and so forth. They left us there, but the guards stayed there, and, as I say, they traded their guns for brooms.

So they bundled us up and, of course, I had pulmonary problems, but there were guys with arms gone, there were guys with legs gone. One of the interesting stories is about my friend, a Britisher who had only one leg and was on crutches. He was wounded at Dunkirk. Gangrene had set in, and they cut his leg off. They put us on those hospital conveyances, the trucks and such, and by that time, they were capturing Germans right and left, and they were herding them back up. Our group got into a convoy. They were going to move us to a landing strip and then fly us to France, to Nancy, as I recall, where they had a hospital for American soldiers. Unfortunately we got into a convoy where one of those drivers had left his lights on, his dimmers or whatever, and in middle of the night, down comes this German plane, affectionately called Bedcheck Charlie, and strafed us. Here are these guys who had been waiting five years for freedom, and here comes this German plane strafing us. As he came down and strafed us, the back of that hospital vehicle that we were in opened and we charged out into freshly plowed farmland. I'm telling you the truth. I ran as fast as I could, an example that we can do things when we have to do it. I hid out there, and who's over right next to me that had run as fast as I had without any crutches? That one-legged Britisher.

Well, the plane came back but couldn't find us, and we got on into our convoy, got to our landing strip, and we flew on into Nancy. I was running a fever. I got to go through the chow line that morning. I remember I went to the breakfast line three times. Why I didn't make myself sick, I don't know, but I went through three times. I had some type of pneumonia, and they kept me there awhile. May 8 was VE Day in Europe, and by that time I had cleared and was headed to Camp Lucky Strike.[13] They named all those places for cigarettes. I went through Paris, France, going from one train station to another, in the back of a truck. I missed the great celebration by twenty-four hours, but all I was interested in was getting home.

I hit Camp Lucky Strike, and my stomach was so hard with hunger. I can remember eating a box of Hershey's. They were three cents a bar. I ate a whole box of those things, never fazed me.[14] There we loaded up at the port of embarkation to head back to the States. They sent us on little old bitsy ships smaller than the one I went over on. Of course, one of the memorable things was coming into New York Harbor and seeing the Statue of Liberty. You thank the Lord that you're back. It makes you proud, it makes you happy, and you give thanks to the Lord that you got back. It arouses all the patriotism.

This exposure to the army and to combat and my experiences as a prisoner of war matured me. It certainly gave me a sense of the value of life itself. I certainly treasured and honored life more than I ever had before. I think I became closer to my family and maybe my friends. You know, you can't do without food for days and days on end and not get a basic appreciation for just a crumb of bread, so I became more conscious of waste. There may have been some bad effects, but I think the good would outweigh them.

Bill Logue's five months as a prisoner of war earned him corporal rank and sixty days of temporary duty at home with his parents. During a short time on reassignment to Camp Crowder, Louisiana, his pneumonia returned and he was hospitalized in New Orleans. There he was discharged from the army on Friday, November 30, 1945. The next Monday he was back in Baylor's business school, where with the help of the GI Bill he completed his undergraduate degree in 1947. After graduating from Baylor Law School in 1949, he served as justice of the peace in McLennan County and had the task of signing death certificates for most of the 114 people who died in Waco's massive tornado on May 11, 1953. Logue married Gloria Shearin in 1951, and they had four daughters. From 1954 to 1960 he served as McLennan County judge. From 1961 to 1999, almost forty years, he was judge of the Nineteenth District Court. For most of that time he volunteered as the county's primary juvenile court judge. He retired at age seventy-five as the longest-tenured state judge in Texas. Because of his devotion to youth, McLennan County's Juvenile Justice Facility was named in his honor.

Judge Bill Logue shared his story of being a prisoner in Germany in the fourth of ten interviews covering his life history for the Waco and McLennan County Project. Bill Logue, *Oral Memoirs of Bill Logue,* a series of interviews conducted by Rebecca Sharpless, February 14, 1994, through April 28, 1997, in Waco, Texas, BU Digital Collections.

Notes

1. US Liberty ships, built quickly as an emergency measure during the war, transported both cargo and troops for the army and the navy

with crews of merchant marines. Richard Snow, *A Measureless Peril: America in the Fight for the Atlantic, the Longest Battle of World War II* (New York: Scribner, 2010), 194–99.

2. US casualties in the Battle of the Bulge in Belgium, December 16, 1944, through January 25, 1945, were 19,276 dead, 47,493 wounded, and 23,218 captured. Peter Doyle, *World War II in Numbers: An Infographic Guide to World War II* (Buffalo, NY: Firefly Books, 2013), 96.

3. Browning Automatic Rifle.

4. The period between capture and arrival at prison camp was the most perilous time for POWs. German policies disclaimed responsibility for adhering to the Geneva Conventions while POWs were in transit to camp. Any suspicion, justified or not, that a prisoner was a spy or saboteur had severe, often deadly, outcomes. Confiscation of clothes and boots, exhaustive marches, and starvation tactics discouraged escape attempts. David A. Foy, *For You the War Is Over: American Prisoners of War in Nazi Germany* (New York: Stein and Day, 1984), 45–47, 81.

5. During and following the Battle of the Bulge, the numbers of Allied prisoners multiplied far beyond Germany's ability to meet even basic shelter, sanitary, nourishment, or medical needs. Arieh J. Kochavi, *Confronting Captivity: Britain and the United States and their POWs in Nazi Germany* (Chapel Hill: University of North Carolina Press, 2005), 97–102.

6. Stalag XIII-C was near Hammelburg, Bavaria. Harry Spiller, *Prisoners of Nazis: Accounts by American POWs in World War II* (Jefferson, NC: McFarland, 1998), 179–80. The near starvation at Stalag XIII-C is verified by other POWs in Kochavi, *Confronting Captivity,* 94, 101.

7. Logue's experiences on work details and his frequent moves just ahead of the Allied advance into Germany were common among POWs captured in the Ardennes in late December. See Robert E. Humphrey, *Once Upon a Time in War: The 99th Division in World War II* (Norman: University of Oklahoma Press, 2008), 234–71; and Saylor, *Long Hard Road,* 64–66.

8. Targeted since October 1943 by the British Royal Air Force at night and the US Eighth Air Force by day, Schweinfurt was in ruins by the time Logue reached there. Sporadic shelling in the spring of 1945 signaled the approach of the American forces, who captured the city on April 11. Martin Middlebrook, *The Schweinfurt–Regensburg Mission* (New York: Charles Scribner's Sons, 1983), 310–11.

9. President Roosevelt died on April 12, 1945.

10. Nuremberg was the site of Stalag XIII-D and Lazarett [Military Hospital] XIII-D. Spiller, *Prisoners of Nazis,* 180. Poor conditions at Stalag XIII-D in April 1945 are described in Foy, *For You the War Is Over,* 141.

11. As British troops evacuated Europe through Dunkirk in 1940, the Germans captured more than thirty-four thousand men. The lot of those who survived the rigors of the first four years of imprisonment deteriorated greatly in the early months of 1945 with the flood of American POWs into the system. Kochavi, *Confronting Captivity,* 3.

12. Trained at Fort Sill, Oklahoma, and Camp Barkeley, Texas, and consisting of national guardsmen from Colorado, Arizona, Oklahoma, and New Mexico, the 45th Division fought its way through Sicily, Italy, and France to reach Germany in late March 1945. The division endured heavy fighting April 16–20 to capture Nuremberg. On April 17, its 180th Infantry liberated 250 American and 450 British prisoners, presumably including Logue. Leo V. Bishop, Frank J. Glasgow, and George A. Fisher, *The Fighting Forty-Fifth: The Combat Report of an Infantry Division* (Baton Rouge, LA: Army & Navy Publishing, 1946), 177.

13. The route home for most American POWs rescued from Germany in spring 1945 was through the nearest field hospital and then one of the "cigarette camps" on the Normandy coast near Le Havre. First used as staging camps for incoming soldiers after the Allies occupied the area in September 1944, the camps bore the names of popular cigarette brands: Lucky Strike, Old Gold, Chesterfield, Philip Morris, Pall Mall, Twenty Grand, Home Run, Wings, and Herbert Tareyton. Larry M. Belmont, "The Cigarette Camps: The US Army Camps in the Le Havre Area," accessed June 25, 2014, http://www.skylighters.org/special/cigcamps/cmplstrk.html.

14. Walter B. Young Jr., taken captive like Logue in the Ardennes on December 16, also confessed to consuming an entire box of Hershey's chocolates at Camp Lucky Strike. The camp's generous offerings of boiled chicken, eggnog, eggs, donuts, and other rich foods was a long-held memory for many former POWs. Spiller, *Prisoners of Nazis,* 25, 49, 58, 76, 127, 169; Saylor, *Long Hard Road,* 232.

JOHN VALLS

On December 9, 1924, John Valls was born into a large and very successful farming family living near Laredo, Texas. His family had a long history in the area. Valls's great-great-great-great-grandfather was the last mayor of Laredo, Mexico, and the first mayor of Laredo, Texas. His parents, both of Spanish descent, married in 1907 and had eleven children; Valls was the tenth. In the early part of the century the Valls family's San Rafael Farm, a large Bermuda onion and tomato operation, prospered. At one time the family even owned the St. Anthony Hotel in downtown Laredo. In 1939, however, the family fortunes turned. The family had planted large orange orchards, but they were lost in that winter's hard freeze. Because the trees were uninsured, Valls's father had to declare bankruptcy. Growing up in Laredo, all the sons were very involved in sports, and Valls excelled at football, basketball, and track before being drafted in 1943 after his junior year in high school.

THE WAR CAME AND TOOK AWAY MY LAST YEAR in high school. I would have swept everybody in sports! But as it was, what would have been my senior year was spent in the army. I took basic training in Amarillo, and I made the football team there. I remember when I faked out and went in and caught a pass, the coach said, "Okay. Hey, you! Stay." So they gave me a uniform and everything. I took the test for pilot—I have always loved model airplanes—and I passed the test. So I was sent for pilot training.

I was transferred to Central State Teachers College at Stevens Point, Wisconsin. January 1, 1944, I marched into Central State Teachers College. During my time in CTD (College Training Detachment[1]) I set the record for the three hundred meters the first month. I broke it the second month and I broke it again the third month. I made the basketball team, and the coach there said, "Hey, when you get through with this, come back and see me because we want you here."

I stayed at Central State Teachers College until March. At that time the program was eliminated without prejudice. We didn't do anything wrong. The whole school was gone because they decided they had too many pilots. They told me, "We are going to send you to a gunnery school. You're going to be a gunner in an airplane." I went before a colonel, and he asked, “What do you feel like?” I thought I’d impress him, so I said, “Sir, if I can’t fly the airplane, nobody’s going to fly it for me.” He didn’t say anything, wrote something down, and then he said, “Next.” The next day I was in the infantry. They transferred me to the infantry!

They sent me to Reno, Nevada. I did nothing but went out in a truck in the sand and stayed in a tent. They were training us to go to North Africa. Fortunately I got my orders changed; I don’t know why. They sent me to Greensboro, North Carolina. There I was in a track meet. I won everything.

Then they sent me to Boston. I shipped out of Boston. Fourteen days to Southampton, England. Out of the fourteen days on board I was seasick thirteen. I was lucky to have a top bunk because the guy at the top would vomit and it would come all the way down. Oh God, I suffered. Oh!

But I made it to England and, as usual, I found a place to run. We didn’t do infantry training on Sundays. So I found a beautiful track field with hurdles and all. I went and ran there. A very well-dressed man saw me. I know it was him because when I got back to the base, Base Air Depot No. 2, the colonel called me in to see him. I went in and saluted, wondering what the heck I did. And he said, “They want you to go run in London.” I said, “Yes sir, that’s fine.” They flew me in a C-47 all by myself. In London they told us, “Hey, the queen is going to be here. We want you British subjects to stand, and when she comes out, you will bow like this. And you, Yank, you don’t have to bow, but you can stand at attention.” When the queen appeared—I mean, the queen was like a god to them—I got the fever, too. When she came out I bowed too, just like the rest of them.

I raced, and I won. I won the 400-meter hurdles. I had never run the 400-meter hurdles before. They even had a kid in front of me, and I said, “Hey! How am I going to pass him?” They said, “Oh, you can pass him. He’s younger than you. These are handicaps.” They say it “’andicaps,” not “handicaps.” I passed him, and I won. The next week the colonel called me in: “They want you to go to someplace else.” I went, and again I won. The third week I flew, again on a C-47, to another meet. And again I won, and they gave me a prize and everything. I sent the prizes to Laredo, and they got here. My sisters all had cutlery sets and this and that. At one of the meets I received a certificate signed by a bunch of lords. They also promised that a medal will be given to me when obtainable. This was during the war, so I understood why it wasn’t available. This was in August 1944.

In England our military training was done well. I remember sitting on the side of a hill, about two hundred of us, when this master sergeant, battle scars and everything, came in shaking, holding hand grenades. He said, "Today we're going to teach you about hand grenades. When you pull this trigger and you let it drop, it will go off in five seconds. So don't ever pull the trigger." Then he pulled it—and he dropped it. Zoom! Everybody left. I was hitting on people, shouting to them to get the hell out of the way. We counted—one, two, three, four, five—nothing. We looked up, and there was the master sergeant saying, "Come on back. There's nothing wrong with me. I just wanted to see if there are any heroes here, who was going to pick up the grenade and throw it away." Not any of us! But it was good training.

We finally shipped out from England to Le Havre in northwestern France. When we came in, Le Havre had already been taken by the Allies. We didn't have to fight for it. Immediately I was assigned to the 52nd Armored Infantry Battalion, to the 9th Armored Division, to the Third Army, with General Patton. Right away we had a lesson. We had to say the words, "Kill or be killed. Kill or be killed." Thirty times a day we said it. Anytime we met a buddy, he said, "Kill or be killed." We were told, "You will not surrender. You will die, but you will not surrender. You will not retreat. You might die, but you will not retreat. Understand that." Patton, I mean he greatly impressed all of us kids.

Soon after that I finally got to see my first German soldier in combat, face to face. I had him with my M-1 rifle off of safety. I was a good shot, but I couldn't shoot him. I couldn't kill him, because I turned cold. I turned cold, and I couldn't shoot him. He threw his gun down and surrendered. I took him in, saying, "I caught a Nazzy! I caught a Nazzy!" I didn't even know how to pronounce "Nazi." I told the sergeant, "Sarge, I couldn't kill him. I turned cold." He responded, "Don't worry, son; next time you will." And sure enough, he was right. From that day on, it was rough. It was bad.

I had the same experience that Sergeant York had: I knew about guns. Back home in Laredo I would go with a friend, Tommy Leyendecker, to his ranch, the Bruni estate, when we were just nine. They had about a hundred thousand acres we roamed in his Lincoln Zephyr car. On the fender we placed our twenty-two to shoot rabbits, all of us kids in the neighborhood. We were good. So when I went to the firing range with an old rifle, a Winchester. Pow, miss. Oh no! Pow, miss. Three times. Pow, miss. I said, "Sarge, something's wrong. I didn't miss." He grumbled "Oh, here's another one. All right, bring the damn thing down." It was all bullseyes. They had not even looked to see. There were some guys from New York in our group that had never seen a gun. I qualified immediately.

In training, the master sergeant was in charge of us, and he gave us instructions every day. When we got to France, however, a captain immediately informed us, "I'm your CO here, and I don't wear my bars because it's nothing but a naming stick." Sure enough, in four days he was killed.

Out of a company of twenty-two that I joined with, two of us out of that original came back. It was hell. It was really hell. You had to dig a hole every night, whether it was raining, snowing, or whatever. You had to dig that hole because if you stayed aboveground, the mortars and hand grenades came in and did their damage. So, I mean *every* night. Many times we took houses—we took towns that did not fight—for shelter.

In our outfit we had an American officer that spoke German. Every time we got to a town, he'd say, "If you fire one shot at us, we will destroy your town. If you don't fire at us, we're not going to disturb you. We're not going to fire either. So please surrender and avoid bloodshed." Sometimes we went in, no problems. Sometimes we went in and met kids with Panzerfaust, rifles with hand grenades—boom! boom!—beat the hell out of us. We lost a lot of people. You didn't make friends. You avoided forming friendships because your friend could be gone the next day.

I don't have the Purple Heart, but I got wounded on my leg and in my arm. If I hadn't been wearing my helmet, I would have been killed. The thing exploded on top of us. I feel ping, ping, ping, ping, ping! The guy next to me began to shout, "I'm hit! I'm hit!" He was covered with blood, all down his front. So we shouted, "Hey, medic! Medic!" They got him, took him off. The next day they brought him back with a Band-Aid. He had been barely hit, nothing but a little thing but enough for blood to run. He was mad as hell! I remember it. That night all of us tried to take our jackets off and I couldn't get mine off. The jacket had stopped the blood. I was hit in my leg too. I didn't say anything, I don't have the Purple Heart, but I was wounded.

Two beautiful things I remember. Number one, I'd lie in my hole at night and see thousands of bombers coming over—thousands, thousands, thousands, coming over. I said, God, we cannot lose this war, because there was doubt when we went in. The United States was number seven in power. Germany was first, England was second, France was third, Italy was fourth, and Japan was fifth. We were only number seven. We didn't know that we could win the war. It was amazing how we produced and delivered so much equipment. We got three little boxes of food a day, and sometimes we didn't.

One night, we were already dug in, and they called, "Hey, Company C, come on out! Come on out, up the hill. They're going to give us a bath." Well, it's nighttime. They couldn't give us a bath then, so we went into a railroad station. There was Jack Leonard, who used to sing for Tommy Dorsey, singing, "Marie, the Dawn Is Breaking, Marie."[2] Every month they gave us a bath. We went, and there was a block square with tarpaulins all over. It must have been ten thousand of us at a time. We had wooden ramps and hot water. You went in there, took all your clothes off, threw them away, they fumigated you, and then you got a bar of soap. Oh man! White soap! With soap you washed and then had a clean towel to dry with.

After the bath, you had your rifle inspected. Just the day before, an airplane was strafing us, and I forgot I had a brush on top of my M-1. I took my gun off, and before thinking I fired at him. Pow! The bullet destroyed the damn barrel because the brush had been in there. Yeesh! And the sergeant asked me, he says, "What in the hell did you do with this gun?" I said, "I don't know, Sarge. You give me another one."

On another instance, we were patrolling an area, and I emptied my gun at a giant German airplane, four engines with an Me 210 on top of it.[3] It had a twin engine with both the big airplane and the little airplane going full blast, taking off just forty or fifty yards from me. Pow! I got my M-1. Pow! Pow! Pow! I landed all eight shots in the big airplane. The smaller airplane had the controls in it. Those were German officers going to Brazil in the giant airplane. The small airplane got up to a certain distance and then went off. It was amazing.

Towards the end of the war we were so tired — mentally, not physically. We were strong but so tired mentally that I prayed — and so did everybody else — to get killed or get this goddamn war over with. That's exactly how I worded it. "Please, please, I've had it. I don't see the end. I don't see the end. I'm here, and I can't do anything about it. I'm hungry, I'm scared, I'm tired, I'm cold." It was bad, bad, bad, bad, bad. One can't imagine.

We also took the town of Dresden, famous for its china. I was assigned to guard one of the factories. I went in there, and I looked around and found no German soldiers or anything. I told a local there at the factory — the guy spoke English very well — "All I want is a room. I want a cot, a bed, a blanket, and water. That's all. And leave me alone." He did that. He brought me everything. And I was already in bed, sleeping, and he knocked on the door. He asked, "What's your address in Laredo?" I replied, "What do you want to know for?" He says, "Oh, I'm going to send you these boxes." He had two boxes. I said, "Hey, you can't do that." He continued, "I can. Just give me your address in Laredo." "Okay, 1004 San Bernardo, Laredo, Texas, USA."

German Messerschmitt, Me 210. *Courtesy of San Diego Air and Space Museum Archive.*

That's it. Believe it or not, those boxes got here. Dresden china, the best china that they make. They made it to Laredo, because later on I wrote a letter to my sister and asked, "Hey, did you ever get a package?" She answered, "Yes, we got it. It's beautiful."

On April 15 I was leading a patrol, and here comes an army of men moving toward us on the autobahn. I thought, That can't be an American army. As they got closer, I saw a big old swastika flying. I said, "Oh shit!" I turned around, and I was going to go and report to Colonel William Westmoreland, the 9th Armored Division commander. Before that, however, out of the mass of soldiers a German jeep appeared over a rise, flying a surrender flag, a white flag. So I stopped, and a young German colonel got out and saluted me. I returned his salute. I held my gun on him. He spoke better English than me, with my thick Spanish accent. He said, "General Model wishes to surrender his army." Wow! So I take him in. At first I said, "Oh okay, I'll drive." He said, "No, I'll drive." Then I ordered, "No! I'll drive." I got in, and the German jeep was not like an American car. I ground the gears and the colonel was cringing. I said, "Okay, you drive!" It was then that I made the biggest mistake in my life. I should have gone in and said, "Sir, I've captured an army." Instead I told the German colonel, "Go ahead and surrender." Westmoreland came out with photographers, generals, and they left me by the wayside. He got all the credit. I learned later that we took in three hundred thousand soldiers that day. It was me!

One day—I don't even remember what my orders were. I know that we were under British General Montgomery. The 9th Armored Division had been loaned to Montgomery, but we were still taking orders from my sergeant. My orders from the sergeant were, "Patrol this area,

Female survivors holding bread, Bergen-Belsen, Germany. *Courtesy of Yad Vashem, The Holocaust Martyrs' and Heroes' Remembrance Authority.*

and go into this area." I was alone, mind you, as I walked, and I saw a giant wall right on the street. I thought it was very strange. I didn't know it was a prison camp. I opened the gate. It wasn't even locked. I opened the gate, and as soon as I walked in I heard a sound like somebody scored a touchdown in a football game, but it was very muffled. I walked into the compound, and everybody was looking at me. Most were standing, but some people were in racks that I could see. They were just lying down. They lifted their heads up and looked and then went right back down. They were dying. It stunk. All of a sudden this man came up to me making sounds I didn't understand, eagerly trying to give me his prize possession, a sleeveless rabbit-skin coat. I replied, "No, no, no, I'm an American soldier. I can't take anything. Go, you're free! You're free. Go!" The man insisted. I pleaded with him. "I can't take anything, please. Please, I can't take anything. Go! Go! You're free!" The man would not relent. I took it, and then he left.

Soon after that the English troops came into Belsen.+ Reporters from *Life* magazine were also there to document the conditions. General Eisenhower got the people in the town to come and parade down to witness the atrocities. Five thousand bodies on the street. I have never seen anything like that. It was gruesome. As a matter of fact I wanted to get the hell out of there because, number one, I couldn't stand the smell, and number two, there were already British troops coming in after me. They were in charge. Let them be in charge; I don't want to have anything to do with it. It was not until later that I even knew where I was. But it was gruesome. I was just a kid from high school that really was very naïve. I didn't know anything. But when I saw that, I thought, How can any people do that to other people? How? It's impossible. It's impossible!

I know I have a guardian angel. I know it. I've been in so many bad things that somebody must speak for me, even now. My guardian angel has gotten me out of some serious trouble that I could have gotten into. I've had offers of a lot of illegal things, and somehow somebody talks for me. Somebody says words, and I ask, "Was that me?" I know it. I've got a guardian angel.

One time we had won a battle, and I was assigned to be in charge of identifying our dead. We had German civilians with mule carts, wagons, picking up our dead and placing them on a wagon. I was in charge of getting their dog tags and making sure they were Americans because in combat you get dirty and everything. Oh, I got so tired of seeing those grey faces, pulling out the tags from several wagons. I got so tired of seeing that I thought, To hell with it. If they've got green socks, they go. From then on I just looked at the socks. If they were grey, take them off. If they were green, leave them there. That experience made an impression on me even though I didn't think about it at the time. When you die, when you're killed, you turn grey—everybody. I remember that was one of my jobs. In the army you did what you had to, everything. It's not like the movies. Audie Murphy was a real hero. They said we were heroes. They call me a hero.

In another instance, we were going to take a U-shaped building. It was green with two stories, defended by bunkers on each end firing machine guns at us. I got under one of the bunkers with a hand grenade—boom—they quit firing. The sergeant comes up and he says, "You stupid bastard! What the hell do you think you were doing? What if that hand grenade hadn't gone in there? It would have killed all of us!" He was right. I shouldn't have done it. But I did it, and it turned out. Rumor had it that the facility was a house for prostitutes for the SS.

At another point I was in charge of receiving some prisoners that were surrendering. It must have been close to the end of the war. In comes a Mercedes-Benz, nineteen-thirty-something edition with a chauffeur and an SS captain, accompanied by his mistress, to surrender. I looked in there and I said, "Das amerikaner uhr." That means, "That's an American watch." He had a watch. The Germans didn't have wristwatches; they had pocket watches. He said, "Nein, nein." I said, "Yes, it is." I got in there, took the watch off. It was US Air Force. My brother Louis had just been killed flying a mission over Italy. I had never been in a rage before, but I grabbed the SS captain and flew into a rage. I got him, and I was pulling him out the little window in the Mercedes-Benz. I was going to kill him with my bare hands. I yanked him out. He had been previously wounded, and the bandage stuck in the windshield causing blood to go all over. A sergeant came and got me, and they took me off. I was fighting the sergeant because I wanted that guy. I wanted to kill him. I was going to kill him with my bare hands because my brother had just been killed, and he had an air force watch. I know my brother had one.

On April 30 we were going to take Berlin. Eisenhower arrived and commanded, "No, no, no. Go south. The Russians are going to take the capital." Thank God. I wouldn't have lasted through another invasion like that. Hitler shot himself that same day, April 30. I was about twenty kilometers from him, about fourteen miles, I think. I figured out where the bunker was and where I was. I was near there. So we went south.

Then we were set to liberate Prague. We are almost at Prague, actually seeing the city. Again, Eisenhower says, "Hey, get the hell out of there. The Russians are going to take it." There was a very pretty girl from there in Prague that begged me and says, "Please, please, please!" She spoke English. "Please, take me back! Please, they're going to kill me here. Please!" I said, "Okay." I brought her with me in the half-track all the way to Rehau. We were at night looking for a little concrete thing that separated Czechoslovakia from Germany at Rehau. It was there, at Rehau, where we met the Russians. The Russians put a rope across the street. The Americans couldn't go over it, but they could come over. I was on a flatbed truck with the girl, just platonic mind you. We weren't sexual or sexist, even though they said that we were. We would not rape them; we didn't do that. All our soldiers were good.

This girl was there with me, and a Russian officer was making points with her, and he came on the flatbed. I told him, "Hey, Ruskie, nein, nein, nein. Fraulein mine. Understand? Verstehen sie? Fraulein mine, not yours. Okay?" And pow! Man, I hit him and knocked him off the flatbed and took his pistol and beat the hell out of him. Nothing ever happened from it, but that actually happened. I had a fight with a Russian. They were dirty. They were bad.

The war ended for me at Rehau. I was only there for fourteen days. I met another girl that was very nice. The locals had no food at that time. Right after the war the troops had provisions that were called 10-in-1. That means ten meals in one. We didn't have the little C-rations or whatever they called them now. We even had powdered milk, powdered eggs—very good. I went to her house and met her father. Her father was a professor. In return for some food I shared, he was teaching me German. Oh man, if I'd have stayed in Germany six months I'd have learned the language. I still know quite a bit, but just enough to hold up infantrymen. "Haben sie das geld?" That means, "Do you have any money?" "Ja, ich habe." "I've got it right there." But the German people were great. I wondered at times if we were fighting the wrong people.

My brother Louis, when he was on the way to Africa and to Europe to fight the war, met a girl named Gladys in Savannah in 1944. They fell in love. They were going to get married. He proposed to her, and she accepted, but they never had a chance to marry. They were in town for about ten days.

After the war, about three years later mind you, my brother Alphonso was flying B-17s, and he stopped in Savannah and met Gladys, too. He went just to pay a courtesy call. They visited, and he invited her to visit our family in Laredo. Gladys came to Texas, to see Alphonso really. I remember Alphonso and I and a friend, Fernando, sitting out on our porch talking. [Alphonso said,] "Hey, this girl is coming to visit us. You take her out, and I'll take her out." And Fernando said, "No, you take her out." I demanded, "Hey, I'm going to take her out!" "But you're already going with a girl," they argued. I had a girlfriend. I replied, "I'll tell her about it and tell her that I'm just being nice to a friend." But, wow, when I saw that pretty little thing, that was it. She had the most beautiful blue eyes, the prettiest turned-up nose, and the cutest butt I'd ever seen. Wow. Gladys and I went together for twenty days. She stayed here and went back, and we got married on Thanksgiving Day, November 28, when I had some time off from Baylor. We have now been married for sixty-five years.

I pray three times a day: when I get up, when I take a nap, and then when I go to sleep. I pray religiously because prayer does do good. I've had my prayers answered so many times. I mean, as ugly as I am, how can I get somebody as pretty as Gladys?

Once, here in Laredo, a survivor from one of the prison camps came to give a talk, and I met with her because they told me, "Hey, we want you to go and see this lady. She was in a concentration camp. She married the guy that freed her, an American lieutenant." I did the same thing at Belsen. The speaker, Helga, knew about that. When she spoke at the local civic center, she asked me to sit at the front because in her speech she says, "I want to mention John Valls is sitting right there, that he was there with me. We didn't know each other, but he was there." She said, "Stand up," and I took a bow and everything. When she pointed me out she stated, "I don't know what his rank was, but to me he's the general." There were about four thousand people there, some very prominent Laredoans. When I came out, they wanted to shake my hand because they knew that I was there.

Valls's father had hopes that John would return to help with the family farm. Valls's dream, however, was to make a university track team. He received scholarship offers from several colleges to run track, including Texas, Texas A&M, Howard Payne, TCU, and Baylor. Valls married Gladys and moved to Waco to attend Baylor University. He experienced considerable success and was named All-Southwest Conference in track in 1949 and 1950. After graduation he played on the Texaco Chiefs basketball team, touring and playing games all around the nation. Along with sports, Valls has had a lifelong passion for writing, publishing several short stories, and building model airplanes, selling many designs to model-airplane magazines. John Valls received the Bronze Star and two Presidential Citations for his service in World War II.

John Valls's interview was part of the Texas Liberators of World War II Concentration Camps Oral History Project, funded by a grant from the Texas Holocaust and Genocide Commission. Copies of all materials were also deposited in the Library of Congress and the four Texas Holocaust museums—Houston, El Paso, Dallas, and San Antonio. See John Valls, *Oral Memoirs of John Valls,* an interview conducted by Stephen Sloan, with videography by Robert DeBoard, March 2, 2012, in Laredo, Texas. BU Digital Collections.

Notes

1. Valls was assigned to the 97th Army Air Force stationed at Central State Teachers College in Stevens Point, Wisconsin. During World War II, College Training Detachments, which prepared candidates for flight-school training, were housed at colleges and universities throughout the United States.

2. Jack Leonard, a tenor, recorded more than two hundred songs with the Tommy Dorsey Orchestra before leaving for military service during World War II. His replacement was Frank Sinatra. See Leonard's obituary from the *Los Angeles Times,* accessed June 30, 2014, http://articles.latimes.com/1988–06–19/news/mn-7647_1_jack-leonard.

3. The Messerschmitt Me 210 was a German heavy fighter aircraft.

4. The British 11th Armored Division is credited with having liberated Bergen–Belsen Concentration Camp on April 15, 1945, pursuant to an agreement with the Germans to surrender the camp peacefully. However, in *Belsen: The Liberation of a Concentration Camp* (New York: Routledge, 1998), 23, Joanne Reilly notes that "survivor testimony makes reference to there being other British troops in the camp before the main liberating body arrived."

HENRY JACKSON "JACK" FLANDERS JR.

Henry Jackson "Jack" Flanders Jr. was born in Malvern, Arkansas, October 2, 1921, and grew up in Little Rock. His life as a youngster centered on playing with neighborhood friends and faithfully attending the Baptist church. He and his best friend, Tommy Bond, enjoyed sitting high in a big oak tree on their street, looking up at the clouds and wondering what it would be like to look down on the top of those clouds from the other side. Thus was born their shared dream of becoming pilots. In his teens Flanders felt called to serve the church as a pastor or missionary, and in 1939 he entered Baylor University in Waco, Texas. By December 7, 1941, he was twenty years old and in love with a girl back home. He was actively engaged in social and service activities at Baylor, was well along in his ministerial training, and served as the pastor of a small, poor, rural congregation near Navasota, Texas.

The news about the bombing of Pearl Harbor on Sunday hit me like a blast. Until that moment, that blooming war was far away to me and my friends, like on another planet. For this to happen at Pearl Harbor just slapped us terribly. I've forgotten an awful lot of things in my life, but I'll never forget that. We were into that war! Oh, how that changed everything for us. The war put me into a bind. I was a ministerial student, but I was also a student pilot. At Christmastime in 1940, the year before the Pearl Harbor bombing, I had told my dad that Baylor had a Civilian Pilot Training Program that I'd just give anything if I could take.[1] I just wanted to fly. I always loved the air. Well, he came up with the money, fifty bucks, which included about fifty hours of flying plus ground school. Across the larger part of the spring quarter, we'd go out to a flying field at Rich Field, in Waco. I learned to fly out there and took ground school on campus.

When you signed that contract to take the Civilian Pilot Training Program, there was a clause down at the close which read just about like this: "In the event the United States finds itself engaged in warfare, I'll volunteer my services." At the time I thought, That'll never happen to us! I got my wings in the spring of 1941, and you know what happened in December. There I was, a ministerial student and a pastor. I'd been ordained, and as an ordained minister I held the 4-D

Baylor men on December 8, 1941, *The Round Up*, 1942. *Courtesy of Baylor University Digital Collections.*

classification, where they had placed ministers. The military couldn't conscript me, a ministerial student, but the war had broken out. Under God, what should I do?

I wrestled with it, and when I got home at Christmas, I met my closest friend across my whole life, Tommy, who had learned to fly at Fayetteville in the spring at University of Arkansas. I decided I ought to go in. So Tommy and I went down to the basement of the post office in Little Rock to get the forms. We found out that we were underage, so we would have to get our parents to sign the forms permitting us to go in. Tommy's dad was dead and had been since he was just a baby. His mother signed his form, and he went in. I went home, and Dad said, "Jack, I tell you what, you go back and finish this quarter, and if you feel the same way, I'll sign it and you can go in." I went back to Baylor, and Tommy would write me from where he was in different California bases, and I'd write him. Then he went overseas to the European Theater.

By the time the close of the quarter in February arrived, I had done a lot of thinking. While talking with my buddies who were ministerial students, not a one of them ever encouraged me to go in. But doggone it, I signed that blooming form! I went on in Baylor over the spring quarter and enrolled in the fall of 1942. I decided I've got to sign up, so as soon as I turned twenty-one, in October, I enlisted in the army air corps. I took my physical exam and passed everything, but we were told that it would likely be six months before we would get called up. Once I finally decided I should enter, I never had one of my friends to put me down. Whether or not I was right in that decision, I will say that I feel comfortable with it. Yet I won't know for sure until I get to the other side.

I stayed in Baylor for the winter quarter, and there was only one more quarter to go before I was to graduate. In early February we who had signed up, about forty or close to fifty, all got orders to report. We were three weeks short of winding up the quarter, and the Baylor president, Pat Neff, said he would give us credit for all the courses we were passing. I had been elected permanent president of the Class of 1943, but I was still one hour short to graduate. My speech professor, Sarah Lowrey, gave me credit for that one hour with Neff's approval, so I was able to wind up my work before I went in. I went home to Little Rock, but a bunch of my friends went down to the Waco railroad station with me and the others who were getting on the same train. They saw us off! That was my departure from Waco. I remember on that train pulling out of Waco, thinking, Man, that's the end of Baylor!

After my visit home to Little Rock, I went to Fort Worth to report for duty. Then we were bused up to Sheppard Field, in Wichita Falls. At Sheppard all of us student pilots from Baylor who got our orders to go into the service on the same day were split up. We'd see one another in the mess hall and other places when we'd get a chance. We had five weeks there that we couldn't even get off the base. From Sheppard Field we went in all directions. I went over to the University of Tennessee, and I was in the eastern command, and others went in various directions. We got split up, and I'd say after we left Sheppard Field I didn't have close ties with any of them. We all just went to the wind, so to speak.

I took basic training for about two months at Maxwell Field, Alabama, and oh, it was rigid training. Had inspections on Saturday morning. Everything had to be in place. If there was anything out of line, even if the inspector would put a finger on the cot there and get dust on his finger, you'd have to spend an hour or two drilling extra on weekends. It was very rigid training, but this rigid discipline was something that, looking back, I realize I badly needed, so it was good for me. It helped prepare me for the future.

We had three steps in flight training: primary, basic, and advanced. I had primary and basic flight training at Malden Field, in southern Missouri, and my advanced training at Spence Field, in Georgia. Throughout the training we had to be inspected, step-by-step physical exams, and we knew they were coming up. One thing I worried about was my left eye. As a kid, I'd had a baseball hit it. I exercised it and, boy, I'd eat a lot of carrots before the exam, but I never had any problem with physicals, nor eye exams. The big thing before you moved to the next level would be your last flight exam when you go up with the instructor and he'd check you out on everything. You passed or you failed. If you failed, you could stay on for a longer period of time, perhaps. It was up to them. You always sweated out those final flight exams. We also had a lot of ground school, but I didn't really worry about that because I'd already had a lot of ground school in navigation and meteorology and so on before. Those flight-training periods I enjoyed because I loved the air, but we'd sweat out the exams and stuff.

Once we got into flight training up in Missouri, we got to fly primary planes, double winged, single engine. I had flown before, but I hadn't flown in planes like those. In the Civilian Pilot Training Program, we had only single-engine and single-wing planes, but it made it a lot easier for me to get through primary flight training. It just so happened that we'd been stood-down for a few days because of weather, and we were needing to begin to log our flight time. There was a field some miles from where we were, but it had a drier landing strip than what we had where the base was. On that morning they needed another plane to be flown over to that other field. There was one instructor and one cadet in each plane, but they needed one other plane. The colonel asked the instructors if there was anybody who had a pilot under him that he felt could fly a plane over there. We hadn't flown many hours then. One of them said, "Yes, I have one." He identified me. So I got out, took off, logged my time in the air, and landed over there. When I went in to land, I had a strong crosswind. When I touched the airstrip—we had narrow wheels—the wing tip touched the ground or the strip, not much, just touch. Any time that happens, the plane can't be flown until it's been checked. I was really in the pits because that happened on that landing. I taxied in, and my instructor was waiting, and he could see the expression on my face. He said, "Flanders, don't sweat it. There were three instructors ahead of you and one that landed behind you, and they all did the same thing." That made me feel a lot better.

That primary flight trainer we flew was a dream! We could just do anything in it. See, you sat in the open air. That was something else that was new. We sat in cockpits on the top of the plane. The things we'd flown before, we were inside the planes in the civilian pilot training. There was no more fun to be found flying than in that primary flight trainer. With those wings, we could do turns of all kinds, and we just had all kinds of fun with it. We felt more like a bird. We were on the outside, looking down. The air there was cold. Oh, it was cold! But still it was a lot of fun to fly. I resisted one temptation there. There's a bridge over a river at Malden. Of course what the guys were tempted to do was fly under that bridge. But they had people in the town who were supposed to report when they saw one of them go under and give the number and the time. I never did do that—that time. But I did later on. Something inside boys that you want to take chances.

About the only instrument we had to help us in navigating was a compass, and we had ground maps. That's what we had, no other help. If you were making cross-country flights, you'd chart your course, then what direction you needed to fly. You'd have to figure the wind direction and the corrections you needed to make. Unless we were following a map in going from town to town, we were flying by instrument, and that was the compass. What we'd do would be to get that plane headed the direction we wanted it to go by the compass. Of course, that compass was dancing. We would try to get the thing set on the course we were to fly, and then we'd look at the horizon and find something out there in the direction we wanted to go, any kind of a marker. If nothing else, maybe a rise of terrain. We wouldn't look at the compass, but we'd fly to that point. It's just another way of flying from the way it is today. Back then a lot of it was flying by the seat of your pants.

While I was stationed up in Missouri, one night I got a call and Dad did the talking. I could tell it was about to kill him to tell me what he was getting ready to tell me. He said, "Jack, I hate to tell you, but Mrs. Bond got word today that Tommy has been shot down over the Netherlands." I remember how upset I was that night and after. I thought, Oh shoot, old Tommy bailed out. We'll hear from him someday. I just figured he'd be a POW or something. Well, they found his body, and it's buried out in Arizona or New Mexico, a cemetery out there. He didn't make it back.

All of my training up to that point was flying and just learning to handle the plane. When I graduated, got my wings and commission, I was kept on as an instructor at Spence Field, Georgia. On that Saturday when we graduated, we were to have our shipping orders posted on the board, with your name and where you were to report in and when. Generally, you had two weeks between getting your commission and the next assignment. My name didn't show up. It bothered me, and I waited until later in the afternoon and went to see my instructor. He said, "Oh, Flanders, we're going to keep you on as an instructor here." That wasn't what I wanted, but that was my assignment, and you have to take your assignment.

I went on to Arkansas, and the following Wednesday I got married and had a honeymoon. At the end of the two weeks, I reported back in and began to instruct pilots and in instruments as well. There was a certain amount of pleasure to it, but I decided that wasn't what I had joined to do. Each morning I would go into the officer in charge and respectfully request transfer to combat. I did that for six weeks, and at the end of six weeks he told me that I had been transferred.

From there I went into preparation for combat. That was a different world. I had to learn how to fly P-40s. That was the first plane I ever took off without having an instructor with me. I flew that for two weeks over at Tifton, Georgia. Then I went to Florida. It was down there that I had to learn gunnery and dive-bombing and strafing. This would be in the summer of 1944. By the way, on the bus going to Eglin Field in Florida, we heard on the radio that D-Day had occurred. I then served time down at Eglin. That was really quite an experience, firing a machine gun. See, they'd pull a mock plane, just a model thing, behind a bigger, real plane, and you'd fly in to shoot it by firing a shell.

Up in Virginia and North Carolina I was flying the P-47. There we did lots of formation flying and dogfights. We'd get in dogfights with F4Us and F4Fs over there in our P-47s. They could whip us in climbing, but our plane had a speed and a strength that they didn't have. It just depended on how you handled it. We did a lot of dogfighting over there with other types of planes. We had ground school all the way through everything.

In the air you had radio communication, and the one in charge would give orders, telling each one, You do this, and you do that, and so on. We learned to fly in formation. Flying in formation for us was four planes in a unit. The leader was followed by two planes on his right side, coming back like an arrowhead, and one plane to his left, behind. In the event of dive-bombing, you'd all get in a row called an echelon. The first one, the leader, would peel off, dive down. At a certain count—it had to do with our speed—you'd fly straight and you'd flip and be going down in sequence toward the ground target. We did a lot of that in training before going over. Then we got our orders to go overseas.

On January 1, 1945, knowing his next assignment was the European Theater, Flanders began keeping a daily diary in a small pocket datebook.[2] *He recorded his activities every day and repeatedly expressed how much he loved and missed his wife, Tommie Lou. Fortunately she was able to visit him for eleven happy days before he deployed. On January 25, Flanders kissed Tommie Lou goodbye at the base gate at eight o'clock in the evening, and at five o'clock the next morning he left Virginia for the deportation base at Camp Kilmer, New Jersey. Five days later, on January 31, he left for Europe on board the RMS* Queen Elizabeth.

We were told that there were twelve thousand bodies on that ship. We were all on the top decks. They didn't have much in the cargo hold.

When there was weather going across, that ship would just weave back and forth because there wasn't a lot of weight in the hold. All the weight was at the top. Because of that, I remember, as we were pulling out of New York and passing the Statue of Liberty, we got orders that we were to move back to the center of the ship to keep from capsizing because everybody was wanting to see the Statue of Liberty from her side of the ship. We ate twice a day on board the ship, and we were well fed. We played bridge and, of course, had a lot of other games going on. This was a British ship, and only the captain of our ship knew the route we would be following. His superiors didn't know. The reason for that was security to keep the submarines from hitting us. He'd chart his own course, and nobody knew where we were going until we got to the other side. He handled the whole thing, and he was boss of the ship.[3]

After we got out of the harbor in New York and into the sea, I don't recall ever seeing another ship. Maybe there was one, but nobody was accompanying us because the *Queen Elizabeth* was about the fastest thing around, unless you were in a military ship itself that was geared for high speed. She traveled on her own, and we were not fired at. We did have one bad storm. I'll never forget that weaving back and forth. There must have been sixteen of us in a small room. The bunks were just stacked one upon the other. You'd get in your bunk, but you had to be careful not to bump your head on the one on top of you. That was just the way it was on the top decks of that ship. The enlisted men were farther down in the ship.

This was my mental vision then as I remember it. In warfare almost everybody at home was doing something to carry on the war: farming, factories, whatever. But the guys on the front, they're the ones doing the job that all the others were working to support and get done. We were to be the arrowhead or the front, the ones to do the job for which all the rest of it was just preparatory and supportive. Just to be out on that front line was where I would like to be. I wanted to be well prepared, trained to do a good job when I got into combat, because that's what the whole thing was about.

The word that best described my feeling was *question,* I'd say. Big question mark. Going by the Statue of Liberty, I bet that most all of us were thinking to ourselves, Wonder how many of us will ever see that thing again? Question mark. All the way through, Will I come back or will I not? When I'd go on a mission, I'd think, Dad-gum it, Jack, put your brain to work! Give it your best! Don't screw up now! But I was living with a question mark.

From their arrival port in Scotland, Flanders and his fellow pilots traveled by train to camp at Hanley, in Stoke-on-Trent, where they waited twelve days for orders. On February 23, 1945, after a few days of sightseeing in London, the group left in the fog for Lunéville, France, to join the 1st Tactical Air Force, a component of the Ninth Air Force. Their specific assignment was the 314th Fighter Squadron, one of three squadrons in the 324th Fighter Group. Their primary duty was to support the Seventh Army, which, under Lt. Gen. Alexander McCarrell Patch and in alliance with the First and Third Armies, was in the fifth month of its arduous march toward the Rhineland. The twenty-four new arrivals in the 314th were replacements for an earlier group of twenty-four pilots, of which only three still survived when Flanders arrived.

It was something I will never forget. My first night in France, I was put on a top bunk in the pilot's quarters at the Château de Lunéville. It was a room just filled with guys bunking there. Just before I went to bed, I found out that the guy who had slept there the night before, who was named Berlin, of all things, had been killed that day.[4] I just stretched out there on the bed and thought, That guy was stretched out right here last night, and he's not around today. Here I am sleeping in his bunk. I wonder who may be sleeping in this bunk after me sometime? Question mark, you see? But you learn not to permit your mind to abide on those things. The questions would come, but then, Now, I've got to do this, that, and the other and not let this get on top of me or it'll have a bearing upon my combat activity.

We had been through all of this training for combat in the States, and after we got assigned over there in Lunéville to the 324th group, we had to unlearn a lot of things we had spent months and months learning to do. You simply do things differently in combat. We learned how to fly in echelon formation and how to make U-turns. You always wanted to keep your plane on balance with the wind and other things. You are always trying to keep the nose straight ahead and not be skidding, sliding in the air. But we learned that when you're pulling up from a target after you've bombed it, you do not want to fly on course. You want the nose of the plane to be going in a direction that you're not actually headed so you'd be at a different direction than your plane indicated. The reason: on the ground, when they are firing at you, they'll fire at you in the direction you're headed. That sort of training you never got in the States, but in preparation for actual combat, learning to do that and to duck was important. You'd do anything you could to keep them from hitting you from the ground.[5]

P-47 Thunderbolts flying in formation. *Courtesy of US Air Force.*

On Saturday, March 3, I flew my first mission, which was across the Rhine. We had been told the target and were heading toward it. All of a sudden I saw, at about one o'clock, a white thing. Oh my, I thought. That's an eighty-eight that exploded out there. It was a long way from me, but I saw it. About that time, boom! my plane bolted up. I didn't have my belt tight enough, and my head hit the top of the canopy. The thought came to my mind, Somebody down there is trying to kill me. It's quite a change in your world. You realize you're what they're wanting to kill. But I didn't dwell upon it. I went through the mission there. When we'd cross the Rhine or get beyond where the front line was—of course, it was still west of the Rhine—as we had it marked in our briefing, and then came cruising back into Lunéville, boy, that was one thankful feeling! I would loosen the oxygen mask and begin singing, "I'm gonna buy a paper doll." That was just a little song I enjoyed singing and just sang it to myself, by George, going home safe.

Between missions we stayed active. We just didn't sit much at all. Now, ping-pong, I did some of that. We'd go out jogging or whatever, but bridge was the big thing because it got your mind on the game. We'd go get briefed early in the morning and then go back and wait to be called, and we'd play bridge. It was a real therapy because it kept our minds on that rather than dreading what the heck we were going to be facing there in thirty minutes or two hours or whatever it happened to be. So we were doing things, and ping-pong was one of them.

I'm not sure they knew I was a minister. I spent evenings in the bar with the guys. That's where they were. They were boozing it up, but I didn't drink with them. They came to respect that. This was another relief at night. Today they don't let commercial pilots fly if they've been drinking, I think, twenty-four hours or forty-eight hours before. But, shoot, getting their minds off of it with the booze at night and then on a mission early the next morning, I never saw any bad effects. But that was a different world of warfare. One night a fellow who had been over there a long while asked me to have a drink, and I said, "No, I don't drink." He said, "Aw, come on, the good guys never go home." I didn't drink with him, but I never forgot what he said. I kept thinking, I wonder if that scamp is right, because we were losing buddies every day, and we never knew who was going to be next.

We'd lose one maybe in a week or four or five days. But one week we really lost a bunch of them. It was eight, I think, by that tally. I just never had a week like that. I recall that from the replacement group that came in ahead of us, not one of them got home. They got killed after we joined them. It was a weird thing. The last one was interesting. He didn't want to go home quite yet. He wanted to wait until a buddy of his could go, but he couldn't stay on the base unless he was in combat, and he was staying on beyond his fifty missions just to wait. He got killed. It's a weird world in which you live. You live so close to death.

Watching pictures of warfare—ground troops, and other things—there is no question about it: We lived in the cleanest warfare that could exist. We had our meals; they weren't luxurious meals, but we had meals three times a day. We had heaters in the room, burning gasoline, but still warm cots. We either got killed or we came back alive. I never saw a pilot come back injured. There were some, but I never saw one. I never saw blood. We did have a German plane that came in and bombed an area close by, and one guy got killed on the ground. But in air combat you either made it or you didn't. That's why I call it the cleanest possible warfare. We'd see those jokers on the ground and what they were going through at times—not often, because we were having to watch for planes. But thinking about it at night when we'd come in, those poor jokers were out there in those blooming holes and whatever they could find, and here we were sitting in this room playing bridge and had a warm fire burning. We could go outside and take a shower in a little room added onto the building there, get a bath, and wash our clothes. We'd get up in the morning, and I remember looking at that cot and thinking, I wonder if I'll crawl back into that tonight.

Easter Sunday was the one day where it really got to me, because we'd been over and bombed a village that had trains in it. We just blew the blank out of it and came back safe. In worship that night, there I was, had had a bite of supper, and we were worshipping together. I thought, My, I wonder what's going on over there in that village, what it looks like after what we did today. After worship was over I didn't let my mind get back on it. You've got to keep looking ahead.

We really missed those of our buddies that didn't come back. That night we just didn't dwell on it too long, but we'd think about them later on. We'd see something in the room or somewhere else: "Oh, so-and-so said this, or he did that, or that belonged to him." We really were careful to make sure that anything that a roommate who got killed possessed, that that stuff was kept together and was sent back to his family. I wrote a few of their families when I could get the address. It was hard to know what to say. Just tell them what great guys they were mostly.

There was one thing that we didn't want to come our way. You see, whoever it was that planned the missions, on up to three missions—maybe four missions, exceptional—had one to three missions all worked out and had it who was to fly in each flight and position. So getting briefed, it's all listed up there. But some guy gets sick; he can't fly. Put another fellow into that place. That's what we didn't want. The reason: if I get killed today on a mission I wasn't supposed to have flown anyhow, it was somebody else's place to die, not mine. If it was our own, that's fine. That was one thing. We all had to do it at times, but we did not like to be a replacement pilot.

When a pilot in our squadron took a hit, mostly I would see them after they had been hit out of marginal vision when you turn and look. But just seeing one actually hit, I don't recall. You see, we were looking straight ahead. You do have your marginal vision, and you've got somebody flying your wing, but you're looking ahead. Or if you're not doing that, you're looking 360 degrees and then up and down to see if there are other planes coming in on your tail or at you. It's strictly concentration once you get into the combat zone.

I lost two buddies one day. This was while we were still staying at the chateau, before we moved out to the cavalry area. I lost two good buddies that I'd gone over with. They were just gone. I'm a walker, and I went out behind the chateau into some woods. The question came to my mind, When's my day coming? I was talking with God, and I said, "God, I don't know if I'll be one of them that'll get home or not," because of all of those that had been in the replacement unit ahead of us, none of them got home. "I don't know if I'll get home or not, but if I do I'm going to give thanks for every day of life I have."

On April 7, on my thirtieth mission, three German jets made feints at us. We had heard about them, and we were on constant alert for them in the air going on a mission. We were trained in a cockpit so our heads were turning back and forth, to the left and right, looking down and then up. All we had to worry about these jets were that they'd come onto our tail. They could come down high from behind us, swoop in on us, and we couldn't see them, or they could come from the ground up, low level and up, and hit us in the tail. If we didn't see them, they had us. It was just that clear cut. But if we saw them, all we had to do was get in a steep bank instantly. They were coming through and firing their shells so fast that they only had just a split second to fire and hit us. As long as we could see them, we didn't worry about them because they just really couldn't hit us because we were at an angle. We did live in the fear of those jets. They were so fast, but they had a short time range with fuel. I'm not sure I'm accurate, but I think they had enough fuel to last them thirty or forty minutes, maybe, in the air; that's all.[6]

Those jets were taking off somewhere in southern Germany and landing. On our missions we were constantly looking to find out where those jets were on the ground and where they were taking off and landing. We were flying over southern Germany and central Germany, and we never saw where they were located. It was amazing because we knew they didn't have a long flight range. All right, the war is over. Some of us were making a trip from Stuttgart, Germany, down to Munich. On the autobahn—their autobahn was the predecessor to our interstate highway—they had double lanes with grass in between. On that autobahn down to Munich we noticed a long stretch on it that was cemented in and painted green. We looked up on the hill in the woods and were able to see where they assembled the jets and pulled them down to put them on a little narrow two-rail track which took them down to the end of that autobahn strip. There they took off and landed. We learned that they had experts in colors, and they'd see that the color on the strip in between was kept the color of the grass at that time of the year. I'm telling you, we were flying over that and we never identified it. You'd just see that wide stretch there.

When you got fifty missions you were supposed to be able to return home, but those ahead of us didn't have a limit like that. I don't remember what the figure was. It was way up. I doubted that I could ever make that many missions because we were losing so many buddies and you don't know when your time is. As long as we were flying every day, we could live with it. When we were stood-down for a few days, the stress built up. By April 30 I reached my forty-eighth and forty-ninth mission, and I just figured, Well, I'm getting close. What if I make it? I just might make it. I really didn't dwell on those things too much, just hoping I could make it.

On May 7, the day the Germans surrendered, I flew my fiftieth and fifty-first missions. See, we were told we needed to fly our missions. The war was not officially over until the next day, so our assignments would be counted as combat missions. We were not to fire unless fired upon. Oh man, that was a different day of flying. After I had flown one mission, I asked to get assigned for another one. Who was going to argue about that? So it just counted, but it didn't matter.

After the fifty-first mission, we did not return to Lunéville but landed at Echterdingen Field, a former Luftwaffe airfield in Stuttgart, Germany. It was a field with a lot of planes. We had bombed and rebombed it I don't know how many times. But we had learned early that they were well armed there. They had bunkers, stacks of dirt and whatever, around the many big eighty-eight weapons. I don't remember how many times I had a mission to there, but I think the first time I went in high, but not real high, over the mountains. There's a range of mountains west of the field, and when we got over them, we'd come in on them. Toward the last, however, we learned so much about them and their armory that we would fly on the deck. I mean we flew right on the ground, at treetop level, and they couldn't pick us up until we came over the hill and then in on them. That caught them by surprise. We were bombing it and damaging the buildings as well as the planes, but we were after the planes primarily. We went in there to live. It was a very strange experience. We weren't fussing about anything then. We'd won. The war was over. We were well cared for there.

At Stuttgart we had a jet. It was there when we took over the field. The war's over. On our field we had a Me 109 Messerschmitt, a Focke Wulf, a jet, and gliders. I had logged my cockpit time in the jet, and I was ready to take off and fly that thing. In the glider we'd be hoisted into the air and just slowly glide around and come in 360 degrees and land that glider back on the field. One guy got a high hoist and he tried to make it a 720-degree turn. He spun in and broke his leg. The next morning we got orders from headquarters: there'd be no more flying of confiscated aircraft. You talk about a fellow being a persona non grata, he was. So I never got to fly that jet.

On May 19 we put on a air show for Charles de Gaulle. We learned he was coming in, so we prepared a good air show. We came in to land, and of course all the troops were dressed up. All Frenchmen were supposed to stand in his presence when he came around. He was riding around the field, enlisted men on one side, officers on the other, and everything was just as elegant as we could make it. We learned this after we landed. A girl was driving his car around for him, and there was a fellow sitting on the bank by himself about halfway out, a civilian, an older man; he was just sitting and watching the show. De Gaulle had the car stop and had that fellow brought to him. He was a Frenchman who had served us when we were in Lunéville before we moved over to Stuttgart, and he had come with us. He was sitting watching the show. De Gaulle had him thrown in jail in Stuttgart. Somebody in our group went and got him out that night, but that's the kind of fellow de Gaulle was. He expected the whole world to stand up to him. So we who were at Echterdingen Field did not have the respect for de Gaulle that a lot of people had.

Leonard C. Lydon was our colonel, and he had been with the group from India. He'd been in India two weeks, across North Africa, all the way through. He had knocked out around two hundred missions. That scamp. Every day his men had to fly he would fly one mission, unless he was sick. That's how he was identified with the men. We admired him. Oh, there's no way to describe it!

The war was over, and we had a ball there on the base at Echterdingen Field. The colonel had managed to have all the nurses that could be found in that area and other ladies to come in. We had one big party, dancing, that evening. It broke up—who knows?—one, one thirty, and he was driving one of the nurses back to her base that time of the night. Driving down the autobahn to the east, going by a little village there on the autobahn, were two American guys—one enlisted man, the other an officer—there at night on the side of the autobahn with their weapons signaling for him to stop. He couldn't know at that time of the night who those guys were, ours or Germans in our uniforms. He had to decide what to do, because the Germans had pulled a number of bad things using our uniforms. These two were out inspecting the power line or telephone line or something for the general. They signaled for him to stop that car. He slows down, gets right there close to them, and guns it. The officer fires in the air. The enlisted man, kneeling on the ground with a machine gun, opened fire at the VW, the car. This is a weird thing. Only one shell hit that car. It came through the rearview window, through the back of his neck, and out his mouth and killed him. The nurse was able to get out to the side. Only one shell.

Here's this fellow who's been through two hundred combat missions, something like that. The war is over. Only one shell. It's just one of those weirdest of all things in life. He was dead. You talk about mourning; that we did. We had this big ceremony for him. We had an air show for him in four groups forming the shape of a diamond, so to speak, and we flew in over his coffin low on the deck with the front point where the first plane would be vacant, right over his coffin.[7]

We decided to make a trip down to Munich to see a big show they were to put on with some people from the States. We went through Augsburg and into Munich. We knew there was a prison camp out there, and we drove off the main road to see what it looked like. There were a few guys still behind the fence. It looked lousy. They were moving them out, but these were the healthier ones and were able to stay behind. I'll never forget looking through that fence at those guys standing there, and going into their living quarters. We went to the place where they burned the bodies of Jews and others. They burned up their bodies. My, the smell of that incinerator! It was a very moving experience. We had been alerted that while the Germans were retreating, they would often retreat behind camps. They would kill off those in the camp rather than have to worry with moving them somewhere else. Our ground troops were trying to get in there so fast that the Germans couldn't kill off those that were in there. They were able to get to Dachau in time to save a lot of them there.

A trip that I took the enlisted men on was a very wonderful experience. I took them from Stuttgart on an R&R trip all the way up to Luxembourg—over into Heidelberg, Luxembourg, and on up into Brussels, Antwerp, and back. There were three of us officers. I had to first make the trip to get it organized, and I was leader of it on the bus up there and back. That was one great experience for me, to see all that country when the war was over. Cologne had been bombed out and just trashed, piled up with debris. The vehicles were driving through, and you couldn't see anywhere and you were just following your road. Trash and debris were piled up on each side, and there'd be an enlisted man there at a crossing to tell you which way to go and direct you where to go. Fortunately, the only damage the Cologne cathedral had was some stained glass windows blown out on one side, but it was kept intact. I learned in that cathedral from a priest that there at Cologne during the war those priests had hidden some Jews in the basement. The beauty of that story of how that Catholic cathedral was hiding out those Jews to save their lives when the priests could have gotten into all kinds of trouble for doing such a thing! It was so strange that that church was not destroyed. When you go back today, it's all a modern setting. When I stand in front of the church, and I have several times, I think of all that mound of stuff that was out there in 1945 on my first visit.

They were taking some of the pilots on to the Orient directly; others were being sent home to prepare to go to the Orient. I had first-lieutenant rank, but I was real close to captain. In wartime the time was contracted by what we called combat duties. I was just short of captain. I just didn't know which I ought to do, go on to the Pacific or what. I was just waiting for orders; that's what it boiled down to.

After some of us went to R&R on the Riviera and came back, we found out that our colonel had picked about ten of us as pilots to go back to the States with him to prepare a new group to go to the Pacific. He was asking each one if we were willing to do it, those he selected. I told him I would. I volunteered to be a pilot leader. We needed to do it. We got the Germans; now we must take the Japanese. The colonel did later tell me, "Why don't you go with me? I guarantee you when we've been in the Pacific one month you'll be a captain." I understood we'd have thirty days' leave at home before getting together with him to form that new group to go to the Pacific.

On July 10, we volunteers left Germany for Paris for processing out. There we learned we would be flying home. On July 16 we left France in a fleet of DC-3s. We made stops in French Morocco, Dakar, Liberia, and Ascension Island. All down both sides inside of the DC-3s they put big fuel tanks. There were little dents in the top of the tank. That's where we sat. They could fly a long, long way, and we were able to make it all the way from Ascension Island to Brazil, seventeen hundred miles, without refueling. From there we flew over the Amazon River to British Guiana and over Trinidad to Puerto Rico. When we took off from Puerto Rico at 6:30 a.m. on July 25, I wrote in my journal, "God be with us now." We'd been flying in the air for two weeks, something like that. We weren't fussing about the delays getting home. We were getting home. Man, when we felt that runway in Savannah, Georgia, under our seats and we were back on our own soil again, it was indescribable.

From Savannah I took a flight to Charleston, where I caught a train to Camp Chaffee, Arkansas. By the way, on the ship going over I started growing a mustache. I kept it all the time I was over there. When I finally got back home, I wanted my wife to see it. The next day I shaved it off! While I was on thirty-day leave—that was in August—the two bombs were dropped on Japan and the war was over.

Looking back on the war, I recall that there is so strange a closeness you can feel to God when you get up in the morning and just don't know whether you'll be back to the bunk that night. It really made a big difference to me when I realized that a lot of dear people suffer and die. It makes you thankful for things. I do believe that's something that taught me to be thankful when you've got a blooming foot problem or back problem or whatever that you can recover from. It's something for which I will ever be thankful.

Following the war, Jack Flanders returned to church ministry. He and Tommie Lou raised two children. He earned his PhD in theology at Southern

Baptist Theological Seminary, in Louisville, Kentucky, and was professor of religion for more than four decades. He taught at Furman University, in Greenville, South Carolina, and at his alma mater, Baylor University. He also taught law ethics at Baylor Law School. He continued preaching while studying and teaching and from 1962 to 1969 was full-time pastor of First Baptist Church, Waco, Texas. And Flanders kept flying! He flew as a member of the air force reserve for a few years, then flew rented planes to keep in practice. While teaching at Baylor, he co-owned a private plane and flew across the US on family and professional trips. Flanders had several opportunities to revisit Europe. Forty years after D-Day he walked again in the woods at Lunéville where he had mourned his fallen comrades. There he remembered his promise and gave God thanks for each day's gift of life.

Jack Flanders shared his life story in twenty-four recorded interviews gathered for the Baylor University Project and the Religion and Culture Project. His third, fourth, and fifth interviews documented his experiences as a pilot from 1941 through 1945. See Henry Jackson Flanders Jr., *Oral Memoirs of Henry Jackson Flanders Jr.*, a series of interviews conducted by David B. Stricklin, September 29, 1988, to January 30, 1990, in Waco, Texas, BU Digital Collections.

Notes

1. The Civil Aeronautics Authority pilot training program sought to create a cadre of available pilots to call into service in case of a national emergency. Initiated by the university president, Pat M. Neff, in 1939 and approved by the board of trustees in 1940, the Baylor program graduated seventy-five student pilots, including Flanders, by summer 1941. Dorothy Blodgett, Terrell Blodgett, and David L. Scott, *The Land, the Law, and the Lord: The Life of Pat Neff* (Austin, TX: Home Place Publishers, 2007), 217.

2. Flanders maintained the journal from January to September 1945 and later transcribed it from the original pocket-sized datebook. See "H. J. Flanders Jr. Log: World War II in Europe," BU Digital Collections.

3. The US Army Air Corps transported pilots, crewmen, and ground personnel — as well as single-engine fighter planes — across the Atlantic by sea in the same large numbers as its ground troops. Their destination was perhaps unknown to troops, but there was only one beginning and ending point for RMS *Queen Elizabeth* in the Atlantic. New York City was the only US port that could accommodate a ship its size, and Gourock, near Glasgow, Scotland, was the only

British deep port beyond the reach of the German air force. US and British destroyers and aircraft protected the ship out of the harbors, but beyond that the *Queen Elizabeth* sailed unescorted. The captain obtained word of the date and time of the ship's departure less than twenty-four hours in advance and received a sealed envelope with the ship's prescribed course only after clearing the harbor. The speedy, zigzag course designed to avoid German torpedoes required shifts of fifty to twenty-five degrees every few minutes. Daniel Allen Butler, *Warrior Queens: The* Queen Mary *and* Queen Elizabeth *in World War II* (Mechanicsburg, PA: Stackpole Books, 2002), 85–87.

4. A. F. Berlin was among forty-one pilots in the 324th Fighter Group killed or reported missing in action in France or Germany between August 28, 1944, and Flanders's arrival on February 23, 1945. Over the next five months, another twenty-two 324th pilots were lost or killed. "Losses of the 324th, March 13, 1943–July 10, 1945," 324th Fighter Group, accessed March 20, 2012, http://www.324thfightergroup.org/324home/html/home-2.html (site discontinued).

5. From 1942 through 1945, the 314th, 315th, and 316th Fighter Squadrons made up the 324th Fighter Group, which was based at Lunéville, France, from January 4 to May 8, 1945. The importance of the specialized pre-combat training for newcomers, like Flanders, is described in James Troy Thompson, "Chapter 12, Flying the P-47" in "Supplemental Comments to the History of the 316th Fighter Squadron 1942–1945," Tales of the 316th, accessed December 9, 2014, http://home.comcast.net/~blueyonder316/JT/JTJChap14.html.

6. German jet fighters destroyed about 150 Allied planes, mostly during the early months of 1945. More than fourteen hundred German jets were built or under construction, but only about two hundred were in operation before war's end, and half of them were lost in combat. Alan J. Levine, *The Strategic Bombing of Germany, 1940–1945* (Westport, CT: Praeger, 1992), 184–85.

7. Col. Leonard Clair Lydon died on May 25, 1945, having served as commander of the 324th Fighter Group since December 25, 1943. An eyewitness described the "35-ship fly-by" as "perfectly done and perfectly timed with the lead slot empty and every P-47 tucked in tight and steady." James Troy Thompson, "Chapter 14, V. E. Day" in "Supplemental Comments to the History of the 316th Fighter Squadron 1942–1945," Tales of the 316th, accessed June 30, 2014, http://home.comcast.net/~blueyonder316/JT/JTJChap14.html.

HANNIBAL "DOCTOR JOE" JAWORSKI

Hannibal Jaworski was born in Halle, Germany, on April 19, 1902, to parents of Polish and Austrian ancestry. When he was a few months old, his parents immigrated to the United States through Ellis Island and settled in Central Texas. He learned the values of education and hard work from his father, a pastor in German Evangelical churches. From childhood on, Jaworski worked to earn his books, tuition, and living expenses as he progressed through high school, college, and medical school. He graduated from the Baylor College of Medicine in 1926 and spent the next four years in Waco as intern and resident at the Central Texas Baptist Sanitarium, later renamed Hillcrest Baptist Hospital. Known affectionately as "Doctor Joe," he then joined a local clinic in Waco as junior surgeon and soon saved enough money to open his own private clinic. Devoted to continuing his medical education, he did postgraduate work in the 1930s under some of the best surgeons in the United States, Canada, and Great Britain. His studies in Vienna, Berlin, and Munich placed him in position to witness the effects of Nazi persecution on the lives and work of renowned Jewish physicians. He was in Vienna in March 1938 on the day when the Third Reich annexed Austria, his mother's beloved homeland.

In December of 1941 I was in Waco visiting one of my very dear patients and friends. While we were sitting at the dinner table, the message came from President Roosevelt that Pearl Harbor had been attacked. This surprised us tremendously. We were both sad and mad. Of course, within a few days the news came that America was mobilizing. We needed lots of help, especially in the medical branch of service, so four of us decided to go to Fort Worth to the doctors' induction center and apply. We drove up there and signed in, and we were told that we would soon hear.

My very dear friend Dr. Herschel Connally was very much surprised that I had signed up, as I was nearly forty years old and had the biggest, largest practice in Waco. "Let some of the younger men go first," he said. I objected to this and told him I had made up my mind and promised my dad that if my country needed me that I would serve, no matter what the consequences or what the sacrifice. In the meantime my brother, Leon, also had applied, in the judge advocate's department, and he was getting ready to leave.

It was July before I got a call. I had wired the adjutant general and told him that I was ready to go, had my house in order, and I had been waiting for several weeks for an order. I remember the telegram from the adjutant general's office telling me to report to William Beaumont General Hospital, in El Paso. I got everything arranged and left, signed in at William Beaumont General Hospital for indoctrination, and was assigned to the general surgery section. Later I became the head of the general surgery section at the William Beaumont Hospital and awaited further orders to go overseas. I was qualified for overseas duty. I was checked and rechecked, and a special investigation was made. I was told to get everything ready and keep my suitcase packed so I could leave in a few minutes' notice to be flown to a European Theater as surgical consultant. I waited for days after days after days, and it became a little bit monotonous.

Finally, one day I was called in to the head of William Beaumont General Hospital's office by Colonel Edwards. He told me, "Colonel Jaworski, we have the greatest news for you, and we are so proud of you and so proud of your assignment." I thought that I would get some large assignment in Europe. I had nothing but Europe on my mind. I asked him, "Where am I going, and when am I going?" He said, "You're leaving as soon as you can get ready, and you're going to be assigned to the surgical service at McCloskey General Hospital."[1] I didn't know where McCloskey was, so after a few minutes, I said, "Well, where is McCloskey General Hospital?" He said, "It's being built. It's going to be the largest surgical hospital of the army." I said, "Well, where?" He said, "At Temple, Texas." I came as close to fainting as I ever did in my life, and finally after a breath or two, I said, "Colonel Edwards, Temple, Texas, is only thirty-five miles from where I live." He said, "I don't care where it is. Colonel Jaworski, you should be proud that you have been assigned to this enormous hospital which we're building. We're going to cut orders and let you leave and get started because the thing is just barely on the ground."

I left William Beaumont General Hospital, stopped at Waco for a few hours, and went to Temple. Nothing but mud roads and half of one building was there, and that was McCloskey General Hospital. I started from the bottom, and we built McCloskey General Hospital through nothing but hard work and sheer fortitude. Later, many buildings were added, and it was a wonderful institution. We had the finest equipment, the finest personnel, and I was our chief of surgery from 1942 to 1945.

I was told that we had orders from the surgeon general to take care of the deliveries of some of the combat soldiers' wives that were stationed at Camp Swift.[2] General James A. Bethea was head of the entire organization at the 8th Service Command. I said, "General Bethea, we don't even have the rooms ready." He said, "Well, in the army we tell you to get them ready." He was a very kind man and one of my dearest friends, later. I said, "General Bethea, we have no instruments. We have nothing." He said, "That's up to you. My order is for you to get ready so they can be taken care of." I couldn't think what to do. Real quick, I remembered I could go to Waco. All my instruments and everything were still at Hillcrest Hospital, and they would be kind enough to help me. I called them. They said, "Sure, Doctor Joe, come on. We'll get everything ready for you." I said, "Get everything ready for a complete delivery, and a few extra instruments. I don't know what I'm going to do." I hadn't delivered anyone since my first experience with the clinic in 1930. I came to Waco and took all the instruments I could, all the equipment I could, and got back to Temple at about two o'clock in the morning. In the meantime I looked over all my members of my staff, probably around one hundred and twenty, and one of them, I found out, was an obstetrician and gynecologist. We delivered our first baby within just a few hours after I brought the instruments, and no one was prouder than General Bethea. They immediately wired the surgeon general that we had our first delivery at McCloskey.

I started early ambulation in McCloskey General Hospital with the okay and the blessings of General Bethea. We had received many hernia operations and many other operations. We got them up, if possible, the very next day. The rule and the instructions were that they must stay in bed a week, then go home for a week or two and recuperate. Then, after about a month, they could come back and we'd start the training all over again. I really don't have any evidence of early ambulation being instituted in any of the larger hospitals, and I remember when I studied at several of the larger institutions, I did not notice any early ambulation. This was, I believe, sort of a project of my own, a belief of my own, which was encouraged later by several of my good friends, by my associates, and especially General Bethea. He and I believed very strongly in early ambulation, and it was very fine for me to have a man of his caliber to stand behind my early thoughts and my early beliefs.

It had become of interest to me when I used to work on the animals in experiments at medical college in 1927 and '28, and I kept good records on it. Later, when I was operated on for appendicitis in 1934, I did not want to stay in the hospital and got up and walked soon after surgery. On the fifth day I went back in the operating room and started assisting and operating on county patients and city patients. That taught me a great lesson. I began to talk and practice early ambulation. My patients were the happiest ones on the hall. If I could make it a little easier for them or a little better for them or help them in any way, I felt that this was my purpose. I had the opportunity at the McCloskey Army Hospital to practice it. Later on we had an outstanding meeting, invited all the doctors from all over the area that could come, and we gave them a talk on early ambulation, early care, early movement, and the use of elastic stockings, which I also started. It was very well received at McCloskey General Hospital, and we saw the evidence and a wonderful esprit de corps there and the good feelings of the men that we operated on who were allowed to be up the next day or the third day and could move about and not stay in bed.

Of course, at first we met a lot of resistance by some of the higher-ups. Surgeon General Norman T. Kirk came to see us. He made rounds with me.[3] He was a former orthopedic surgeon. He was very much pleased until we came to some of the orthopedic wards, especially the surgical ward. He would visit with the boys. They were very friendly. He was a very hard, rough-talking, strict general. He asked two or three of the boys, "When were you operated on?" They said, "Yesterday." He said, "What? Yesterday?" They said, "Yes, yesterday." He immediately turned to me and said he wanted to talk to me. He said, "What are you doing? You should have read the orders that they should stay in bed for at least a week." About that time, General Bethea spoke up and said, "Colonel Jaworski has started an early ambulation here at our hospital with my consent. You would be surprised at the happiness that these boys have shown by being able to get up and move about." He said, "Orders are orders, and my orders have not been rescinded." Later on, General Bethea took General Kirk by the obstetrics and gynecology ward. One or two of the patients had deliveries the day before or the night before, and they were already up. They told him how much better they felt and how happy they were, and they were so thankful that they had a chief that would allow them to do this.

Later on he told General Bethea, "We have to get this young surgeon out of here. His ideas have not proven at all." Of course I shook in the boots. General Bethea was very kind and talked to General Kirk a long time and said, "This young man has really developed something of which we are very proud. I wish you could stay a week and just see how well these boys do that are really sick, how well they get up, how happy they are, and how happy they are to get home and come back." To make a long story short, after he threatened to send me off, get rid

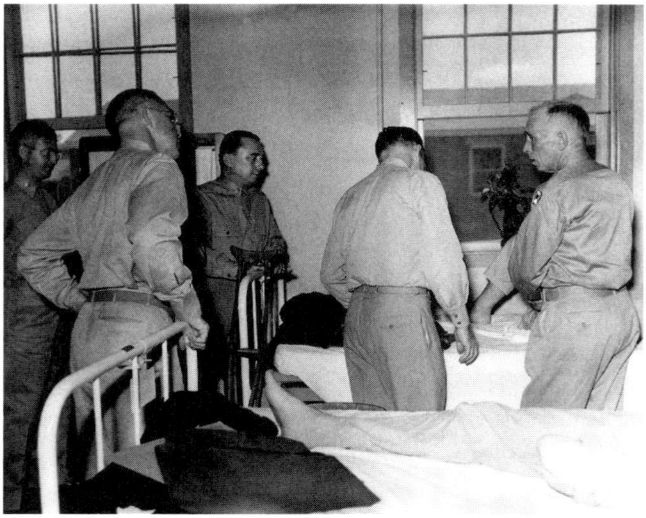

Maj. Gen. Norman T. Kirk, Surgeon General of the United States (far right) visits recuperating soldiers at McCloskey General Hospital in August 1943. Col. Hannibal "Joe" Jaworski (middle) pays rapt attention. *Courtesy of The Texas Collection, Baylor University.*

of me, he rescinded and wrote the orders that we must start early ambulation on all of our patients. I think, knowing Surgeon General Kirk, being a man of vast experience and also a man who believed in new ideas, that he began to study this problem, and when he saw the good results, he was proud to start this program then in the large hospitals. This was part of my greatest success while in the army.

Then I experimented with penicillin a year or so while I was at McCloskey. We were designated by the surgeon general to be one of the hospitals to study the use of penicillin. Penicillin was brought to us from England. It was first discovered by Dr. Alexander Fleming, who did not have all of the facilities to study it, and the English, when the war broke out, were unable to further study the use of penicillin. They contacted America and designated a pharmaceutical company to make penicillin and ship it to us in an armored car, under protection, and we were designated, then, to try it. I remember so well that we started with very small doses, maybe five or ten units. Then, of course, we began to study bigger doses and bigger doses. We had to be extremely careful for reactions. We had to carry the antidote with us to use in case of a reaction and carefully instruct all doctors in its use and how to prevent reactions and, if they did occur, how to treat them.[4]

We did a tremendous amount of work at McCloskey. We served the local camps, Camp Swift and some of those nearby, but we received many transfers from nearly all over the different areas of the United States. Later, when evacuation procedures became easier, we received nearly all of the evacuees from the European theaters, as many as we could handle in the surgical field. Many times we would have twenty, thirty, or maybe even more planes land at Temple airport during the day and some even late in the evenings, bringing in casualties directly from the small field hospitals, and we were able to take care of them. The order for the field hospital was do as little as possible. If it had to have a lifesaving procedure, to go ahead and do that, but temporize, or temporarily do as much as you think is necessary and then immediately obtain and induct transportation. It was a very fine arrangement and very well carried out. It turned out to be a lifesaving procedure when we could get to some of these severely injured people so early after the initial procedures had been attempted or done, and that we could go on and proceed to take care of them.

Our organization and care was tremendous, and our mortality rate was absolutely remarkably low. The boys that we saved and the boys that we took care of and the boys that would leave McCloskey recovered was really a remarkable experience. When you think of five or six thousand people being taken care of and a mortality rate very low, you feel like the entire personnel worked awful hard and did the right thing at the right time to take care of the lives of those young boys. We would receive the wounded direct from the battlefields of Europe by air transportation, sometimes as many as forty or fifty planes a day. We took care of them the best we could. We received three presidential citations and were complimented by the surgeon general.

In May of 1945 the surgeon general said they needed someone to organize a group of hospitals in the Philippines, where the casualties were expected to be extremely high.[5] That's when I received my assignment: I was to leave McCloskey, fly to Dallas to take a plane to San Francisco, and be flown out to the Philippines the next morning. I left McCloskey, and they were really sad and disappointed to see me leave. I was extremely honored to be the head of the surgical service. We all were proud to work together in our organization and achieve our goal. The officers' and the patients' relationships were the finest. I was given a farewell dinner and ceremonies by all my officers, and after the dinner I left for San Francisco and registered in a hotel there to await my flight to the Philippines.

During the night I thought we had a thunderstorm, which the clerk told me later it wasn't a thunderstorm but a light earthquake. I checked on my plane flight to the Philippines and was told it had left the night before. Arrangements were made for me for further assignment to an army camp close by, Camp Beale. It was hot and dry. I had fifty medical officers who I would have to take to the Philippines. Later I had to show that I could use a rifle. I was feeling rather bad with high fever from inoculation shots, but I made it through the rifle range, scored perfectly. The rifle man told me I had to shoot a pistol also. I told them I really did not feel like doing this and left. I passed the examination. I was issued a pistol, and I was ready to leave when orders were issued we would leave by ship.

Early one morning we were told to get ready. I assembled the officers under my command that I was to take over, all casualty experts, and we lined up to enter the ships. They played "Sentimental Journey." I never will forget that. We boarded the ship, and I was ordered by the commander that I outranked all officers and would be in command. I told him I couldn't care less. I arranged a place where the officers and I could have daily meetings to get better acquainted. I told them what was expected from us. All the officers were extremely nice and cooperative.

We expected trouble from the Japanese submarines which had surrounded the Philippine Islands, and so we had to go by way of Australia. Life on ship was quiet, the food was fair. I met some of the other officers up on deck. I remember one time I made a bad mistake prior to landing by calling the ship a boat. I gradually learned the use of the navy vernacular and made a good sailor. We finally approached Manila, but due to the Battle of Manila we were unable to proceed and had to go to Batangas, about sixty to ninety miles further.[6] This was most difficult.

We finally arrived at Batangas. We could not unload directly, so we had to put in to get to the shore in boats. Part of the way we had to wade through the water to get to the shore. From there we slowly made our trip to a small field hospital located close by. I was very fortunate because the executive officer of this field hospital was one of my former McCloskey General Hospital associates. He was very glad to see us. Food rations were very low, though, and Manila and the Philippines had nothing but K-rations. We were told to make ourselves at home. We were delighted to do this as we had walked for some time to get to this field hospital, and we were tired and hungry. We stayed there a day or so, and the executive officer asked me if I had come to replace any of their personnel. After I told them that I had a group of medical officers and we were making our way to Manila to take over some of the executive offices there and that I was to be surgical consultant[7] for the Pacific Theater, he realized that he would not be replaced or any of his men would be replaced. So he very quietly, in a nice tone, told me that we would have to move as their rations were so low. We would have to make our way to Manila.

We finally arrived outside of Manila in what they call the mesa, and I was told that they had an old, partly destroyed building which were the colonels' or high-ranking officers' headquarters, and I could go there while my men would have to stay in tents at the mesa. I did not like this very much, so I decided to stay with my men. We unloaded and made ourselves as comfortable as we could in the tents. That night a terrible monsoon arrived and our tents were flooded. Part of the tents were blown away, and I remember well that I had to place all of my equipment and my locker up high as the water was rushing through my tent. At early dawn I could barely see what was going on. I heard a small frog making quite a noise, and I located him sitting on my locker. I thought that he was probably my guardian angel, so I left him there. Later on, some of the men arrived in trucks, and I was moved to the colonels' or higher-ranking officers' quarters.

I was assigned to reorganize the 4th General Hospital. The 4th General Hospital was in what had been the Japanese general headquarters until General Yamashita was run out of Manila [in March 1945]. Before the Battle of Manila the Japanese had taken over the harbor and city of Manila. Our infantry and several divisions of our army crossed the river at Manila and destroyed most of the headquarters of the Japanese and Philippine army and had them cornered up behind the old walls of Manila. I was told that they had used the 110 mm cannons and were shooting pointblank at the remainder of the Japanese army. Finally, the remainder fled towards Baguio.

The equipping and repair of our hospital area took quite awhile, but we progressed very nicely. The casualties were coming in rather rapidly, and we had many men injured or contaminated with infections. We also had quite a number of men with hepatitis, and we were trying to get them out of Manila as soon as we could. Hepatitis is very hard to treat in a generalized war hospital or army hospital, and we realized that to save the boys we should ship them in to the mainland as quick as we could, or to Hawaii, where they could be treated. This we accomplished with very little loss, and I was very proud that we could take care of these boys. We organized the 4th General Hospital into a very nice hospital unit. It was the largest hospital unit in the Philippines. The Far Eastern Air Force Command had a very nice place organized at Clark Field, and I was also consulting surgeon for FEAF. The progress was, like I said, extremely difficult, but we progressed very well. We had the hospital and hospital units in our different areas of convalescence in good condition, and we were able to take care of the boys in a superior manner.

We had quite an experience in reorganizing and re-evaluating the areas which we could use for our own soldiers and our own casualties. Later a group of Australian prisoners, former prisoners of war, were shipped to Manila, and we took care of them on their way to Australia. We did not receive too many Japanese prisoners of war in Manila. We had quite a number of them which we didn't have much privilege to treat as they were usually put into compounds, where they were taken care of by the military as prisoners, although we were in constant communication with them and took care of the ones that really needed attention.

We had many incidents that happened. Some were harsh and terrifying. On a trip between the hospitals, we were shot at by sniper fire. Later on, of course, the snipers were totally annihilated. Many of them were captured; many of them were killed. We had a group of Japanese prisoners that had to clean up the area around our general hospital. One time one of them struck a field mine with his garden tool or hoe. It exploded and part of his legs were removed, and the rest of the Japanese would just keep on working, left him lying there. One of our men saw it and ran over there and picked him up and carried him into the hospital, and we took care of him. I often wondered how cold-blooded these people were and how little respect they had for human life, but I imagine that was their teachings and their beliefs. They were not afraid of danger. They were not afraid of losing their lives. They had a philosophy of life that was absolutely, totally indifferent to death or to danger or to suffering.

We had many incidents of torture and cruelty that happened from Japanese that were still in the islands. I was at Clark Field one time and the pygmy tribe brought in a Japanese sniper that they had shot out of a tree. These Japanese would tie themselves up high in a tree and wait for the American soldiers or American officers, especially an American high-ranking officer, to go by, and then they would kill him. These pygmies watched them as they tied themselves in the tree and, as they were expert climbers, they waited until this Japanese soldier or sniper, through exhaustion, would go to sleep, and then they would crawl up the tree and shoot him with a poison arrow. They'd untie him and quite often would bring the body to some of us or some of the headquarters and ask for a peso in money for them. I soon realized that sometimes they brought the same body back four or five times to get four or five pesos! I got along fine with them. In fact, they gave me a few arrows to take home.

I had a chance to go to Corregidor when they were getting rid of the Japanese occupation of Corregidor. As we went towards Corregidor, I was shown an area just outside of the islands where the Japanese had dumped millions and millions of Filipino pesos which they had acquired in their capture of Manila. They had put them on barges and dumped them into the sea so the American army and navy wouldn't get hold of them. Later, divers went down and recovered most of them. I still have one of them that they gave me as a souvenir.

Life in Manila was hard. We did the best we could. I finally was moved into a small house with Colonel Worrell, the commanding officer in Manila, and he and I shared this small house together. The walls were all rather air conditioned by bullet holes, but it was a place to stay and a place to sleep.

Food was scarce and hard to obtain. We lived on K-rations the first weeks, which were extremely hard on most of us. The Far Eastern Air Force Command at Clark Field, after we had fairly well organized ourselves in Manila, would fly some steaks and hamburger meat and lettuce and tomatoes and a few things from Australia. They would call us and tell us to come over as soon as we could so they could serve us steak, which was absolutely nonexistent in Manila. We'd drive sixty miles in a jeep, over shot-up areas and territory, finally arrive, and the steaks were always gone. I finally told one of the officers in charge that I hoped that I would treat them better when I was the consulting surgeon than they treated me with their food! But we were glad to obtain whatever we could.

One time we brought some lettuce and tomatoes home, no meat. I put it in the refrigerator, which I had obtained from the many large depots of supplies that were shipped into Manila for organization of the hospitals which we were supposed to organize to take care of the casualties resulting from the combat it took to conquer Japan, which later, of course, we did not use. We obtained one of those, and we put our supplies in this refrigerator, hoping the next day we could have some fresh vegetables with our meals. My commanding officer always slept with a burp gun under his pillow, and I slept with my .45 under the pillow. Many times I would get up at nights and work, especially when I couldn't sleep or my back would bother me. I would go and relieve the officer in charge at nights and operate most of the night and then also the next day. That night I was rather tired and went to sleep. I locked the screen door, it was just so hot, and locked the doors in front. When I woke up the next morning, I noticed the doors were unlocked. I went straight to the refrigerator and all our food was gone. We had slept through while a man had slipped in, taken all of our supplies, and went out, without us even noticing or hearing him. I thought what a folly it was to keep all the guns under the pillow when you didn't even wake up to see the thief or hear the thief!

We finally organized ourselves well enough. I had a small office in the hospital. I had several of the Filipinos work for me, some of the professors of their Santo Tomas University who we employed in our organization, and most went very well. When the bomb exploded and we knew that the war was nearly over, it became just a matter of organization and taking care of the casualties the best way we could and getting them home as fast as we could. The Filipino people, especially the educated ones, were extremely easy to get along with. They were so anxious to help us, as they felt that we were their saviors.

Of course later, after the bomb, MacArthur then wanted to repay his respects back to Manila and his love for Manila and the Filipinos, and he ordered that most of the food that we could spare and some of the food that we wanted for ourselves should be given to the Filipino people. He ordered that as many of the new jeeps as possible should be given to the Filipino people, and we could see them ride along or pass us in one of the new jeeps while we were still driving the old jeeps. He was very fond of the Filipinos, and he bent double backwards in giving them whatever he could, even if it handicapped, to some extent, the improvement in our condition in the Philippines.

I remember so well when Yamashita, the Japanese general who had fled [Manila in March 1945] with probably sixty thousand of his men towards Baguio, finally decided, due to our surrounding them and not allowing any food to come in and slowly starving them, that he would surrender. He marched with what was left of his army and people under his command and people who had joined the Japanese army in fleeing from Manila back to Baguio [in September 1945] and gave up. It was the most horrible sight that I hope I will ever see: thousands of people starving to death, very many of them unable to walk and being carried as best they could — Japanese soldiers, Japanese nurses, children, and some foreigners who had joined in fleeing from Manila.[8]

I obtained as many cots as we could, and we kept them out on the mesa. We took care of them as well as we could. Often two and three hundred would die overnight out of the probably forty or fifty thousand that returned. We had to put the Japanese medical personnel in charge of them. They could handle them and had been handling them in Baguio. I would make my rounds in the morning, and I'd see that some of the Japanese sick had been removed, and I would question them about them. They would tell me through an interpreter that they

Japanese Gen. Tomoyuki Yamashita in prison during his trial, in late 1945. *Courtesy of National Archives and Records Administration.*

found the sick unable to get out of bed to take care of themselves, so they clubbed them to death. I immediately left orders that this had to stop and anyone caught doing this would be court-martialed and shot.

The Japanese commander-in-chief, Yamashita, was put in the New Billibid Prison. He was kept there for later court-martial. I remember many times I would go by and see him, visit him, and check the New Billibid Prison, which was part of my command. He would, through his interpreter, want to talk to me, and he begged me on several occasions to please not allow them to hang him, but to rather execute him by shooting him because then his soul would be free to join the ancestors. If he were hung, he would be treated like a criminal, his soul would never be allowed to be accepted by his forefathers or his ancestors. He offered me his gold watch. He offered me the epaulets and his insignias. I told him I couldn’t do a thing, that it was against the court-martial proceedings and it was against the army rules and regulations, that I could not accept anything, but I would take care of him until the day that the court-martial trial was over and they would decide what to do with him. He later was hung by the army. I felt sorry for him, but I knew that he had also been a very hard, torturous type of general and that many American boys were tortured and treated very severely under his command of the Japanese army. Before he died he gave me a Japanese bill, paper bill, and signed it and thanked me for everything I had done for him.[9]

Close to Christmas [1945] I decided if possible to do something nice for my officers. I knew my secretary, a former professor at the University of Manila, would help me plan some nice surprise. We finally decided on a chicken dinner. We had lived and dined mostly on K-rations. The Filipinos were known for their fighting roosters, as most of them had one or two or more and would have regular cockfights, betting heavily on them. We both hoped to buy some whose fighting days were over, and we succeeded. He took them to our mess hall and turned them over to our Chinese chef. The day of the dinner arrived, and I could hardly wait for them to serve our surprise. The Chinese chef and helpers brought in the fried chicken. Everybody cheered. I soon noticed, though, that nothing but thighs and drumsticks were on the plate. I immediately called the Chinese chef. He appeared, and in no uncertain tones, I asked him, "Where is the white meat, the breasts?" After a few minutes' silence, and his head bowed, he said, "We were hungry, and we ate all the breasts." Being chief of the court-martial board, my first thought was to have him and his crew executed, but my kindness overcame my grief and disappointment. We laughed to ourselves and ate the chicken. We had some sad moments and we had some happy moments, but we made the best of it.

My personnel worked hard day and night to take care of the casualties, and I had things well in hand. I was told that I would be possibly ordered to Seoul, Korea, to open up a large hospital there to take care of some of the casualties. Soon after that, though, I was told that the Russians had blocked the harbor of Seoul, and we would not be allowed to send a hospital ship in. We would not be allowed to embark. After I found out that I could not go to Seoul, and my work at Manila had progressed so well, I then asked if I could not be sent home. I went to the headquarters to apply for a relief of duty, and a Colonel Stewart came over to interrogate me, looked at me for a minute, and he said, "I have orders not to grant you this request, but I'm going to grant it anyway. You probably don't remember me, but I was one of your students at Baylor College of Medicine. If it hadn't been for you, I never would have become a doctor. Many times I was at the time of quitting, and you would talk to me and help me pass my courses. So today I'm going to do something for you. I'm going to sign your release." Well, that was really a joy to me, as I had served as long as I could. I was not feeling too good. I had lost probably forty pounds or more, and I needed some better food and better care. I had developed duodenal ulcers, and I felt like I should take care of myself. He signed my request and told me that I would get my orders in a few days, and I would be flown back to the States.

When I came back from the Philippines, my dearest friend during my army days, General Bethea, head of the 8th Service Command Medical Corps, insisted that I stay with the medical corps and go with him to Japan. He was ordered to take over the organization of the medical corps and hospitals in Japan after Japan had surrendered to the United States. He talked to me several times about it and assured me that if I'd go to Japan with him, he'd see to it that I was well taken care of in the medical corps, both as far as assignment was concerned and also promotion. I thought of it many times, worried about it, but I finally decided, after I had returned to Waco and started again, that I was happy that I did not go with him to Japan.

Many things were changed during the war. If any good came out of a war it was the improvement in medical care and surgical care and procedures and attempts at saving lives. We were able to introduce programs and care of patients with diseases, sicknesses, also injuries, which were new to our profession. Improvements were made especially in surgical procedures and in anesthesia. I believe that the greatest improvements in anesthesia were developed during the war, in closed intratracheal type of anesthesia especially. We were able to operate on pulmonary conditions and chest injuries under closed types of anesthesia which were hardly heard of before World War II. The operation on injuries to the brain was also perfected, which later on saved many lives. Our treatments of lung injuries and chest injuries were perfected to such a way that we were able to save many lives. Our treatments of empyema, a pus infection of the chest cavity and the lung, were perfected in such a way that it was a common thing to get these people well, and many of them died before. We had nothing for pneumonia before the war except for a trial rabbit serum and things like that, which many times did not work. But after the use of penicillin, many cases of pneumonia were saved before they ever got into any difficulties. Many other infections, like osteomyelitis and infections of the bone or infections of soft tissues as well as other tissues, were treated, and the results were tremendous. Use of penicillin in the treatment of venereal disease was like a big eye-opener. Many of the dreaded diseases and dreaded infections—strep throat, meningitis, postoperative complications—were completely removed.

I did not have to go into the war. But as a young child and then a youngster, my father would tell us, "If you can ever do anything for our country, you must do it, as they were good to us to let us come here." He also impressed us that if the good Lord gave you something that you can do and return to your fellow man, or an ability to do something for your fellow man, or an ability to relieve the suffering, that you must do it whether there's any involvement concerned for reciprocation or not. That is what you must do. This impressed us ever since we were youngsters.

And it was, to me, an opportunity to do something for our country. I have never regretted it. I've been proud to do it. I was very proud to receive citations, commendations, medals for what I had done, although they did not amount to a thing as far as I was concerned. I was happy within my heart to know that I did something for my government and I repaid, in a small way, the opportunity that this country has given our family. That's the way I felt about it. My brother, Leon, felt the same way. We often talked about it. We often gratefully acknowledged the fact that we carried out what our daddy wanted us to do. I'll always think that when you do something in return, and later on know that you did the right thing, that it makes you feel good. It's just a feeling of satisfaction. All the bitterness that you might have had or encountered, all the sadness you might have encountered, all the sacrifice that you encountered doesn't amount to much at all. Time takes care of all that.

In 1946 Colonel Joe returned to his life as Doctor Joe, practicing as a general surgeon in Waco, Texas. In 1948 he married a former patient, Madge McReynolds, and they enjoyed thirty-seven years of marriage before her death in 1985. Both Jaworski and his wife became well-known golfers and big-game hunters. Jaworski never gave up his quest to aid people in need. In November 1950 he pulled two fishermen to safety when their boat capsized in Lake Waco during a storm. For his bravery he was awarded the Carnegie Hero Award. When a massive tornado struck downtown Waco on May 11, 1953, Jaworski called upon the skills he had learned in wartime medicine to help organize the hospital's emergency response. He received many honors throughout his career, including distinguished alumnus awards from both Baylor University and Baylor College of Medicine. He established the Jaworski Society for planned estate gifts at the medical college and endowed a scholarship to help support graduates of the university who attend the medical college.

Dr. Joe Jaworski shared his life story in ten interviews contributing to the Waco-McLennan County Project. His experiences in World War II appear in the third, fourth, fifth, and sixth interviews. See Hannibal (Joe) Jaworski, *Oral Memoirs of Hannibal (Joe) Jaworski,* a series of interviews conducted by Daniel C. Lyman, November 10, 1989, to June 17, 1990, in Waco, Texas, BU Digital Collections.

Notes

1. Originally named for Maj. James A. McCloskey, the first regular army physician killed during World War II, the hospital was activated on June 16, 1942, and turned over to the Veterans Administration in May 1946. In 1979 it was renamed for Congressman Olin E. Teague. Ida Jo Marshall and Cheryl Ellis Vaiani, "Olin E. Teague Veterans Center, Temple," *Handbook of Texas Online*, Texas State Historical Association, accessed October 30, 2013, http://www.tshaonline.org/handbook/online/articles/sboak.

2. Camp Swift, located about sixty-eight miles south of Temple, was also new in 1942. It became Texas' largest army training center during World War II. Art Leatherwood, "Camp Swift," *Handbook of Texas Online,* Texas State Historical Association, accessed June 27, 2014, http://www.tshaonline.org/handbook/online/articles/qbc27.

3. General Kirk visited McCloskey in August 1943. Photographs of his visit and other special events at McCloskey from 1942 through 1945 are available in the Hannibal "Joe" Lucas Jaworski Papers, The Texas Collection, Baylor University.

4. The US wartime Office of Scientific Research and Development contracted with both commercial and academic laboratories to refine penicillin under a secrecy pact with Britain after its first successful use in patients in England in 1941. Throughout the war, as researchers continued to experiment with penicillin and develop antidotes for allergies to it, hundreds of thousands of Allied and US troops received the drug. By war's end, US drug manufacturers had captured the majority of the world's penicillin production. David Wilson, *In Search of Penicillin* (New York: Alfred A. Knopf, 1976), 14–15, 205, 271.

5. Preparing to care for casualties that would come in the planned invasion and occupation of Japan required a massive buildup of medical personnel, facilities, and supply lines in the Philippines through the late spring and summer of 1945. See Mary Ellen Condon-Rall and Albert E. Cowdrey, *The Medical Department: Medical Service in the War against Japan* (Washington, DC: Center of Military History United States Army, 1998), 418–25.

6. The Battle of Manila concluded in March 1945, several months before Jaworski's arrival, but the Japanese had left the city in ruins. Pockets of Japanese troops were still in the area doing all they could to distract

the Allies and delay their plans for invading Japan. Stanley Falk, *Liberation of the Philippines* (New York: Ballantine Books, 1971), 157.

7. Surgical consultants were senior physicians who managed the selection of surgeons and their assignments to the various medical units, supervised compliance with established surgical procedures, updated surgeons on new techniques as they developed throughout the war, and made recommendations for improving practice in battlefield surgery. Cowdrey, *Fighting for Life,* 19–20, 164–65.

8. About fifty thousand of Gen. Tomoyuki Yamashita's Shobu fighters and other followers subsisted in the mountains near Baguio until giving up on September 2, 1945, the day of the signing of the Japanese surrender in Tokyo Bay. The next day, September 3, in Baguio, Yamashita signed the surrender of his command. Falk, *Liberation of the Philippines,* 157–59.

9. Yamashita was sentenced to death on December 7, 1945, four years after the attack on Pearl Harbor, and was executed on February 22, 1946. A. J. Barker, *Yamashita* (New York: Ballantine Books, 1973), 147–59.

JOHN FRANK "JACK" ONION JR.

John F. Onion Jr. was born five minutes before his twin brother, James Wesley Collins Onion, on March 27, 1925, in San Antonio, Texas. Five years later, their father, Judge John F. "Pete" Onion Sr., a prominent lawyer, justice of the peace, and future district court judge, bought the historic Huebner farm and stagecoach stop on the Bandera Road outside San Antonio so that his sons could benefit from country living. The boys, nicknamed Jack and Jim, grew up on the prosperous Hill Country farm with a working dairy and a stable of saddlebred show horses. They attended a three-room rural school through sixth grade before continuing their education in San Antonio, where they completed Jefferson High School in 1942. In high school they both earned the rank of first lieutenant in the ROTC. The Onion twins spent the next two years on their father's cattle ranch in Frio County earning a temporary exemption from military service by raising beef for the war effort. In 1944, at age nineteen, they volunteered for active duty, hoping to serve in the navy. Their assignment, however, was the marine corps. Because they were twins, Jack and Jim were allowed to stay together when they reached boot camp at Parris Island, South Carolina.

I GUESS IF I HAD TO LOOK BACK AND PICK OUT three months that I would not want to relive, it would be that three months. We got a lot of good training, but there was a lot of it that was just plain mean. I didn't realize that one human being could be that mean to another. Knock on wood, I knew how to do close-order drill. I had seen country boys who had never been near a military base, and they would show them one time how to right face, and then they'd tell them to do it. Of course, they didn't do it very right, and they got a fist in their stomach. They'd show them one more time, and then another fist when they didn't do it right. I can always remember hoping that it got time to go to sleep, because when I was asleep I wasn't aware where I was.

It was normal in the military, at four thirty in the morning, the drill instructor would yell, "Hit the deck!" Marines use the navy lingo. From that moment we had to get up, get dressed in a skivvy shirt and our dungaree pants and our shoes, make your sack so you could bounce a quarter off, and be outside the barracks building in formation ready to do calisthenics. Within three minutes you were doing side-straddle hops or other things. Then you were run through what they call the head, which is another lingo, and you were seventh or eighth behind some guy at one mirror trying to shave. Then you marched through the dark streets to the chow hall, and they told you to take all you want but don't leave anything. To me, I always thought they were going to come around and check my plate. I lost twenty-four and a half pounds in boot camp. We were the oldest boot platoon for some reason, and we had to stay in KP for three weeks.

When we finished, they sent us up to Camp Lejeune, North Carolina, for what they call secondary training. We were not far from the coast, and it was cold. They moved us out of prefabricated huts, where you had a big potbellied stove, into tents, and it would solidly freeze every night. You'd wake up and your face would be caked with ice. One day they announced, We're going to march you over to quartermasters. We got over there, and they gave us an extra blanket, and we cheered. The only stove we had in that tent was just a little coal-oil flame, which was nothing. We had one night with the extra blanket. Next morning they got us in formation, got our extra blanket, marched us back to quartermasters, and we returned the extra blanket. We asked why. "We heard you all were shipping out," was the response.

We were shipped out to Camp Pendleton, California, on the train. There we were, on the West Coast, waiting to get on board a ship. We were there at Pendleton a lot longer than we anticipated. We were told the ship we were leaving on kept breaking down, being repaired, and then didn't work. They shipped us out on December 23, 1944. The second day they announced that there would be no drinking water available; the ship's equipment for turning salt water into fresh water had broken down. If we wanted water to drink, we had to line up at eight o'clock in the morning, stand in line, and get hot water that came out. You had to leave it in your canteen all day, walk around with it all day to get it cool enough. At six o'clock in the evening, you needed to get back in line to get more. Oh, by the way, no more freshwater showers. There is saltwater soap and salt water. If you want to clean up, you have to clean up on it.

Then, the third or fourth day, the ventilation went down in the hold below decks. I slept down there. I woke up the next morning, and I was sloshing around in my own sweat that was caught in the hammock. There was no ventilation. They decided to allow everybody that could to take a bedroll and get in a line on the stairs coming up out of the ship. After the evening meal they'd open the hatches, and you could run and try to find a place on deck to put your bedroll down. I really worked and got on a good position on the stairs with my bedroll. They opened the hatches, and I ran around and got a place on deck, and, oh, that ocean breeze was so great! I woke up the next morning, and the smokestack had kicked out all these little black specks of dirt or coal or something all over your face, all over your bedroll. Any time you tried to remove one of them, it smeared. You try to get all that off your face with salt water; saltwater soap doesn't help. You had all those smears on your bedroll. I spent the rest of the next month sleeping down in the hold, despite the heat, because it was just too much of a hassle.

It took us seven days, to December the thirtieth, to get to Pearl Harbor. Here we were in Pearl Harbor, and it was, Look, but don't touch the merchandise. They left us onboard ship all the time. Hawaii was only for viewing. The sunken battleships in Pearl Harbor itself could be seen. After a week we joined a convoy and went and stayed about a week in Eniwetok. Then we took off, and our ship started breaking down. First time, the whole convoy stayed with us; the next time they left one destroyer escort behind. The next time after that they left a destroyer escort a second time. We were stopped one time fifty miles off Truk, which was still in Japanese hands. Fortunately we finally got it started, and we got into Saipan on January 23, one month after we had left San Diego.

We were a replacement draft.[1] They kept us separate and apart. I don't know why they didn't assign us to regular units at that time. They didn't break us up; they kept us together. We had rifle-range practice and different things—digging holes, close-order drill, cutting away the jungle—you name it. Finally, after a month or six weeks, they told us that they were breaking us up. I was always fearful that they'd count down the list and draw a line between my brother and me and one of us would be sent one way or the other. But they sent both of us to the 2nd Division, 6th Marines, 2nd Battalion, Fox Company.

I remember going up to Fox Company with my sea bag and bedroll and rifle, and we went in to talk to the gunnery sergeant, who was in the office. They had wooden platform steps and wooden flooring and then a tent. The gunnery said, "You're what?" "We're the two new marines assigned to Fox Company." "Oh well, good thing you arrived. Now, just put your gear down outside and get up to the mess hall." They had kind of a Quonset hut that was used as a mess hall up there. He said, "They're having a meeting up there now. Get up there and tell them that you're the two marines from Fox Company."

My brother and I put our gear down inside, went up to the mess hall, which wasn't really too far away, and the meeting was going on. As we walked in, I could hear the major saying, "If you're not a volunteer, we don't want you here." I thought, Well, now what is this? So we sat down. He said, "Now, for those of you who may have come late: this is a unit that's going to be trained to go in to the next island that we're going to be invading, before the invasion. We are going to be cutting telephone wires, cutting throats, killing snakes, and trying to pick up as much information about troop movement as we can. I repeat: we don't want you if you're not volunteering. I think maybe we should start with the pictures of the snakes that're going to be on the next stop." They showed us some of these big snakes with long Asiatic names that I had never heard of in my life. I thought, Golly. They started talking about how poisonous they were and how you better get to them before they got to you and that you would also be doing sharpshooter work by climbing trees and shooting with silencers. I'm sitting there, saying, How did I volunteer for this? He went on, telling us about it. What he was talking about was Okinawa. In fact, I think he used the term "Ryukyu," the islands that Okinawa's in.

When it was all over with, I went up to him with my brother and said, "We have just been assigned to Fox Company, and the minute we got there we were sent over here. We had no briefing or no background. We just walked into this. We didn't volunteer, and we don't want to volunteer." He says, "Well, I don't want you." I said, "Well, good." I thought, Mutual meeting of the minds. So we went back to Fox Company, and surprisingly, the gunnery sergeant didn't have a violent reaction. I said that he didn't want us, so we were assigned to a tent.

Shortly thereafter, the company commander came into our tent. The officers were not supposed to read our mail. Officers in some other company were supposed to read our mail. But my brother had hurt his back in California, and from time to time it flared up on him. He apparently had been on some work detail throwing sacks around and his back had given him some trouble, and he had written home about it. Well, the company commander walked in and said, "Which one of you Onion boys have the bad back?" Well, I knew he'd been reading my brother's mail. My brother raised his hand, and he looked at me and said, "You are now the new BAR man"—Browning Automatic Rifle. That is a much heavier weapon that doesn't use clips; they use magazines. It's the heaviest firepower in a platoon. The only thing I had had in boot camp was: "Get in line. When it comes your turn, lie down, sight up the BAR, and pull the trigger. Get up, and let the next guy lie down and shoot." So I didn't know any more about the Browning Automatic Rifle. But I did find out that when you went out on these fourteen-mile hikes, when you carried all of that—extra magazines and bullets and stuff—around your waist and your extra weight on your shoulder, it did make a difference.[2]

I can always remember the guy that had the BAR had had it for some time. I remember we'd gone through one inspection, and we were coming up for another. He was sitting there in the tent with me one day, and he said, "Oh! I didn't tell you, but you need to really clean down here in the stock. You lift up this little thing and pull this metal out." Well, gee, I didn't even know it was there. Didn't seem to have anything to do with firing it. I opened it up, and, being there on an island in the Pacific, it was already rusty as it could be. He helped me clean it up really fast so that by time of inspection no one knew that it'd gone rusty.

We then were sent aboard ship to go to the Ryukyu Islands. Our troopship was the *Bayfield*. I did not know it at the time, but the *Bayfield* had been carrying troops on D-Day, June 6, 1944, off Normandy. It is mentioned in many D-Day stories. We generally knew that it was someplace called Okinawa, but among the troops there still wasn't a lot of talk about where it was. We didn't want anybody else to know, including the Japanese. We were on board ship, and the 2nd Marine Division was surrounded by a number of cruisers and destroyers and destroyer escorts. We drifted in on the southeast corner of Okinawa, and we made no pretense that we weren't there. It was obvious we were floating in. When we got there, on April 1, the battleships closer in to the land were shooting at the landing. I had never seen a battleship shooting all of their guns. The battleship would jump back; the recoil pushed the whole ship back. From time to time they'd hit a oil depot or something, and there'd be a big flame.

After an hour or so of that, we unloaded all of the assault boats. They had filled the assault boats about half full because they didn't want any Japanese planes flying over and seeing empty assault boats. We were going to make a fake landing on the southeastern side of Okinawa. The main landing at that same time was being made around on the Inland Sea, closer to China. That's where the landing craft got in rows after rows from all the different troopships and started in toward shore. As they got closer to shore, then the marine pilots came in and laid down a real heavy smoke screen between the shore and the assault boats. In the smoke screen the assault boats turned around and came back out to the troopships, and they all got back up on the troopships and then we moved back out to sea. The second day we came in, and that same operation was repeated. Battleships bang-bang-banged, and then we put the assault boats in the water again, smoke screen, and then we backed out, went back out to sea. We were actually able to hear on

Second Division Marines board attack transports in Tanapag Harbor, Saipan, bound for Okinawa. *Courtesy of US Marine Corps.*

the ship's radio Tokyo Rose saying there wasn't enough left of the 2nd Division to fit into a telephone booth. Of course, all of this had been fake landings.[3]

The 2nd Marine Division was scheduled to go in to relieve the 1st Marine Division on line on the other side of the island, the Inland Sea side, on L plus 6. Instead of D-Day, they called the landing L-Day. When I tried to find out what *L* stood for, I was told it stood for "Love." That never has satisfied me. You don't talk about landing day; the enemy might pick that up and figure out landing day.[4] We had heard that the 1st Marine Division was doing well, that they had advanced well beyond their expectations. Then through the grapevine we got another message onboard ship that they had continued to make great progress, and we suddenly looked up and saw that the 2nd Marine Division was afloat with nobody to protect us except two or three destroyer escorts. There was one whole marine division afloat with very little protection on the open sea.

We were told scuttlebutt that we were the bait for the Japanese battleship, the great big battleship, *Yamato,* that was going to be lured out by us. I think maybe we were just part of the picture on this, I'm not sure, but this is what we heard at the time, that here was a whole marine division afloat with very little protection and that this battleship could sink us but we would really be protected. They were all out there, coming to our protection. I think it was the next day after that we heard that the *Yamato* had been sunk, had come out of Japan and been sunk.[5] I've seen stories on the *Yamato* being sent to Okinawa to do as much damage as they could, and the Americans, having broken the Japanese code, knew they were coming out. The stories didn't mention us at all. We didn't get proper billing. But then I've read other stories that factor us into it. So I don't know.

At L plus 10, they announced to us that we were going back to Saipan, that the battle at Okinawa was going so extremely well that we weren't needed. We went back to Saipan, and the 6th Marine Regiment, of which I was part, stayed onboard ship for ten days to two weeks, something like that, because they said the 6th Marines were going back to Okinawa in case there was any need for reinforcements. After that period of time they removed us, sent us back to where the rest of the Fox Company was, which was our old tents and everything that were left standing there before.[6]

Not having expected us to come back, the food wasn't very good, needless to say. Over the hill from us on Saipan, the 8th Marine Regiment had gone back into their old tents. As soon as they opened the PXs over there, they, in protest of the kind of food they were getting, went to the PXs and bought candy bars, which marines call pogey bait. They ate the pogey bait and didn't fall out for the meals. The 2nd Division commander got incensed and came down and got up on a platform after he had the whole 8th Marine Regiment assembled and told them, "Look, we didn't know we were coming back either. Food may not be as good as you would like or as good as we would like, but it's not going to waste. You are going to fall out and eat."

Well, a few more fell out to eat, but a vast majority of them continued to eat their candy bars. The division commander said, "Well, they don't seem to like it here on Saipan. So if there is a need for reinforcement, the 8th Marines and not the 6th Marines will go." Sure enough, when the battle got down around Naha, the 8th Marines had gone back to Okinawa. Some of the 8th Marines I talked to later said when they were getting ready to jump off to go into battle, they saw a civilian-type car but painted khaki color with flags flying on each fender coming along a road. They said, "We didn't know who that was, but it sure must be somebody important. It came up on a little mound above us. We know it was someone prominent." Shortly after that, the Japanese mortars zeroed in on that car, and they killed General Simon Bolivar Buckner Jr., who was the Tenth Army commander.[7] The moral to that story is: Eat what food is given you; don't fall out for pogey bait. That story is in the marine corps annals, but, as it affected me directly, I felt close to that story.

There were six marine divisions during World War II. Each division had four regiments. There were three regiments out of all regiments that did not see hand-to-hand combat after I went overseas. I happened to be in one of the three regiments that didn't see hand-to-hand combat, although I was at Okinawa. We had a kamikaze plane plow into the ship just back of us at Okinawa. I sometimes think back and remember when we told the recruiter we wanted to be in the navy to be near the water and he said, "You'll be near the water. You'll be good marines." Maybe God had something to do with it because I was hell-bent to go another way: the navy. God works in mysterious ways.

While we were on Saipan, we were to start training in earnest to invade Japan. Somehow it seems like to me that we knew in advance that we were going to hit Japan at Kagoshima. Later I saw pictures on the short beaches where the volcanic mountains rose up at Kagoshima, where the Japanese had cars on railroad tracks and guns loaded on the railroad tracks where they could come out and fire and then go back into the mountain. Part of the mountain would raise up, the guns could come out on the railroad tracks, fire, and go back in to protect them. In training on Saipan, we had long, fourteen-mile hikes. I crawled through the jungle vines, trying to figure out some way to get those magazines up over the vines. They always wanted you to be up towards the front with the greatest firepower, the BAR. We realized the invasion was at hand.

When we were first there at Saipan, the B-29s bombing Japan would take off in the late afternoon from Saipan and Tinian. You would see they were heavily loaded. They left Saipan airfields, and they would just barely fly over the top of the water. In fact, once or twice they pancaked into the water, but most of the time they finally gained altitude. We could see the B-29s also taking off from Tinian, which was across the way. When I was still in the replacement draft on Saipan, they would come back from bombing Japan about four thirty in the morning. They'd come very low over our tents, and of course you might as well get up then. Most of them had dropped their loads, and they were not full. They continued the bombing of Japan, and we continued to train to go.[8]

Then one night we heard this excitement, a loud noise, and we heard that the atom bomb had been dropped on Hiroshima. We hadn't heard about the bomb. Of course we felt, if this can shorten the war, more power to it. Several days later the bomb was dropped on Nagasaki. It had come from a plane that had left Tinian, which was right across from Saipan. After the second bomb was dropped at Nagasaki, I can remember one night that we heard a low, dull roar. I didn't know what it was. It was in a distance, and it was a strange noise. Pretty soon it got a little louder. It sounded at first like some machine, and maybe the machine was coming this way. But then you said, No, it's too loud, too massive. It just started roaring and roaring. Finally we were suddenly aware that everybody on the island was yelling and screaming. About that time, somebody rushed in and said, "The Japanese have surrendered." Well, we started yelling, too. It was quite a moment to send shivers down your spine, to think that the war was over.[9]

I guess I'm kind of hard-nosed; I still have had a hard time in my later life hearing people talking about how immoral and unethical we were to drop the bombs. I'm saying, "Do you realize that Japanese were being killed every night with these firebombs and things? Would you have rather sacrificed hundreds of thousands of American lives assaulting Japan? Those people would be fighting for their home, their homeland. They would be killing hundreds of thousands of Americans, and we would be killing hundreds and thousands of them. This is by far the best." Nevertheless we have people today that continue to say, "Oh, it was a horrible thing; we should have gone ahead and fought a regular war." Well, somebody forgot to tell them that Russia was through with their war and had entered the war against Japan and were poised to enter Japan and take their share of Tokyo and their part of Japan, which would have instigated communism right into Japan in a big way. I didn't agree with him on a lot of things he did, but I take my hat off to Brother Harry Truman, and I get a little emotional about it because it meant my life.

After we learned that Japan had surrendered, then we realized that we were going to be the troops to go in to the occupation. They put us on troop ships, and a bunch of new marines had come in from the United States a day or two before we left for Japan. They put a bunch of new marines into our Fox Company after we were already on board ship, ready to leave for Japan. Lo and behold, there was this one young fellow who was told he was the new BAR man, and they told me to give it up. Well, they didn't get much opposition from me. I gave it all over to this young man, and then I said, "What's my weapon?" They said, "Take his." Well, he had a carbine. I'm not sure how good a weapon it is in battle, but a lot of the officers wore it because they didn't want to carry too much around. It was light.

We landed in Nagasaki on September 23, 1945. The bombs had been dropped in August. We got outside the harbor, and they unloaded us by cargo net onto assault boats, which are the low boats. We started into the harbor, and people have to realize that the bomb was dropped on the main city, which was some distance away from the harbor.

Second Marines arrive in Nagasaki in September 1945. *Courtesy of US Marine Corps.*

Nagasaki has some hills, and some of the city was built in among these hills, and the valleys between the hills ran down to the harbor. A lot of the buildings between these hills suffered damage, cracks and other things, but they were not hit like the atomic bomb had hit the main area. The harbor area was generally protected. Some of the area around the harbor was not too badly damaged. They had told us before that we couldn't go into that area. When we were still on Saipan, they said no one can go in for seventy-five years. Well, it was a little daunting to think that we were going to go in there before the seventy-five years had run. We went in with these low assault boats and were going towards these great big white concrete piers where big cargo ships and even cruise ships could've docked. We were way, way down below.

I'm sitting up there, and I didn't see any American forces on the docks anywhere, in any direction. I'm saying, Well they could come out of the blue and start machine-gunning us, and we're down here in these little assault boats. It was unusual. Then to add to it, on the dock where we were going, it was sort of comical because there were two Japanese there in top hats and cutaway coats—morning suits, I guess.

They were there, the two, alone. They didn't appear to be harmful. I guess they were supposed to welcome us or something. I'm not sure what they were doing. It was surreal.

Somehow, after we got to the piers and were riding in the assault boats, some of our people got up and got cargo nets dropped down from the piers to our ships, and we had to climb up with all our gear on these cargo nets and get up on the pier. They took us a few hundred yards from the pier where we landed to a vacant factory that had obviously had some machines there that had been removed. It was concrete floor, except where the concrete was raised for a machine. They told us to throw our pads down on the concrete floor because that was where we were going to spend the night. One fellow in our unit had somehow gone down to the harbor at Saipan and acquired a monkey, and he still had the monkey with him when we got to Nagasaki. The monkey got loose in this warehouse and was way up in the beams, and he stayed there.

Sometime toward early morning, somebody was shaking my arm, and I looked up, and it was some sergeant I had never before seen. I knew that he was not in my outfit. He said to me, "You're on guard duty." I said, "Where?" He said, "Come. I'll show you." I had to get up and dress, put on my clothes, and I followed him. He took me outside the warehouse and about two blocks away at what appeared to be an intersection. Above the intersection were some houses. There I was with my carbine, which was the only weapon I had. He said, "This is your guard post." Here I was in a foreign country, and I'm here with a little carbine. I said, "What are my instructions?" He said, "Well, they didn't tell me. But I suppose you're supposed to keep any Japanese from going from this point further down towards the warehouse." I said, "Well, I guess that's a good guess." So he goes off and leaves me.

By that time, it's eight o'clock in the morning. I'm at an intersection in a strange city that's been bombed, and I'm standing there. All at once, here comes a Japanese along. He takes a second glance at me, and then he starts bowing and bowing. Then here comes a second Japanese and he starts the same thing. Soon I have fifteen or twenty people standing there, bowing at me. Well, I wasn't going to bow back because that's not my culture, and besides that, we're here as conquerors, aren't we? We're not supposed to bow back. Finally, several of them retreated; some would turn and go another way. Up above me, on the left side, a woman came out of one of the houses and into the kind of backyard, and when she saw me, she ran quickly back into the house. Well, I stayed there for four hours, encountering these passing Japanese, thinking, I don't think with this carbine I could stop many people. Around noontime, here came some people who were not in my outfit at all and said, "You're relieved." I said, "What do I do?" "Go back to the warehouse." I went back to the warehouse and subsequently during that day got back with my unit.

They moved us out to a part of the town where they had some Japanese army barracks that were built on the side of a hill. There'd be a long row of Japanese barracks, and then below that there'd be a staircase coming down another row and another row down till they got to the ground floor. Must've been seven or eight rows there. There was a house at the bottom, where either the commanding officer or somebody lived. They told us we could not drink the water. We had to put pills in the water that we were able to acquire, but the pills had to remain in the water for forty-eight hours. So for a number of days we had no liquid; we could only drink coffee at a mess hall. And of course the Japanese toilet facilities were not any kind that we had seen. They were ceramic, but they were just little holes in the floor with a little ceramic—not a real cover too much. While we stayed there at those barracks they had honey dippers[10] come in, and that was a day that you'd rather be away from the barracks. I guess we were there about two months in those Japanese army barracks.

We were taken on tours of the bombed-out area. I think it was the first or second week they put bulldozers down in there to clean off some of the areas. Some of the buildings were just gutted. Some of the frames were up, but the entire inside of the building was gone. Some places you could see there was a bridge across a river. You could see the concrete imbedded into the bank on either side and maybe some steel sticking out, but the bridge was gone. You could see in other buildings that were once there, no longer there, complete rubble. They had some kind of steel-framed factory that ran almost a mile and a half that the bomb had just taken everything on the inside and leaned it over. The Japanese were still going around with the masks on to protect themselves, but they did that also for colds, so it was hard for us to tell.

My brother was much more athletic than I was. He was more coordinated, and he got on a baseball team. They bulldozed out some of this dust, ash, and made a baseball field. He went down there nearly every day with some team, and they slid bases in this homemade baseball field and everything else. Years later they determined that he had thyroid cancer, and they determined I did not. They thought that was rather strange that one identical twin would have it and the other one didn't, and there was a lot of debate and back and forth. Finally, after going through a bunch of tests, they gave him 10 percent disability because they thought that he could possibly have contracted the thyroid cancer malignancy due to inhaling that atom-bomb dust.

At Nagasaki we were just holding the thing. The emperor must have had a greater influence on the Japanese people because our experience there was that the Japanese were rather docile. They had been very difficult people to fight against—the banzai attacks and the kamikaze and all of those things that had gone with it. We had in occupation very little trouble with the Japanese.[11] We didn't have them sneaking onto the base or wherever soldiers were. Sometimes we had Japanese workers who came on base during the daytime, but they had to be off by a certain time and usually were. We had rumors one time when we were at Saga that there was a group of kamikaze pilots that apparently were going to make a kamikaze-type attack on our regimental headquarters there, which had been a Japanese army base. That never materialized, and we just never heard any more about it. We never had any of our American soldiers being mugged or killed.

After we had been in Nagasaki for two months, they got us out of the barracks one morning about four thirty, took us down to the railroad station, and told us that we were going north to the regimental headquarters at a town called Saga. I got separated from my brother. He had been taken off some work detail. I remember getting the worst cold in my life and my feet freezing on that Japanese train. We got to the town of Saga, and they immediately put our Fox Company on DUKWs,[12] which could run on water or land, and we went on some very dusty roads for about thirty miles to a little town called Tosu, which was the main railroad hub for all trains from the lower island of Kyushu on to the main island of Honshu, which included some of their bigger cities and Tokyo. You could stand on your tiptoes and look as far as you could see and there was nothing but railroad tracks. I often wondered, from a military standpoint, why they hadn't done something about that because seemed like to me it could've been bombed so easily and tear up their rail traffic. We were sent to this town and placed into two or three schoolrooms in a Japanese school, and we formed our so-called guard duty.

We had our main guard duties at the railroad station because there were trains coming through there all the time. We also had a guard duty at the school and several of the highways or roads coming into the little town of Tosu. We were there, I suppose, for about four or five months at the town of Tosu. It was an experience. We were told to take all military insignia off of any Japanese we saw passing through the streets or passing mainly through the railroad center coming through on trains. However, they did not tell us that the Japanese wore insignias designating their profession: a nurse or some kind of engineer or something else. To us, we didn't know one of those from military insignia. I felt real badly about it later. We'd catch these young Japanese, tell them to take it off, and it was something they were proud of. When they didn't take it off, we'd pull it away from their headgear. I felt badly about that, but all the months we were there, nobody came down to correct us on the thing. Occasionally we would see a few troops going by, one or two troops, and we did make them take off their insignias.

I remember one time my brother and I were on duty together at the railroad station, and a train came in from China. There were cars full of Japanese marines. These Japanese were large men; they were six foot and taller. They had on very fine uniforms and woolen coats and were, I guess, from northern China. They had most of their equipment still with them. I decided that maybe the better part of valor was to let that train go on to wherever it was taking them, that they had those cars full of Japanese military. My brother and I were the only guards at the station. I didn't know what firearms they may still have had. So on that one occasion, I didn't do that.

The Japanese railroad stations were poorly equipped. They were cold. They had no heat. We had a little guard booth there at the station that we had heat in, and I can remember a Japanese who was bringing his family back from China. He had a little girl and his wife. They were having to wait over for a train there at Tosu. He came around to the guard post, spoke beautiful English, and asked if we could take his wife and little girl into the guard-post booth because it was so cold. Well, of course that was impossible. I tried to explain to him in English: if the guard post got blown up by a little girl with a bomb—and many times there were stories about enemies having bombs and things—that we could get ourselves killed and we would have violated our instructions. He said he understood and went back. Later, when we were making the rounds, we saw him in the railroad station sitting there in the cold with his wife and young daughter. It was quite an experience.

While we were there at Tosu, we had guard duty, and we rotated guard duty among the people in the company. It finally got around to your graveyard shift, from twelve midnight to four in the morning and from twelve noon to four in the afternoon. Of course, that wasn't the most popular shift, and we did have a corporal who came and talked to the company officers and said if he could choose his men, he and his men would volunteer to permanently take the graveyard shift. Well, the bad thing about that shift was, that you no sooner got to bed at night that they were waking you up to be able to get you to your post at midnight, then you came back at four o'clock in the morning, and you hardly had time to sleep till you were up. You had to go to close-order drill or something else that didn't have anything to do with guard duty, then you had the whole afternoon to spend on guard duty.

He said he would volunteer if he could pick his men, and he did. The company officers let him do it. I began to notice that they would leave before eleven o'clock to get to their post at twelve, and I noticed they didn't come back any time close to four. It was after five o'clock. But I thought, They're the volunteers. Well, I suddenly found out that what they were doing was going around trying to find Japanese abroad at those hours of the night. If they were on bicycles, they would break up their bicycles and beat up the Japanese. It pretty soon got to be knowledge among the whole company what these people were doing. I guess they got their kicks, jollies, or whatever you want to call it, but I thought it was just uncalled for, and I thought the officers should have known about it. But that went on until we left. Then they told us that we were having to go back to Saga, which was regimental headquarters. When we got back there, we started guard duty again—for what else do privates in the rear rank do?

After several weeks one of the fellows came in and said, "Didn't I remember that one of the Onion boys can do some typing?" I had had junior high school typing. I didn't have it in high school, but when I was in boot camp I took a typing lesson. I think I got thirty words a minute, and it was very horrible. I never heard about it again until we first got to Nagasaki. Some officer said, "We need some help on personnel records, and does anyone here volunteer to work on it?" I thought, Well, working on personnel records is better than guard duty. So I raised my hand. The upshot of that was, they never called on any of us. But somebody remembered I'd volunteered, so they said, "By the way, there's an opening over in Headquarters Company, the 2nd Battalion, for a typist. It's in a disposition outfit." "Disposition?" "Well, they're disposing of Japanese war materials, and they're keeping records of it, and they need a typist."

I went over there, and they sat me down at a typewriter, which I hadn't seen in a year or longer, and I couldn't even remember where to press down to make the capital letters. Finally some guy said, "Oh, right here." They said, "Okay. Put in caps up here, FLEET MARINE FORCE, so and so and so." Well, I typed that point up there. I had a captain and a gunnery sergeant and somebody else standing over me, which was enough to make me hit the wrong letter every other word. As soon as I got through, the captain said, "You've got the job." I said, "What?" "You got the job." Well, it ruined my typing because I started trying to teach myself how to hunt and peck or start over this way and that way.

By the time I had been there a week or two, they came in and asked me, "Do you know anybody that can draw maps?" I said, "Maps? Draw maps? What do you mean?" "Well, you take these maps, and then you have to put this onionskin paper over it and you trace the thing so the people going out in the field looking for the Japanese war material can find the locations." I said, "You know, my brother took mechanical drawing in junior high school." He came over and drew a map for them, and he got a job. So we were both transferred to Headquarters Company.

When the disposition unit work was done, Jack served stints as a prison guard in Saga and as a general clerk in the company headquarters. The Onion brothers transferred to Sasebo, where they waited about five weeks for their return to the States. In Sasebo, Jack continued to do clerical work, and Jim became a bartender in the officer's club.

When I got on board ship to come home, I felt free. It was a big general ship, and we had five thousand troops on it. We had three meals a day. By the time you got through with breakfast, you better go get in line for lunch, or else you may miss out on lunch because the lines just wove all the way through the ship. Well, along they came, and somebody caught me and said, "They've set up company office in the fantail, in the back of the ship. They're looking for you. They're working on personnel records, and they want you to go find these different individuals." I said, "There're five thousand people on this ship, and they're scattered everywhere." Well, I got called upon to go find this fellow. I would spend four hours walking around, telling everybody I could think of who knew him. I'd walk here, and I'd walk there. Then the next day I'd go through the same thing. So I always claim that I walked home.

We were not all that great of soldiers or marines. The marine corps was very reticent to promote anybody. We were overseas for over a year on Saipan and then for a year after that. They never promoted an officer or an enlisted man at one point for over a year overseas. I couldn't believe it. I didn't expect to rise to a major general from private, but it just seemed like to me *somebody* would've been promoted. The day they discharged us at San Diego, they told us that we were being promoted on the day of discharge to corporal. You're private first class; now you're going to be promoted. These people they talked into signing over for another four years somehow thought that was the greatest thing, and

I think that was part of the plan: You're going to be a corporal. Well, they promoted us to corporal and issued us paper, even though we never even got the stripes or cared about it because we were going home and being discharged. Some of them did sign over, but Jim and I got on the train in San Diego and came home to San Antonio.

Upon discharge, Jack and Jim Onion both went to the University of Texas at Austin, where they graduated from law school in 1950. They returned to San Antonio to different jobs in the district attorney's office. Jack served as justice of the peace for two years and, at age thirty-one, became the youngest elected district judge in the state. In 1958, while he was district judge, he married Nancy Lee Vogelsang, and down the years they had three children and, eventually, six grandchildren. In 1967 he was elected a judge on the Texas Court of Criminal Appeals, and in 1970 he became that court's first presiding judge to be elected by Texas voters, a position he held until his retirement in 1988. In retirement, Judge Onion continued to sit by designation on various Texas courts.

Judge John F. "Jack" Onion Jr. was interviewed for the project Here and There: Recollections of Texas in World War II, funded by a grant from the Texas Historical Commission. See John Frank Onion Jr., *Oral Memoirs of John Frank Onion Jr.*, an interview conducted by Stephen Sloan, May 17, 2010, in Austin, Texas, BU Digital Collections.

Notes

1. The Onion brothers were among eight thousand replacements taken in by the 2nd Marine Division in 1944–1945 following the division's service in Guadalcanal, Tarawa, Saipan, and Tinian. The division trained in Saipan to perform various roles as a "strategic reserve" unit in the intended invasion of Japan in late 1945. Joseph H. Alexander, *The Final Campaign: Marines in the Victory on Okinawa* (Washington, DC: Marine Corps Historical Center, 1996), 7.

2. The Browning Automatic Rifle (BAR) weighed sixteen pounds.

3. The feint proved successful in focusing the attention of major Japanese infantry and artillery units on the southeastern coastline of Okinawa during and for several days after the real invasion on the southwestern coast. Alexander, *The Final Campaign*, 12.

4. Official sources disagree on the meaning of the code name L-Day. Roy E. Appleman, James M. Burns, Russell A. Gugeler, and John Stevens, *Okinawa: The Last Battle* (Washington, DC: United States Army

Center of Military History, 1948), 28, claim it meant simply "landing day." Alexander, *The Final Campaign*, 10, states that Love-Day was "selected from the existing phonetic alphabet in order to avoid confusion with 'D-Day' being planned for Iwo Jima."

5. The battleship *Yamato* was sunk on April 7 (L plus 6) in the East China Sea as it and a convoy of nine other warships headed toward Okinawa. Appleman et al., *Okinawa*, 99.

6. The 2nd Marine Division, minus the 8th Marine Regiment, "would languish" in reserve on Saipan during most of the eighty-two-day battle for Okinawa, a situation at least one officer considered a waste, since the division was "trained to a gnat's whisker." Alexander, *The Final Campaign*, 27.

7. The 8th Marine Regiment had a close view of General Buckner on June 18, 1945, when he stopped to watch the fighting from an observation point on the southwestern tip of Okinawa. The general was one of more than seven thousand Tenth Army troops who fell in the battle for Okinawa. Appleman, et al., *Okinawa*, 461.

8. From its bases in Saipan and Tinian, the US Air Force flew more than twenty-six thousand bombing missions over Japan in 1945, including the March 9–10 bombing of Tokyo, the deadliest air raid of the war, resulting in a hundred thousand Japanese deaths. Doyle, *World War II in Numbers*, 169.

9. The first atomic bomb was dropped on August 6; the second, on August 9. The emperor's surrender came on August 15; the formal signing of the Japanese Instrument of Surrender, on September 2.

10. Persons whose job it was to burn the human excrement collected in latrines.

11. Official sources corroborate Onion's impression of the population of occupied Japan as "a docile people anxious to cooperate," a situation which greatly facilitated the disarming and demobilization of the Empire's military by the marines, who in turn were recognized for being "kind but firm" in their conduct toward their former enemies. Charles R. Smith, *Securing the Surrender: Marines in the Occupation of Japan* (Washington, DC: Marine Corps Historical Center, 1997), 44.

12. Manufacturer's model name for amphibious trucks built by General Motors Corporation for use in World War II.

INDEX